BUDAPEST 1944–1949

GYOR — Passed through on the way to border, Dec. 1949
SOPRON — Wagon ride towards border, Dec. 1949
SZOMBATHELY — Hearing prior to sentencing, Dec. 1949
BALASSAGYARMAT — Manci and Pista, Feb - Aug. 1950
SATORALJAYJHELY — My parents' imprisonment, Dec. 1949 - Dec. 1950

SZOLNOK – transfer from train to horse drawn wagon - May 1951
KOTELEK – Internment May 1951 - Jan 1953
KUNSZENTMARTON – Jan - Sept 1953
BUDAPEST – Return from internment Sept 1953 - March 1957

Susanne on her 5th birthday, 1949

PURSUIT OF FREEDOM

Susanne McReyts

PURSUIT OF FREEDOM

**A TRUE STORY OF THE
ENDURING POWER OF HOPE AND DREAMS**

Susanne M. Reyto

JET PUBLISHING
Los Angeles, CA

PURSUIT OF FREEDOM
A True Story of The Enduring Power of Hope and Dreams
Susanne M. Reyto

First Edition | Copyright © 2004 by Susanne M. Reyto

Published by:

JET PUBLISHING
LOS ANGELES, CA

www.jetpublishing.com | books@jetpublishing.com

SAN   243-931X

**Publisher's Cataloging-in-Publication
(Provided by Quality Books, Inc.)**

Reyto, Susanne M.
    Pursuit of freedom : a true story of the enduring power of hope and dreams / Susanne M. Reyto.
        p. cm.
        Includes index
        LCCN 2004090251
        ISBN 0-944581-20-X

    1. Reyto, Susanne M. 2. Hungarian Americans--Biography. 3. Political refugees--United States--Biography. 4. World War, 1939-1945--Personal narratives, Hungarian. 5. Fascism--Hungary. 6. Communism—Hungary. I. Title.

E184.H95R49 2004   973'.04945 11'0092
                                            QBI04-200047

$21.95 U.S. | $32.95 Canada
Printed and bound in the United States of America

10 9 8 7 6 5 4 3 2 1

Cover and Book Design: Dotti Albertine | Cover Photograph: Getty Images

*This book is dedicated to my parents
who have been my lifelong inspiration.*

*"You taught me the meaning of love,
survival and the power of positive thinking."*

C O N T E N T S

ACKNOWLEDGEMENTS

I am grateful to my friend, Marilyn Browar, who after hearing some of my stories, felt the rest needed to be told. She encouraged me to write, and her constant prodding became my daily inspiration. With such encouragement and support, I did not want to let her down.

A big thank you to Johanna Schwartz who helped me focus on the story and initially edited my words without changing their meaning. To Peter Harris who guided me and helped to make my life's journey more significant. And my gratitude to all my caring, supportive friends, in particular, Iris Chester, Carol Redston, Denny Oberman, Myrna Feinstein, Paul Belvedere, Renny Klein, and Sally Bennett, who all gave me insightful feedback which made my story more meaningful. I am most grateful to Carmen Culver for her invaluable, professional advice, and many thanks to my editorial and design team: Terri Navarra, Laren Bright, Dotti Albertine and to Ellen Reid, my book consultant, for helping to coordinate it all.

As soon as I began to put my thoughts on paper, I realized that without my mother's assistance I would not be able to tell my story. Indeed, without her strength, concern, and tenacity I would not have survived to tell the tale. Rose, my mom, a youthful eighty-three-year-old with an alert mind and an incredible memory, immersed herself in this venture and became an indispensable participant. In turn, the project gave her an enormous lift, allowing her to search her mind and soul for memories whose recovery proved to be very meaningful. Her excitement about being an essential and integral part of this book has given me the utmost pleasure and satisfaction. I am eternally thankful to her for reliving all of her experiences with me, even those that were painful and unpleasant, and which we rarely talked about before. My respect and admiration for my parents increased enormously, having learned in depth the grim details of their survival. I always knew that I was fortunate to have such role models.

Last but certainly not least, I am forever thankful to my husband, Robert, who has been a constant source of inspiration and support. He immersed himself in my story, helping to bring out memories that were still painful but needed expression. Although it was difficult and uncomfortable at times, his curiosity and gentle but persistent prodding ultimately resulted in a more complete and genuine memoir.

This exchange brought us even closer together. After many of his inquiries, I realized that although Robert had lived in Hungary and knew of my family's great suffering at the hands of the communists, he really was not aware of the details of our hardships. He now knows more about the experiences that molded my life and personality, and, as a result, has a greater respect for my sensitivities and strong feelings about certain issues. Through this experience, we both felt a deepening of the bond between us, and I now have the strength gained from finally sharing these stories with my life partner.

A final thank you to Leona Brauser for giving me permission to include her poem, Legacy, which so aptly describes my experience.

LEGACY

The heart has hiding places
And the mind has subtle ways
It tucks away our memories
And thoughts of bygone days.

They do not age or wither
These memories of old
They stay there in their secret place
With stories never told.

You may find yourself quite busy now
With all the tasks at hand
Of course I understand this
You're leaving footprints in the sand.

But if someday you stop to rest
And you feel very bold
Take pen to hand and write and write
Your stories should be told.

— LEONA BRAUSER

PROLOGUE

This is 2003. Almost sixty years have passed since the end of World War II and in my experience, I have found that most people believe suffering in Europe ended at that time. However, it is the farthest thing from reality. Worse yet, history keeps repeating itself in various parts of the world. In only sixty years, we are now faced with the third major global confrontation.

Kyle, my fifteen-year-old grandson, is a history lover, so he and I often discuss what is going on in the world today, and how these issues relate to my growing up years in Hungary. There are a lot of parallels between that time and today's political climate in some countries. I am concerned about the depth of his awareness, and what young Americans are learning at school today.

The weekly visits to my daughter, Michelle, her husband, Steve, and their children, Nicole and Kyle are always delightful. We usually have a lot to discuss over lunch, dinner, or scrambled eggs, warm cinnamon rolls, and freshly brewed coffee, whether it's Nicole and Kyle's schoolwork, family, business, or politics. On this particular Sunday, after brunch Michelle took Nicole to a birthday party, and the rest of the family left the table. Only Kyle and I remain, engrossed in conversation about the state of the world today. He is only two years older than I was when my parents and I left Hungary in 1957. When I relate to him that my childhood was filled with Nazi persecution, imprisonment, kidnapping from my parents, then later deportation camp and daily psychological torment at the hands of the Communist regime, he becomes eager to learn more about my firsthand experiences. His questions soon evolve into stories about my family's struggle to survive these two tyrannical regimes, and our attempts to escape our homeland. I always tell him about our unstoppable dream of living our future in freedom.

"Zsuzsi, guess what?" he exclaims. Kyle calls me by my Hungarian name, pronounced JUJI, which he finds more endearing than Susanne. "We are studying *Anne Frank's Diary* in English class!"

"That's great, Kyle. I am glad your class will know about the evil of the Nazi era, but I hope your teacher will also tell you about the secrecy, misinformation, lies, terror, and deception during the ensuing regime, which was Communism.

"We survived the Nazis, and afterwards experienced the horrors of Communism, but at that time we didn't know facts and the reasons relating to our suffering. We became aware of the details only recently when documents surfaced after the fall of Communism in 1989."

"How did you find out?"

"Purely by chance, during a recent trip to Budapest, in May 2002. Robert, your grandfather, and I had an amazing, unexpected experience. "Haven't I told you this story?"

"No, I don't think so. Tell me!"

"The most dreaded address in Budapest was Andrassy Street 60. That large building was used for interrogation and torture of thousands of people by the Nazis during World War II, and unfortunately was continued in the same manner by the Communists. The building has since been converted into a museum called HOUSE OF TERROR. While we lived in Hungary, we knew that most people taken to Andrassy Street 60 never left alive. Now, at long last, we had the opportunity to see the inside for ourselves. It was a truly memorable experience: people whispering, some wiping tears from their eyes while reading documents and seeing photographs. Seeing the cells in the basement where the torture and hanging took place certainly made the horrors come alive. One of the floors is dedicated entirely to Communism.

"Susanne, come quickly, look at this!" Robert yelled. My heart raced and for a moment my legs wouldn't move. "These are actual documents of your deportation! This is amazing! We must get copies."

I was stunned. Two walls are completely wallpapered with copies of official documents and newspaper clippings relating to a period in my family's suffering. They served as the blueprint of the plan and execution of the Communist prescription for horror. As my eyes scanned the walls full of images, I felt I was drowning in emotions. I didn't know where to look first. Every document seemed important, exposing one of the darkest periods in Hungary's history.

"You know, Kyle, it is inconceivable that I had to wait fifty-five years to learn the facts about my own life, but I am grateful that it is now there for all to see. I was determined to get copies, I knew they would mean a lot to Rozsi, my mother."

"Were you able to get them?" he asked with curiosity.

"Yes, but getting them was almost impossible. There was a lot of red tape and security checks just to enter the Hungarian Archives. When we finally reached the right department, we had to twist arms and sweet-talk the staff into doing it for us. Forty-five minutes later when they finally located and brought us the file, one of the women explained that this formerly large dossier was originally Prime Minister Rakosi's personal file, but now consisted of only 115 pages, a very scant reminder of that era. Many of the papers disappeared or were burned during the uprising in 1956 and the fall of Communism in Hungary in 1989."

"It's unreal," Kyle says, shaking his head. "It's really cool to find part of your personal history displayed in a museum. I wish you would come to my school and talk to my class about it."

I smiled. I was touched.

"It would be my greatest pleasure, Kyle! If it's all right with your teacher, I'll be there. You can count on that. Let's talk to her and find out when the school schedule will permit it."

It seemed I had opened a small window for him to look into the past. A past that was not just a textbook filled with statements and dates, but a past he could see, feel and relate to.

Suddenly a friend of his arrives, and he gets up from the table and says,

"Thanks, Zsuzsi, I got to go." He rushes toward the door, but stops suddenly. "Can we continue this later? I want to hear more. I want to hear everything!"

As he walks away, I cannot help but think about standing in front of his class and making a meaningful presentation. I realize that over the years I have rarely discussed my childhood with my parents. While many things I remember clearly, I would still need to ask Mother to fill in many important details. I wasn't sure how she would respond. Would she be angry? Upset? Would she be calm and willing? I thought a lot about how to approach her.

Driving home from Michelle's I started to tell Mother about Kyle's invitation and asked her to help me with some facts. I was amazed at her reaction. Mother is an astute, quick-thinking eighty-three year-old, who feels strongly about the importance of telling young people how we managed to live and survive under two brutal regimes. She was so positive and exuberant! Her spirit sprung to life, she truly surprised me. She immediately started to tell me stories and images she had stored in her memory for over fifty years. I had to hold her back to grab some paper and pen to make notes. She was eager to talk. As we got closer to home she didn't grow tired—instead her words came faster. I thought of a racecar driver approaching the finish line: to someone who survived what she did, I guess this was the finish line. She hopes the children of Kyle's generation realize how fortunate they are to grow up in the United States in freedom.

Our children live in Thousand Oaks, thirty miles from our home in Westwood, a lovely suburb on the Westside of Los Angeles. During our weekly drive to visit them, my husband, Robert, Mother, and I reflect on our experiences. Robert was also born in Hungary and we knew many of the same people. We wonder how different these families' lives turned out. Robert was a university student in 1956 and was exposed to a more radical perspective, the outspoken viewpoint of students during the uprising. Many of Mother's and my comments came as a revelation to him, despite living in the same city of Budapest.

Because of the secretive environment, he had no real knowledge of how many Hungarians, like us, were suffering at that time. We often listen to each other in shock and disbelief.

The drive on the five-lane freeway reminds Mother and I how very different it was riding on a country road in Hungary in December 1949 when my family tried to escape their cherished homeland, first soiled by the Nazi reign of terror, followed by the desperate life forced upon us by Communism. At that time we were only thirty minutes from freedom but didn't reach our destination. It would be another eight dismal years before we had the good fortune to make it to the West.

CHAPTER 1
CAPTURE AND ABDUCTION

IT WAS FREEZING COLD. The train finally stopped and we got off. It was dark, 10 o'clock at night. I didn't know where we were, but noticed my parents frantically looking up and down the platform—searching for someone. Mommy held my hand and we all walked outside the station toward a horse-drawn buggy with a man standing beside it. He looked at us and called, "Fekete bogár," which means "black bug" in Hungarian. That scared me. I didn't know what it meant. I thought it was crawling on me, but Mommy grabbed my hand and pulled me away. Our name was "Fekete," so Mommy and Daddy understood that. Daddy nodded at the man and Mommy said, "Let's all get on the wagon. Zsuzsika, you hop on the front seat next to the driver."

She looked worried. I didn't understand it, but I didn't say anything. I was five years old, excited to be riding in the front seat. Mommy, Daddy, Grandma Bertha, Grandpa Wolf, Auntie Kato, and my three-year-old cousin, Kati, all sat in the back of the open wagon. Without another word we left the station. It was scary in the dark and I was getting tired. It was late, way past my bedtime, but the adventure kept me awake. The only noise I could hear was the clickety-clop of the horse's hooves on the dirt road. It was bitterly cold, but I was all bundled up so I didn't feel it. Before leaving home, Mommy and Daddy told me we were going on a vacation, so to me this was an exciting beginning.

I had never sat in a country wagon before or even been that close to a horse. I had to hold my nose because the smell was so strong. It was a bumpy ride as we trotted along in the dark. I could not see a thing. It felt like we were in the middle of nowhere. We had only been riding for a short time but I was already getting restless.

"When are we getting there?" I asked the driver. He didn't answer. Mommy and Daddy were silent too. I looked around in the dark and the only thing I could see were red sparks floating around. I didn't even have a chance to ask what they were, before a flashlight glared in my face. We stopped. I was so scared I couldn't say a word. Suddenly a soldier appeared at my side, the red sparks flying from his cigarette. I looked back and noticed two other men standing at the back of the wagon. They were big and burly, dressed in heavy, dark uniforms, and holding large rifles in their hands. I was the first person the soldier spoke to. The other men were talking to my family in the back of the wagon. I had no idea who they could be, or why we had stopped.

"Where are you going?" he asked me.

I began to tremble. He sounded so mean. He kept looking at me as he puffed on his cigarette.

"Get out!" one of the soldiers yelled.

We got off our wagon and I ran to hug Mommy. She picked me up and whispered in my ear,

"I'm sorry we had to lie to you. These men are border guards, and we are not going on a vacation. I'll tell you more about it later."

I didn't know what border guards were, but as we stood there, we heard a noise as another wagon rolled up next to us. They ordered us to get into it. Mommy quickly explained that the guards were bad people who didn't like us and that we were under arrest.

This was in Hungary, December 1949.

We all sat in the back of the wagon and one of the soldiers guarding us sat next to Mommy. She struck up a conversation with him. As opposed to the others, this one seemed friendly and was willing to talk to us. He was admiring Mommy's fur coat, leather handbag, and gold pin. He said that if she gave him these items he would make arrangements for us to be released, and we would be free to return to Budapest that evening.

After we arrived at the police station, however, another patrolman came over and the guard stopped talking to Mommy. They couldn't make the final agreement. The deal was off.

Inside the police station we were gathered into a large room. We joined a group of adults and children who had tried to escape the country the previous night. We all had to spend the night there, sleeping on the hay-covered floor. Mommy and Daddy lay side by side, and I laid my head on Mommy's tummy.

While it was freezing outside, it felt warmer inside, but only from the breathing of all the people. I cuddled up to Mommy; her warmth comforted me. We were surrounded by armed guards who looked at us with so much hatred that being cold was not even important.

~

Mother's recollections are vivid. She often wishes she could have forgotten some of it:

As soon as they finished taking our names and looking at our I.D's, I saw one of the guards pick up the telephone. They did not waste any time. The border patrol contacted the authorities in Budapest, and the officials there immediately confiscated our home and all of our belongings. All of our real estate, as well as business and personal belongings were seized. Gaining possession of our car, a rare item in Hungary in those days, along with our business and real estate holdings, made our capture another fine treasure for the Communist Party.

∿

As I listen to Mother who remembers so clearly, I realize that many of the incidents left an indelible mark in my mind as well.

Early the next morning, the guards banged on the door. They woke us up. They gave the grownups coffee, which looked like muddy water and a piece of stale bread, no butter, no jam. We children got a watery hot chocolate.

We were still hungry when the guards ordered us out. They led us to a waiting bus and announced that they were taking us to a larger police station in Szombathely, a two to three hour drive. We clutched our mothers' hands. The women and children were kept in a group by several guards, and the men were separated from us; their hands and feet chained together. I was so frightened. I had never seen handcuffs or chains before. I could not imagine what was going on. I started to cry at the sight of my Daddy. I had always spent a lot of time with him, and wherever he and I went, he was respected and admired. And now he looked sad and ashamed. I didn't know which was worse, the sight of him shackled to the other men, or the sound of them shuffling with the metal clanging. I was also afraid for Mommy and me. If they did that to Daddy what would they do to us? Mommy held my hand tight and talked in a soft voice to comfort me.

They made us get on a local bus. There were some village people sitting there already. They put the male prisoners on the bus first, then mothers with children. I sat in Mommy's lap in a seat across from Daddy. I couldn't take my eyes off him, but he didn't look at me. I kept crying, but Mommy's warm body made me feel safe. During the bus ride we were not given any food or drink. I was very hungry, but didn't say anything.

We happened to sit next to a woman who kept looking at Mommy and me with great sympathy. Mommy had a unique talent of being able to read people, and was able to connect with them even under these conditions. She noticed this woman's sympathetic expression, and began to talk to her. Mommy asked if she would do her a favor.

"Would you contact my mother-in-law in Budapest?"

Mommy explained to the woman that Grandma Riza was probably worried, waiting for our telephone call that we had safely crossed the border. She gave the woman Grandma's name, address, and telephone number and asked her to tell her what she saw, and that we would try to contact her after we arrived at the prison. The woman seemed to understand and promised she would do it. Mommy thanked her and prayed that she would.

We got off the bus in Szombathely. Mommy held my hand real tight. A moment later she squeezed even tighter and gasped.

"What is it?" I asked.

She shushed me. From the look on Mommy's face I knew something must be wrong. Mommy was shocked to see the woman she had talked to on the bus gave a big hello and a warm hug to a man dressed in uniform. She thought she had made things worse by asking for help from somebody who was possibly connected to the government. She had only intended the phone call to ease Grandma's worry, but was now frightened that she might have gotten Grandma into trouble as well.

Mother continued:

I deeply regretted having acted so foolishly. I realized that I should not have trusted a soul; I learned my lesson.

After our arrival in Szombathely, the authorities held a brief hearing at the police station. The room was sterile; walls were painted an ugly yellow-beige, with a large photo of Minister Rakosi and various propaganda slogans hanging on the walls.

"Viva Rakosi, Viva the Party!"

"Reach for Socialist Victory!"

There was a large filing cabinet against one wall, and a long, light-colored wooden table and chairs in front of it, on which sat several papers and a telephone. On another wall was a washbasin with a dirty towel hanging from it. The "judges" were two Communist officials who looked at us as traitors for wanting to leave the country. While they sat at the table we had to stand in front of them during the interrogation.

They simply asked, "Are you guilty or not?" But they didn't even listen. Our answers did not matter, because everybody who was caught and brought in was found guilty. Every member of my family was sentenced to various lengths of time in prison.

We had known several people who, not too long before our attempted escape, were also captured but released within a short time. So we also had hopes of being released soon. That didn't happen. Your grandfather, who was 57, was sentenced to seven months. Grandma, age 52, was sentenced to six, and Kato, my sister, to three months. Your father and I received the longest sentences: twelve months for him and eight months for me.

My sentence was the longest among the women, because I was the official owner of a large apartment building in Budapest, and considered to be the "wealthy one"—a crime in the eyes of the Communists.

When the verdict was announced, we were shocked to learn the length of our sentences. It was then that we realized what a mistake it was for so many members of one family to attempt to escape together. We were always a close-knit family, and when we made the decision to leave the country we did not want to leave anyone behind. We should have known that a large group would draw more attention and appear more contrived. We took our chances, but now paid the price.

During the hearing, I stood next to Mommy, gripping her hand so tight it hurt. I didn't understand what was going on but it felt serious. As the sentences were handed down, the women began to cry. Male guards appeared and handled the men, and female guards approached the women, one for each person. I didn't understand what was happening. I didn't dare talk, or even move. I looked around quietly. The guards held something silvery and shiny in their hands. I was scared, still clutching Mommy's hand. Suddenly, a female guard appeared from behind and pushed me away so she could place the handcuffs on my Mommy. I was horrified! I started to tremble and shout, "Mommy! Mommy!" She began to cry. I began to sob uncontrollably. The male guards started to yell, ordering the women to move to the side. In the commotion, another female guard grabbed me and quickly yanked me away from Mommy's side. She had clammy hands and smelled like that horse I sat near the day before. All I wanted to do was run away but I could not, she held me very tightly. Then she shoved me to the side toward the other children.

I started to scream. Before long, all the kids were howling. From all the pushing and shoving we screamed even louder. Suddenly we realized that we were not only snatched from our parents, but were pushed into another room with the door locked behind us. We were all petrified and became more terrified with every passing second. Why did they take me away from my Mommy and Daddy? The guards kept yelling at us to be quiet and stop crying, but we couldn't. I could only think of Mommy and Daddy. I wanted to be with them more than anything! All I could think of was, will I ever see them again?

CHAPTER 2
PRISON NURSERY

THE GUARDS DIDN'T WASTE ANY TIME. Almost immediately, they herded us from the police station room to the prison nursery, normally an orphanage. It was in the next building a few feet away. There were six of us new children, including cousin Kati and me. Twelve others were already there, all between the ages of three and eight. We had no idea where we were or what was going on. We were terrified, shaking, cold, and screaming. The other kids were silent; they just kept looking at us.

The image of Mommy and Daddy shackled and chained never left me. One of the guards tried to calm us by saying, "You'll see your parents soon." I didn't believe her. She was a stranger. She was the one who took me away from my parents and put me in this scary place.

It was bitterly cold. We were freezing and hungry and there was no one to comfort us. Just looking at the guards was frightening. The male guards at the orphanage were big and tall with mean expressions. When they spoke they sounded angry and smelled of food and cigarette smoke. The female guard who brought me in had sweaty palms. I wanted to get away to wash my hands.

The orphanage was one big room with bunk beds against the walls and low, rectangular tables with chairs in the middle. This is where the eighteen of us lived; we slept, ate, played, and survived in that one room.

The smell of food cooking in the nearby kitchen filled the air all day. To me it smelled awful; it upset my stomach and I was miserable. No matter how hungry I was, I had trouble eating anything. I never liked mushy food, and almost everything they served was mushy and disgusting. Breakfast was the only tolerable meal of the day: a watery hot chocolate and bread with lard. Lunch was almost always smelly and mushy; usually a tasteless soup with bread, or some kind of a stew with dumplings to make it thick. They always looked the same ugly brown; even the potatoes were dark and probably old. We had no green vegetables, and rarely ate meat. Once in a great while they served breaded veal, but they would always remind us that it was a "treat." It wasn't for me. It used to be my favorite food but not there. It didn't look appetizing. The yellow, uncooked look of it made me nauseous. I remembered the way my mother served it; crisp and reddish, and the potatoes were white and delicious. Cousin Kati wasn't so bothered by the food. She was younger than I and everything was new to her. Even if she didn't eat much, she ate most meals.

Because I often wouldn't eat, sometimes they would force me. They threatened me, saying that I would never see my parents again if I didn't eat all of my food. I was scared, but I still had a hard time eating. I always felt I was going to throw up. The evening meal was easier. We were served bread with lard, just like at breakfast. Sometimes in the morning we would have jam, and at night they would give us scallions or green peppers with it, the customary way in the countryside.

Bathing was another miserable experience. I was accustomed to having hot and cold running water in Budapest, and bathing three or four times a week. In the orphanage we had a bath once a week, and I wished we didn't have even that. There was just one tiny tub of water drawn for all eighteen of us, and no running water. They had to bring it in, boil it on a stove, and cool it with cold water. The water became dirtier and colder with each child. I didn't want to bathe in that ugly, smelly water. When I was climbing in the bathtub I had to look away and hold my nose. I didn't want to sit in it or get my face wet but they forced me. The soap was a pukey color; smelled like rotten egg and made me nauseous. It made me feel worse than not bathing at all. The ring inside the tub got darker with each child. Whenever I could, I tried to get to the front of the line. I dreamed I could somehow run away.

During the first day, a doctor examined the new kids. They claimed they needed to keep us healthy so we would not infect the other children. After our exam, they lined us up and stuck needles in our arms. They told us it was a vaccination, but instead of staying healthy, all of us got sick a few days later. Each one of us got a different illness from these injections. I developed chicken pox; cousin Kati got German measles. The others got various diseases, some more serious than others.

Every day we were taken back to the doctor's office to be examined. I was really afraid of the doctor after that first visit, and became more frightened every day. The doctor was a mean man; he ordered us around: stand here, lie down, open your mouth, turn around, go back to your room! Every morning when one of the female guards gathered us I was sobbing, didn't want to go, but nobody cared. The more I cried, the angrier and meaner the guard became. She would grab my hand, drag me, and spank me.

We were scared, lonely, and felt neglected. We cried a lot. Missed our parents terribly. When we were not abused, we were bored. There was very little to do to pass the time. There were only a few toys and some paper and colored pencils. We made up games, cut out paper dolls, made airplanes, which we threw into the air, or boats, which we floated in the washbasin. There was always a female guard watching us, looking mean and angry. She never played with us. We did no schoolwork, no writing or arithmetic. Some of the older children sat by themselves reading and writing. If I had fun at all, it didn't last long. Thoughts of my parents in chains and other sad memories always haunted me.

We hardly ever went outside because it was either too cold or raining. We were locked up inside for days and cried all the time. Sometimes they spanked us just for crying. We pleaded for our parents. But their answer was always the same:

"If you behave and do as you're told, they will come and get you soon."

CHAPTER 3

POLITICAL CHANGES

DRIVING HOME FROM MICHELLE'S the freeway traffic was bumper-to-bumper and took much longer than usual. After a few hours of playing with Nicole and the long ride, Mother was tired but still eager to talk about the past.

I am not a youngster, I don't know how much time I have left, but I want to make sure I tell you about the events that happened many years ago. I hope it will help you better explain to Kyle and his class how we were forced to live and managed to survive.

We didn't have enough time to hear everything while driving home. So we decided to have dinner together the next evening so she could continue. When I picked her up, she was excited but concerned that she might not recall everything that had happened so many years before. I sensed that this was the first time in the past fifty years that she had talked openly about her experiences during those dark days in Hungary. She didn't want to forget anything important; she even made some notes. I reassured her that any important dates she could not recall we could find on the Internet. She impressed me with her courage to relive all the details after so many years. As she spoke, her recollections rekindled unpleasant memories, but I believed that this process would also bring her a sense of closure. For me, learning so much gave me a deeper understanding for my mother's courage during the tremendous upheavals in my life, and increased my respect and admiration for her strength and tenacity. This became the guiding force in writing about it.

"Mother, Communism affected our lives so drastically but it didn't happen overnight. How did you recognize the signs of what was to come?"

The changes were slow and subtle at first, but by 1948 the communists won substantial political power. While we were thankful that the Soviet Union liberated us in 1945, three years later they turned the post-war good life into a severe, state-controlled domination. They changed laws, brought in new ones, and arrested people to silence the opponents. It began with all-day propaganda announcements on state-controlled radio stations and newspapers denouncing the capitalists' exploitation of the workers. Within weeks this gave way to the government illegally appropriating businesses, the process known as nationalization, and promising to give the workers more than they had before. Of course, this never happened. Eventually, everybody had to work for the government in one way or another and everyone made the same amount of money. Small business owners were forced to give up their ownership and location, and were forced to become simple workers in centralized government-controlled facilities known as collectives. The managers and supervisors were government appointed party members, sometimes without much

*previous experience. The authorities instituted addi-
tional daily propaganda sessions in factories where they
not only promoted the communist dogma and its virtues,
but threatened those who opposed the process. The
country changed from capitalism to a form of socialism.
Of course, we were all afraid to speak out. Vocal opponents were not only arrested, but often killed too.
However, those who declared themselves Communists
were given power and security for the future, and
promised great improvement in the quality of their lives.
Party membership became extremely significant, an
essential ingredient for a better life.*

"Was Dad ever a party member?" I asked.
"Never!" Mother replied.

*He refused, but a lot of Jews did join. Because of all
the atrocities the Nazis committed against them, and
with Russia liberating them, many Jews became loyal
party members. Considered enemies of the previous
regime, the Communist Party gladly accepted them. Dad
and I often discussed what it would mean to us to join
the party, but he felt he just could not do it. I felt the
same way, particularly because I was a property owner
myself, and considered a capitalist, which was contrary
to the party's guidelines. It was so contrary to his beliefs,
and he knew he would not be accepted. He was a businessman, in charge of his own destiny. This was not the
communist philosophy.*

*The Communists declared that the only people qual-
ified for leadership were those who didn't have a "bourgeois" background. Laborers, landless peasants, and
intellectuals who had been previously "exploited" by the*

rich were now trusted and groomed for higher positions. Former businessmen were not trusted either. Power was placed in the hands of inexperienced people whose only qualification was their loyalty to the Communist Party.

Remember Zsuzsi Benko? Mother asked. Her parents owned a large automobile accessory business which was nationalized, and her father was demoted to a low-level employee. Instead of running the business as before, his new government-appointed boss became his supervisor, giving him orders. Sanyi Benko was now forced to report to a man whom he previously would not have trusted.

Despite the Communists' promise of a classless society, a whole new class of people emerged. Interestingly, those who were appointed to high positions began imitating the behavior and lifestyles of the former upper class.

At the same time, life for the rest of us in Hungary was becoming more and more restricted and degrading. We were isolated and forcibly closed off from the West. We were not allowed to read books by Western authors, or listen to popular Western music, because it was considered decadent or "reactionary" (in their vernacular). We could not travel abroad, nor have any foreign money in our possession. Merely owning or even handling foreign currency was considered a serious crime. Art that did not depict the glory of Socialism was declared decadent and unacceptable, and anything that represented an all-Western lifestyle was forbidden.

"I know we didn't have a choice and learned to live within the limitations, but how did you adjust to such restrictions and constant fear? Now living in freedom in the United States, it's hard to believe that political changes could alter life so drastically."

We certainly didn't have much choice. We had to learn to live within those limits which were cruelly and forcefully imposed on us. Little by little, private enterprise ceased to exist, and opportunities dwindled for those who attempted to remain independent from the Party. I remember Robert's parents, Gizi and Laci Reyto, complaining that on his first attempt to get into dental school in 1952, Robert was refused because his father owned a small dental laboratory, thus he was considered an "exploiter," a person who didn't work in a collective. Laci tried to retain it as long as he could, but he realized that the only way Robert would have a chance was if he closed down his laboratory and joined a collective. Reluctantly he gave it up, hoping that this would enable Robert's admission. Nothing was for sure, but after waiting several months, and losing a whole year, he was accepted into dental school.

"That's unbelievable, Mom, because Laci had a tiny business with only one employee, but I guess it was still privately owned. How did Dad manage to hold onto his business?"

Your father had renewed his contacts in all the ministries and hoped this would provide him protection, or at least give him warning if trouble was brewing. These people worked in various capacities in government offices and were very loyal to Dad, but their positions were not secure. The political atmosphere was constantly changing, and we were always fearful it would be stopped.

We felt the pressure closing in on us. The first signif-
icant impact Communism had on our personal life was
when they closed your nursery school. The school's only
crime was that the curriculum was taught in English, and
its philosophy leaned toward Western thinking. This was
unthinkable and not permissible. When the school
closed—despite the risk, we arranged for a tutor to come
to the house to continue your English lessons secretly.
We prayed no one would find out and report us to the
authorities. You were only four years old but we had to
explain to you the danger and the importance of keeping
it secret.

"I remember that every time the teacher came you reminded
me to be quiet about it and not to tell anybody about learning
English."

Yes, I did. It's funny that you still remember. Mother
smiled. The 'single party' political monster was rapidly
growing and conditions were deteriorating daily, partic-
ularly for those with bourgeois background. We were
automatically considered to be in conflict with the
regime and not to be trusted. Your father was a manu-
facturer and labeled an "exploiter," so we were placed in
that anti-regime category, and subsequently our lives
became unstable and uncertain. We never knew when
and what the next restriction or decision would be, or
who would be affected. The number of your father's con-
tacts dwindled, and those few who remained were no
longer in a position to help. We soon became as vulner-
able as everyone else.
We still lived in our beautiful home, but we knew it
was only a matter of time before some envious person in

*power might want it for himself. We kept saying, "We
cannot be careful enough, we must watch every word we
say, and more importantly, watch who we talk to.
Congregating illegally, speaking to the wrong person, or
saying the wrong thing was a serious crime, as serious as
receiving communications from the West, or listening to
Radio Free Europe. People were arrested and interrogated without valid cause. We had to be particularly
careful because my sister, Ica, and brother, Imre, had
managed to escape to Austria earlier in June 1949, when
the borders were more open. They were now living in
Vienna. Having relatives in the West automatically
placed suspicion on us. We had to communicate with
them through a code language, which was very risky. We
feared our conversations would be intercepted. People
were being arrested for their political views or for having
an opinion about anything that was different from the
official line. They didn't need valid reasons.*

*So many people were unhappy and fearful—they
wanted to leave the country, but it was impossible to
obtain passports legally. Even applying for one put them
in jeopardy and placed them on the 'undesirables' list.
Those who desperately wanted to leave the country tried
to do it illegally, but an elaborate spy network prevented
many people from escaping, and they were arrested—or
worse. Some wound up in prisons, and others were killed
in the process.*

"When did you and Dad know it was time to leave? Why
didn't you leave when Ica and Imre did?"

*There is no simple answer. Looking back, we were
simply stupid.*

Mother keeps shaking her head.

Our name and business were very prominent, we had to be extremely careful. We had to think through every detail. Your father came up with a plan; he arranged for our help to be away from Budapest during the last few days before our escape, send money out to Switzerland, and make final arrangements with Ica and Imre to help us with the border crossing. They had to make contact with the person who helped them during their escape a few months earlier. Dad also wanted to complete an export shipment in the hopes that when he was living in the West he could reconnect with that source.

Looking back, it was unreal that we even took the chance, because by then it was more dangerous and we were risking our lives. Unfortunately, our carefully devised plan didn't work.

CHAPTER 4
IMPRISONMENT

WE LEFT THE DINNER TABLE. I decided to clean up the kitchen later. Mother, with her notes in hand, sat down on the living room sofa. Her thoughts focused as she reviewed her notes. I sat down next to her, and after a deep sigh, she continued—beginning with the misery we endured after our arrest for the attempted escape.

> I was horrified when I realized my Zsuzsi, my only child, was kidnapped from me. Worst of all, I was totally helpless to find you and ease your pain. I burst out crying. My demands to know about your whereabouts were cruelly dismissed.
>
> "They are in goods hands," the guards said gleefully. Some even laughed.
>
> After they took you and the other children away, they pushed us adults into an empty room next to where we had been and locked the doors. We were kept there all day; miserable, angry, frustrated, scared. We sat there ... staring at the wall and sometimes yelling out uncontrollably. When night came they unlocked the door and

forced us to walk surrounded by the guards, to the AVH prison facility, a short distance away. This 'transfer' took place at night to avoid being seen by the public. The AVH was the State Secret Police, the branch of the government that everybody feared most.

Over one-thousand women and fifteen-hundred men were held separately at that small prison facility for ten days. Resting or sleeping was out of the question because we were so cramped that people were forced to sit or lie on the floor so close to one another that it was difficult even to breathe. There were some benches, but no beds in the cells. The interrogations went on all day and all night. We got little food, a single cup of coffee in the morning, and at night another cup of coffee with some bread or a watery soup. We were starving, exhausted, terrified...and above all humiliated.

Inside the facility someone had written on the wall names of attorneys who might be able to help us get released. At that time some attorneys were still allowed to continue private practice, but soon after they were all forced to become employees of the State. I didn't know when I would see your father, or if I would ever see him again! I knew I had to handle this myself, and hoped that the authorities would respond more mercifully to a mother. There was only one telephone for all the prisoners to use. It took hours before it was my turn. As soon as I was able, I called and hired one of the attorneys. He was aware of what was going on, and became my only connection to the outside world.

For ten days Dad and I had no idea where you were, or what had happened to you. We were worried sick. Through this attorney, Geza, thankfully I was able to

learn of your whereabouts. The attorney also appealed
both Dad's and my sentences, although it was doubtful
that we would ever receive a chance for a new hearing.
But, most importantly, the attorney contacted Edith
Helfer, our friend from Budapest, who was all too famil-
iar with the circumstances in Szombathely. A few months
earlier she had spent some time in the same prison for
the same crime. The Helfers were fortunate. The laws
were less rigid at that time and they were released after
only a brief imprisonment.

Edith needed little explanation after the attorney's
call, and immediately departed for Szombathely. As soon
as Edith arrived, she arranged for daily kosher food, the
only outside food that could be brought into the prison
at the time. Thanks to her help, we ate our first true meal
after many days of near starvation. And my biggest

Tommy Helfer and I, Fall 1948

prayer had been answered! She had firsthand informa-
tion about where all the children were being kept. Her
son, Tommy, had also been taken away when she and her
husband were arrested. Eventually they found him at the

same orphanage. Hearing this news was the greatest relief to our hearts, after ten long days of constant anguish and sorrow.

While in Szombathely, Edith managed to make special arrangements to take you and cousin Kati out of the orphanage and back to Budapest. But before they released you, the guards told her that you could not leave until you had fully recuperated from your illness, an illness they refused to explain. Edith had to leave you there for six more weeks. Finally, six weeks later she returned to take you and Kati to her home. Once in Budapest, Kati stayed with a family friend until her mother, my sister Kato, was released from prison, and you stayed with Edith for a short time.

"I'll never forget the moment when I saw Edith. I burst into tears and ran to hug her. So many years later, I now find out that she had come for me a few weeks earlier while I was sick. I never knew that until now. I didn't see her the first time. We were not allowed to leave our room, never saw anybody but the guards.

"The first question I asked her was about you and Dad. She reassured me that you were all right, and her I believed. I wanted love and attention so badly that I constantly sat in Edith's lap. I didn't leave her side. After a couple of days, I calmed down a bit, and slowly became my old self again. But I became so attached to her that she felt she was unable to give enough attention to her own two children. She knew our relatives, Uncle Pista, Dad's brother, and his wife, Manci, lived near Budapest, so she contacted them to make arrangements for me to stay there. I wished I could have stayed with Edith. I felt safe with her; she 'saved me!' She explained to me that their home was not big enough. I couldn't understand it; I kept thinking that she had rescued me, but suddenly she was taking me somewhere else."

While you were living with Manci and Pista, prison life took its toll on Dad and I. Besides the horrible conditions, it had a tremendous psychological effect on us. The future looked bleak and hopeless because we were told nothing, we knew nothing. The only thing we knew was uncertainty. A great, dark cloud now hung over us personally, and as we found out later, the whole country.

More people tried to escape. The prison was full, but they continued bringing in more people who were captured. To control the overcrowding, the authorities decided to move about five hundred prisoners to another facility far away, at the extreme eastern border in a town called Satoraljaujhely. Yet another adversity to face. Would our family stay together or be separated? Fortunately, they kept us together. Your father, my parents, and my sister, Kato, were in the first group to be transported out by train.

They herded us into freight cars for a journey that took a full day. This would have been difficult under normal circumstances, but that day there was a heavy blizzard and the snow fell thick and cold. The men and women were separated again and forbidden to talk to each other. The men were shackled and chained together as before, and the noise of the chains clanking, together with the sound of the train, was grating and jarring. Once we got settled on the train, we were all silent; it was almost eerie. We were freezing, uncomfortable, and physically and mentally exhausted. Even if we could have, we didn't want to talk. We didn't know where we were going or what the future held for us. We were never told anything.

When we finally arrived in Satoraljaujhely, they made us walk a couple of miles from the train station to the prison. Wet and freezing from the heavy snowfall and without food all day, we were near collapse. They were not prepared for us. The prison facility was old and dilapidated, with no heat or blankets for the prisoners. If this was our fate, we now had even greater fears of what had happened to you.

The guards jammed as many people into the small cells as possible. At least our body heat helped to keep us warm. Sleeping here, too, was out of the question. Again, no beds or bunks, and new inmates arrived in the dead of night—waking the few who had escaped in sleep. In time they gave us some food. Hunger made us too weak to withstand the cold. We asked the guards if we could contact our families at home to have them send blankets. Surprisingly, permission was granted and in a week or two, blankets and coats arrived like angels from heaven.

With about twenty women in our cell there was never a moment of privacy. The guards were vigilant in watching our every move, especially when we had a visitor. Everyone was suspected of smuggling in items like cigarettes. Even though the prison staff knew your grandmother, Kato, and I never had visitors; they still harassed us. Time passed very slowly. Some prisoners made playing cards out of paper, but even that was considered a crime, and they destroyed them. They didn't allow us any diversion, repeatedly told us that we were being punished, and were supposed to suffer.

We had absolutely no contact with the outside world. The days dragged by very slowly. At times, some of the women became delirious or hysterical from staring at the walls. I began to fear that I too might lose my mind. One day, a guard asked if any of us knew how to embroider. I figured I had nothing to lose, so I said 'yes,' and they immediately put me to work. I had to embroider slogans on small Hungarian flags that were given to certain factory workers to keep at their workstations as an incentive to increase productivity. This job put me in a privileged position. The lights were turned off at 8 p.m. in the cells, but I was allowed to use an office to continue working as long as I wanted. This was a welcome diversion, helping to pass the time more quickly.

Your father and I saw each other only once a week during religious services which were still allowed at that time. Other than those brief periods, we could never speak to one another during our incarceration. Jewish inmates gathered on Saturday and we had a visiting rabbi for a service, while the Christians had their service on Sunday. The rabbi, as well as the priest, always gave a little pep talk, but they had to be careful what they said, because everything was scrutinized. They risked their lives by helping us a little. In their cautious ways they were able to pass along some information from the outside. The best part of those get-togethers was the opportunity to exchange a few words with people in the other cells.

Unfortunately, the services didn't last throughout our imprisonment because the Communists were espousing atheism, and by April 1950, all public religious practices were banned in Hungary. Without the clergy's *visits, we were once again cut off from the outside world and our confinement seemed soul destroying and interminable.*

As hopeless as it seemed, we still prayed that we would be granted a hearing to reduce our sentences. We were stunned when three months later the appeal had been granted, but we would have to travel to Gyor, a town far away in the Western part of the country, the same as we were before. While we dreaded the horrendous train ride back to the opposite end of Hungary, we would do anything for a chance to possibly shorten our sentences.

Before we left the prison, we were handcuffed to individual guards, a female for me and a male guard for your father. The long journey began in the morning and lasted all day and night with a transfer in Budapest. The next morning we arrived in Gyor, and were immediately taken to the courtroom for the hearing. Your father's case was heard first. Instead of reducing his sentence— they raised it from 12 to 18 months, without explanation! The same was true for every prisoner whose case was heard that day. I assumed my fate would be the same.

While waiting my turn, I noticed a sign: "A child is the greatest value! For girls to bear children is an honor, and for women it is an obligation!" I was thrilled to discover this. Perhaps being a mother separated from her child would appeal to their sense of compassion.

As I stood before these cold, heartless officials I knew they cared nothing for me, or my child. Following their controlled doctrine was everything. To their surprise, I quoted the slogan at the beginning of my hearing, and then asked them to release me or reduce my sen-

tence. Their reply was a flat "no." But they decided to be 'generous' and leave my sentence at the original eight months. This was a significant gesture of goodwill considering that everybody else's sentence had been increased.

As soon as they finished with us, they wasted no time. The guards took us back to the train station for the long journey back to prison. It was the same freezing weather and uncomfortable conditions, sitting for so long handcuffed and chained to our separate guards.

When we got back, we knew we had no other choice; we would have to serve out our sentences. We gritted our teeth and kept our mouths shut because we knew that each day brought us closer to freedom. The days went by very slowly and conditions somehow got even worse. Yet, each day we were getting more worn out, losing weight from near starvation. As winter turned to spring and the weather got a little milder, we were forced to give up our warm coats. We lost even that tiny comfort.

In time, as the prisoners' sentences were up, they were released one by one. When my turn finally came, I thought my miserable ordeal was almost over. I was so wrong. In the eyes of the regime, I was still an outcast, a criminal until I got back to my original place of capture. I was still a prisoner until my actual release. There was still more condemnation and punishment...

Two guards escorted me on the arduous train ride from Satoraljaujhely back to Szombathely, from one end of the country to the other. This time it took two full days and an overnight stay in a Budapest prison. The cell they put me in was filled with prostitutes and disgusting bugs crawled everywhere. I barely survived the night. It seemed the torture would never end. Then, when we *finally arrived at the same AVH office in Szombathely where we were originally sentenced, the agony continued. The process to my freedom moved painfully slowly, forcing me to stay two more days. The prison conditions were the same deplorable ones as in the previous year. The memories of that miserable experience filled my head like thick, black smoke. I felt numb and weak. The only thing that kept me going was the thought of being reunited with you in Budapest.*

During our prison days my family managed to get some money to us in case we needed to pay for dental treatment. There was some left in my name and the officials released it to me when I left Satoraljaujhely. I bought the train ticket to Budapest with it. Now after so many months of confinement—here I stood gripping the ticket in my hand. Before boarding, I called Pista and Manci to tell them of my release and asked them to bring you to Budapest. We tried to time our arrivals simultaneously at Grandma and Grandpa's apartment.

I cried when I got on the train. How different I felt, a human being for a change. At long last I was free!

CHAPTER 5
REUNITED

AUNTIE MANCI AND UNCLE PISTA lived in Balassagyarmat, a country town about three hours north of Budapest. They had a lovely home, and on one of our visits there, I remember going into a pretty room in their apartment, which was to have been the baby's room after Manci gave birth. But Manci had lost her daughter in Auschwitz during the war, and they never changed the room. She always wondered how it would be if her daughter had survived. She never bore another child, and when I asked her, she simply said she couldn't have children. They loved the idea of having me stay with them for a while. I think I brought a bit of sunshine into their lives.

Uncle Pista owned the main hardware-sundry store in town and they lived comfortably in a spacious apartment. I had my own room, which looked a little bit like my room in Budapest. It was already furnished for a child with a bed, a small table and chairs, and a rocking horse. There were lots of stuffed animals and colorful animal pictures on the walls. Manci cooked a lot; she wanted to make sure I was well fed and healthy when my parents returned. I could smell her cooking all the time. While the smell was different than at the orphanage, it still reminded

Manci, Pista and Susanne—a few years later

me of it and didn't agree with me. I wasn't a big eater, didn't eat many things, and any food smell made me nauseous.

A month later, on March 13th, I turned six and they wanted to make it special for me. They invited their friends and a few children for me to play with. The rest of the time there were few children around, only Manci's niece who was a year younger than I. Three mornings a week I went to a preschool, until the end of the school year in early June. The rest of the time I was usually by myself, sad and lonesome for Mommy and Daddy. Manci and Pista didn't know what to do with me; nothing seemed to console me. Even going to the park didn't make me happy. I would be on the swing, and suddenly I'd burst out crying. I kept asking for my Mommy and Daddy. The separation was a long time, and I didn't understand when Manci said, "Mommy will be back in three months." I had no concept of time. It just seemed terribly long.

They were very strict, making certain I went to bed at seventhirty every night. I had to practice my writing and arithmetic tables every day. But no matter how well I did it was never good enough. They were never satisfied. They constantly reminded me

Above: Photo postcard sent to
my parents in prison, Feb. 1950
Below: back of postcard,
marked "HOLD"

to use good manners and proper behavior. They didn't have children, so they did everything they thought parents should do, and thought Mommy and Daddy did. They wanted to dress me like Mommy did. They even had a sailor-collar dress made for me just like the ones I used to wear. They had professional photographs taken of me that they sent to Mommy and Daddy in prison, hoping that they would received them. Manci and Pista tried their best and meant only good for

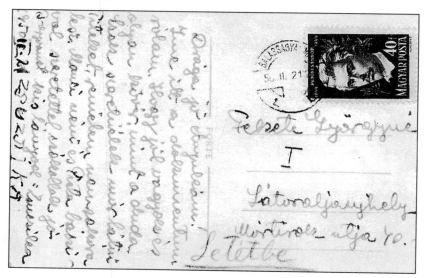

me, but I was always longing for my parents; wishing I could be with them.

Manci and Pista tried to console me, but adjusting after the orphanage was difficult. Manci knew I loved to help set the table so she often let me do it. They used similar china and the same silverware and water glasses my parents had. It reminded me of our home. At first I was excited to sit down at the beautifully set table in the kitchen, but after a few days I wished I didn't have to. Eating was a daily battle.

Everything was unfamiliar to me and they didn't understand it. She cooked special foods but I didn't like them and couldn't eat them. I had developed a lot of dislikes at the orphanage which they didn't understand, and they were very intolerant of my eating habits. Balassagyarmat was in the "country," and people ate heavier, different foods than in the city. While Mommy and Daddy used to make me taste new things, they always let me decide whether or not to eat them. Manci and Pista gave me no choice.

They ate lots of cheeses, which were unfamiliar to me. One of them was a soft cheese that Pista spread on bread or sliced apple. He loved it and wanted me to enjoy it, but it smelled so strong, I had to hold my nose just to be near it. He couldn't understand why I didn't like it. Manci often prepared foods that made me sick to my stomach, like chicken with the skin left on. I had never eaten it like that before; it looked gross to me. I would resist and they would become angry. Lunch was the main meal of the day and was the worst. Evening meals were easier because they were lighter, and included more familiar foods, such as cold cuts, which I liked.

Each meal became a tug of war, and I always lost. They forced me to eat every morsel. The plate always had to be left clean. They often yelled at me, looking angry and mean. Almost every meal I would be slapped or end up with a spanking, either because I had not wanted the food, or because I didn't eat it all. They did not understand that I couldn't eat their way; and they considered it misbehaving. At the end of most meals, I would vomit, and then they punished me. I was sent to my room and often cried myself to sleep.

Many nights I would wake up screaming, "Mommy, Mommy." At first Manci would come in to comfort me and I'd go back to sleep. But these nightmares were almost every night, so after a while they ignored it. I felt sad and alone, but I couldn't complain to anyone. I had no choice but to wait for my parents to return from prison. At times I didn't even believe that they would ever return. The days went by very slowly.

Then came the middle of August 1950. I was told that I'd be seeing Mommy soon. I couldn't wait for the day to come. I had not seen my parents for eight months. It was a long time for an adult, but it was an eternity for me. On August 18th, 1950, Pista, Manci, and I took the train to Budapest to meet Mommy at my grandparents' apartment. Mommy answered the door when I rang the bell. I burst into tears. After hugs and kisses, Mommy and I cried and laughed at the same time. I clung to her, and didn't want to leave her side for any reason! She made me hug and kiss my grandparents, Auntie Kato, and Cousin Kati. I quickly did, but then ran back to sit in her lap. I hugged her and couldn't stop crying. All I cared about was having my Mommy back. There were so many things to tell her, I didn't know where to begin. I also had a lot of questions. Where had she been? What did she do? Where was Daddy? I couldn't forget seeing him taken away in shackles. Did the handcuffs and shackles hurt him? How long did he have to have them on? I wished he could be with us. I also wanted to know what was happening to Kato and Kati and what my grandparents were doing during that time. As Mommy tried to answer my questions, comfort, and reassure me, I clung to her skirt—I just couldn't get enough of her.

Manci and Pista left soon after. They took a train back to Balassagyarmat. I could hardly wait to tell Mommy about living with them.

When I stopped sobbing, I told her everything. I felt so relieved. I knew that all the abuse would be over. Mommy promised to cook me all the things I liked. I knew that everything would be better now that we were together.

We sat and told stories for hours. She wanted to know all about the prison nursery; what we did, what we ate, and what they did to us. She also wanted to hear all the details about Edith Helfer who brought us back to Budapest. Then I asked her about Daddy and living in prison.

Dad and I mainly talked about you and dreamed of the moment when the three of us would be together again. He coped with the hardships of prison life a bit better than I. You know he always handled difficulties easier and he's always been stronger than I. Despite this, he was anxious to return to us. I didn't want to tell you so much about the ugly days in prison; I preferred to focus on the thrill of our being together.

I'll never forget the night of our reunion: it was getting late, but you didn't want to go to sleep. To tell you the truth, I felt the same way; I just wanted to be with you. I was praying for the end of my nightmares. I could hardly believe our ordeal was over. It took a while for it to sink in. Eight months was such a long time to be separated, especially because we had no contact at all. I was relieved to find you in good health and quite a bit taller. But when you told me about everything that you had to endure at Manci and Pista, my feelings and gratitude toward them soured. I do believe though, that Manci and Pista were genuinely trying to do their best for you—but remember, they had no children of their own. They wanted to make sure that when we returned you would be a robust, healthy child. They probably associated thin children with the deprivation of the war years.

I safely tucked away in the back of my mind the ugly memories of our separation and your stay with Pista and Manci. Now that it was over, I kept my mind on the future. We rarely talked about that period, though there were a couple of constant reminders, which we learned to live with. The most important one had become a life-long struggle to protect your stomach from problems. You had to learn to eat carefully and avoid certain foods. The other, I will never forget: the battles I faced whenever I had to take you to see a doctor.

The first major incident happened when I took you for custom-fitted arch supports. It was a cold December day. After entering the street-front store, I removed your socks and shoes so they could make the plaster of Paris mold of your feet. When the technician appeared in his white coat you jumped up, burst out crying, and ran out of the store without shoes or a coat. I panicked because it was cold and at that moment I couldn't imagine why you had done that. As soon as I was able to catch you, you were still sobbing, but tried to explain that you were scared because you thought the man in the white coat was going to do the same to you as did the doctor in the orphanage. That's when I became aware of your great fear. After this I tried different strategies, but none were successful and it was always a real struggle to get you medical care. You would burst out crying the minute you realized where we were going, and you got even worse when the doctor appeared in his white coat. Most of the time you managed your fears, but when certain issues surfaced, the agony of those days always came back to haunt us.

Your Daddy and I were so happy to leave prison, but as we tried to settle down, we didn't regain our 'freedom' as we had expected. Again we had to start all over. Everything we owned had been confiscated; we had no place to live, no business, or income. We had to eat, but from what? And you had to go to school, but where? Your father's mother lived alone in a lovely apartment behind the beautiful State Opera House and I asked her if we could stay with her until we found a place. To our surprise, she refused to help. She feared for her own life, and as bad off as we were, we understood. Sheltering a dissident, someone who had attempted to escape from the country, could jeopardize one's life, even if they were family. We asked many people to help but they all refused. I found myself in a real dilemma and didn't know whom to turn to.

I was desperate. Then Grandma's friend and neighbor, Nellie, offered her home, but only for a few days. I was so grateful even for that. I assured her that we would keep very quiet and draw no attention. Once we moved in, we kept our comings and goings to the bare minimum to avoid the attention and curiosity of other tenants. Nellie saw that we kept to our promise and was kind enough to let us stay longer.

I truly appreciated her kindness and told her how much it meant to us to have people like her and the officer's wife, who cared. I related to her my first conversation with grandma Riza after my release from prison, when I asked her whether anyone had contacted her after our capture at the border. Grandma said that a soft-spoken woman had called and related the story to her. Even after so many years, I am thankful to that woman, who acted apparently without her husband's knowledge, potentially risking her own life and safety for trying to help us. Fortunately, my fears of what I had done were proven wrong.

Respecting Nellie's wishes was extremely important, but living there was very difficult. Although no longer a prisoner, I felt like one. All the fear and restrictions we had to comply with were destroying us from the inside. In desperation, I contacted Karoly, Kato's former husband, who was an attorney, and asked him to find a way to get back the money left in our bank account prior to our ill-fated escape attempt. Although there was a substantial amount, prior to our leaving we wanted to avoid drawing attention to our activities, and didn't withdraw very much. Of course it was confiscated. But before we left, we also stashed a sizable amount of money with a friend, but until I legalized it, I could not use it. All of our assets were frozen, so according to government records we could not have had any money.

Because we had committed a crime against the regime, the government legally confiscated all of our property and getting anything back was a long shot. The only possible way to get anything back was to have your father acquitted of all charges.

Karoly and I formulated a plan to twist the facts in an attempt to prove your father's innocence. We presented the case to a judge in Gyor, arguing that it was I who had planned and pushed the family to escape—not Daddy. "He would not think of leaving behind his elderly mother, who was close to 100 years of age!" I *told them. In reality, it was he who had wanted to leave, knowing that his brother, Pista, was staying to look after their aging mother.*

We knew it would take time before our case went to court, but in the meantime I had to find a more immediate solution to our money problems. I also had to solve your school situation, as this was September 1950, and you were to enter first grade. Without having the money legally, we were not in a position to purchase an apartment.

Our dear friend returned our money to us as promised, but in those days, solving one problem often produced another. I had to make the money appear legal before I could actually spend it. Remember, we were not supposed to have any money. I followed Karoly's plan, and advertised in the newspaper to sell many valuables. But when people called wanting to see an item, I told them that it was already sold. I worked feverishly to legalize the money, and get us a home of our own, and perhaps finally feel 'free.' Once I found the apartment, I could register you for school.

At the end of September 1950, I managed to find and purchase a small apartment, which was actually half of a large one divided in two. This was very common in those days. Dividing and selling half of their apartments allowed people to supplement their meager state salaries, but more importantly it helped to relieve the housing shortage. Politically it was also wise to support the Communists doctrine that frowned upon the bourgeois lifestyle, a large home, and the success and wealth amassed by a single family or individual. Our apartment was in Furst Sandor Street 9, not too far from the Sziget

Street Elementary School, close to where we used to live and familiar to me.

The rebuilding of the apartment took several weeks because it needed a new kitchen and bathroom. Once it was ready, I had to furnish it. We had nothing, only a few decorative items. We were hoping to get back some of the furniture from our previous apartment, so I contacted the former custodian and asked for her assistance. Not surprisingly, the answer was 'no.'

A short time later your father befriended a man who worked at the office of the Interior Ministry, and through him we were able to get information contained in our personal file. There was a notation that the Interior Ministry had warned the custodian that if she dared contact them again on our behalf, she would be placed on the list of undesirables and her name would also be placed on the deportation list. Naturally, she was frightened and didn't even want to have any contact with us.

Now we had a small apartment but no furniture. Buying furniture was not an easy task in communist Hungary. Most manufacturing firms were nationalized, or had gone out of business. There were, however, several so-called "National Antique Shops" in Budapest, where all the property previously confiscated from dissidents were sold to line the Communists' pockets. As we walked into one of these shops near our home, we were shocked to find our old furniture for sale! It was painful to have had them stolen in the first place, and now more painful and humiliating to have to purchase them back from the government. And yet, we bought some of these pieces for they offered a glimmer of light from the good *old days, and a sense of home for the future. We were grateful to have these pieces, although many were damaged, just like our lives.*

After this experience we were curious about what could have happened to the rest of our belongings. I found out that Bela Biszku, a very important man, now lived in our confiscated apartment. He had moved in very soon after our unsuccessful escape attempt and kept whatever he wanted. He was the head of the AVH, the Hungarian equivalent of the Russian KGB. Biszku was the country's second-in-command from 1948 to the early 1980's. While Prime Ministers changed often during that period, Biszku always retained a powerful position. He was head of the Communist Party, and then became head of the AVH. From 1962 to 1978, he was secretary of the Central Committee of the Hungarian Socialist Workers Party. In our hearts, we didn't wish him well.

We moved into our new apartment in late November 1950. It was exciting to start a new life in our own new home, but I kept thinking of your father and praying for his safe return. I know you did, too. This time our prayers were answered.

Despite the odds, the plan to clear Daddy's name worked; the judge proved most understanding. We discovered that this was his last case prior to retirement—a blessing for us, at last. Whether he believed our story or not, he acquitted your father. It was truly unbelievable.

The news was doubly exciting because he was not only acquitted but would be released immediately. He didn't even have to go through the messy procedures before his release, like I did. He was freed directly from prison and arrived back in Budapest that same evening, having served only 12 of his 18 months. I'll never forget the wet, cold December day it was, and by the time he arrived it was dark, but our excitement could have lit up the sky! He arrived home December 31, 1950. When the doorbell rang, you and I ran to open the door. The minute you saw Dad you jumped into his lap. He was weak and needed to sit down, but you didn't want to let go. You held onto his hand as you sat in his lap. We just sat, talked, hugged, and kissed.

Finally, after what seemed like an eternity, our little family was together again. Now that Daddy was back we could begin to live a normal life again. For so long, we had wondered if each of us would live or die, and now, thank God, that was behind us.

Life was now our most precious possession, but amazingly, a few items that held great sentimental value were returned to us by our former employees, who had bravely rescued them. Auntie Rosa, as you endearingly called her, and Bela were more like family, and were so happy to return them to us. Among the items were a silver flatware set and a miniature silver tea service, both of which we carried with us everywhere, and to this day remain among our most valued possessions. There were several other items, as well as a crystal vase, which had been given as a very special gift on our wedding day. Each piece has special meaning, particularly since we had risked our personal safety to carry them, and they have since traveled the globe with us. A photograph album was returned as well, and we still consider that to be "the most valuable treasure ever found."

I missed my Daddy so much while he was away. After his return, I spent as much time with him as possible. We loved to go to the Budapest Puppet Theater, or walk and window shop, and I always held his hand real tight. Sometimes I was afraid to let go.

"This is the best," Daddy would say to me, and squeezed my hand even harder. "I hope you will be my little girl for a long time."

I clung onto him like I did with Mommy when she returned from prison. On our walks, we would stop to sit and rest and enjoy my favorite ice cream, or hot chocolate and a piece of delicious cake. One of my favorites was kugelhof, a coffee cake baked in a pretty shape and filled with cocoa and raisins. Other times, I would eat gooey creamy chocolate cakes topped with whipped cream. We loved walking and eating together. It felt like those fun afternoons we had spent together before all the terrible things happened. I could hardly wait for the moment when we would stop at one of the chocolate shops and he bought me my favorite dark chocolate candy.

I didn't want these walks to end, but a week later I had an accident on the ice at the rink near our apartment. A big man knocked me down; I broke my leg and these special walks had to end. At first it was difficult to move around with the cast on, but after a few days I got used to it. I got around by sitting and sliding on the floor. I stayed home from school for the first three weeks. Mommy brought home the school assignments and helped me with them. I had a lot of time, so she also taught me to knit, crochet, and embroider. After three weeks the doctor put on a new walking cast and I was able to hobble around. I could go back to school, but in the afternoons I had to stay at home. Friends came over to play. Four weeks later the cast was removed and I did special exercises. Daddy was the athlete in the family, so I did them with him. I did different activities with Mommy and Daddy, and they were all special. I wanted to be with them all the time. I prayed that we would never again be separated.

Daddy and I had to recreate our lives. Again he established himself as an indispensable person in the fire safety industry. He became an important figure, recognized by the government, and was able to operate his small business within the parameters of the regime. I, on the other hand, worked in a collective, which manufactured small leather goods. Collectives were businesses that were nationalized and became government-run workplaces. Daddy and I could have worked together, because I was also certificated in fire prevention, but he decided it was safer ' politically' to work apart.

In Hungary, children attended nursery school or preschool, and from there entered first grade. Starting in September 1950, you attended Sziget Street Elementary School located a few blocks from our apartment. You loved school, loved to learn, and always loved spending time with other children.

By now it was the spring of 1951, and we were enjoying what felt like a normal life again. Of course 'normal' was not the same as before. Our lives were seriously governed and changed by the Communist philosophy. There were so many limitations and restrictions, and always the constant surveillance, but at least we were together and determined to make the best of it.

But it was only a mirage; it didn't last very long. Our period of relative ease lasted only five months, from January to May of 1951. You were seven years old.

CHAPTER 6
MY FATHER

IN 1993 MY DAD WAS EIGHTY-SIX and in failing health. He was five foot three, with medium brown hair and a light complexion. Despite his height and medium build, his presence was always felt upon entering a room. He always exuded warmth and charisma.

He valued family life, and deeply loved his own. He adored children, but had only one daughter—me. I often heard my parents say they wished they had had another child, especially since Dad always wanted a son. But due to circumstances there was never a right time.

When my daughter, Michelle, and Steve announced their engagement in March 1993, Steve's son, Kyle, was six years old.

Kyle lived with his mother, but on the weekends when he was with Steve they often visited my parents. During the last few months prior to his death in 1994, Dad relished these moments with Kyle, the first boy in the family. During that short time they developed a loving relationship, and Kyle's memories of him are warm and tender. Dad's dreams of having a boy were answered when Kyle joined our family.

After Dad died, Kyle would ask about him, although some of his questions I could not answer. I realized then that I didn't know much about Dad's life as a young man. When I asked Mother, she was happy to talk about him; after all they had been married for fifty-three years!

Mother and I are sipping cappuccinos in an Italian restaurant on a sunny afternoon in August 2001. The more Mother tells me, the more questions I seem to have.

Your father and I were very different personalities. I admired his positive attitude, which was one of his greatest assets. I am so glad that much of that rubbed off on you. I remember him saying often, "The pessimist sees a problem in every opportunity, while the optimist sees an opportunity in every problem." He always teased me, and whenever I said 'yes' to something, he was surprised. He used to say, "I'm so glad, I expected to hear a 'no.'"

After surviving World War II, and before our attempted escape in 1949, your father started his own business again and built a very successful enterprise. During this period we had a wonderful life. But the time Dad and I had spent in prison drastically altered our security, and by then we were also living in very difficult political times. We had to begin all over again. He was determined to succeed, but had to adjust his business skills to conform to the rules and regulations of the new regime. By that time, private business ownership was out of the question, and since the Communists were in full force, everybody had to work in collectives.

Although your father was a well-known businessman and a renowned person in his field, he would have become just another worker for the State. But through his connections, the Ministry of Interior issued a certifi-

cate stating that his professional experience and expertise were indispensable, and his employment by the government was essential to the well-being of the country.
They recognized that fire prevention was vital in all areas
of the workplace, and the newly appointed managers
had very little knowledge on the subject. They needed an
expert to achieve their goal. As a result, both he and I
became state certified "Fire Fighting Equipment
Specialists." With this we could train others in the handling, use, and servicing of all fire-fighting equipment.

Your father became responsible for fire prevention
and training in the entire city of Budapest. The city officials wanted to insure that all equipment was opera-
tional, and that sufficient people were trained to use and
repair it.

While Dad was technically an employee of the State-
run collective, he had a lot of authority, and with this
came autonomy and prestige. The government soon realized that fires and related damages were reduced by a
large percentage due to his expertise and hard work.

Because of his value and essential accomplishments,
Dad was allowed to set up a small private enterprise to
service the Hungarian film industry. This was most
unusual in 1951. Since films were of great value to the
regime as propaganda, the government encouraged and
promoted the industry. In the 50's, motion pictures were
filmed on celluloid, a highly flammable material, and
using it, and especially storing it, required extreme care.
Your father wisely made himself an indispensable spe-
cialist who serviced all the fire-fighting equipment in the
film studios, and supervised its use and handling. In
short, he became the advisor to the film industry for all
their fire fighting needs.

Mom and Dad worked together so she was proud of their accomplishments and familiar with the professional aspects of their lives. In the midst of our conversation, Mother tells me that Dad had written a short diary about his early years prior to their marriage in 1941, ending with details of his heroic tales of survival during the war. This surprises me. She puts her cup down and begins to fiddle in her purse. As she shakes her head, she becomes frantic.

"What are you looking for?" I ask.

"I brought you something but with so many papers in my purse I can't find it... Oh, boy." She smiles with relief as she pulls out a few sheets of folded paper and holds them up.

"Look what I found among all the stuff at home."

I can't wait to see what it is. As I take it from her, I notice my father's name typed in the first line and immediately realize it is the diary! I am dumfounded. My first reaction is, 'Oh my God, Mother has another treasure!' She keeps surprising me with new things all the time. I'll never know how she was able to collect and save everything over the years. Emotions flood my thoughts about my father. I am so happy that despite having had a stroke, he had the strength to put his thoughts on paper. Mother tells me that he wrote it specifically for me; he wanted to share with me his most important experiences and deepest feelings about his life and his family. He wrote this soon after he first fell ill in 1987, and it was the best gift he could have ever given me.

I knew that all of his aunts and uncles were highly respected in their own professions, many graduating from foreign universities. This was a big accomplishment, particularly around the turn of the century when traveling was not all that common. I tell Mother that Dad shared little bits and pieces about his family, he was very proud of them.

Since it's written in Hungarian, I know it will take me a while to read. Although I speak Hungarian, my reading and writing is not so great. So I put it in my bag for a later time. Mother then shows me two old, yellowed brochures from my father's fire-extinguisher business. One was written before World War II and the other written after. The pre-war brochure is in two languages, German and Hungarian, while the post-war version is only in Hungarian. I can't believe that Mother was able to keep these items; after all we had lived through.

I couldn't wait to get home. I drove Mother home and agreed to get together the next day. Then I drove home as fast as the traffic allowed, and the first moment I had to myself, I read my father's diary:

"After my basic schooling, in the late 1920s, I, George Oliver Fekete, began to work in the family fire-fighting equipment business. I learned the business and apprenticed with my uncle, Wilmos Biro, who received his engineering degree from a University in Germany at the turn of the century.

"While studying for his engineering degree, Wilmos discovered that fires had 'personalities;' each type responding differently to various chemicals and methods of fire-fighting. At that time, firefighting was quite primitive; basically, only water was used. As a result of his findings, Wilmos invented portable fire extinguishers as we know them today. After completing his education he returned to Hungary, and introduced the new technology there.

"He patented the various types of extinguishers, each one appropriate for a different type of fire. The dry chemical extinguisher, powder type, is the most common, because it is effective on all types of fires. Carbon dioxide extinguishers are generally used in areas containing sensitive electrical equipment because carbon dioxide, a gas, leaves no residue and will not damage materials. These were new revelations and in time every person in the fire extinguisher business in Hungary learned the profession from Wilmos. His two real protégés, however, were my younger brother, Janos, and I. We became the leaders in this exciting new field in Hungary.

"I started my own business in 1935, after finishing my apprenticeship at Wilmos's plant. My business flourished, and by the time war broke out in Europe in 1940, my company was a household name in Hungary. I named my business *NOVARA* after the famous ship of the Austro-Hungarian fleet. Commanded by Admiral Miklos Horthy, the SMS Novara was a living legend. The ship was considered a cutting-edge vessel, so I called my business "Novara," since I was on the cutting edge of my industry.

"I became the supplier of fire extinguishers to the government and the military. My company equipped official buildings and public transportation vehicles, like buses, streetcars, and the underground railway. Among my many customers were the Hungarian Army and Navy, and numerous private companies, including Shell Oil. With hard work I was able to build up the business within a few months. I was very familiar with important officials, as well as military and police officers.

"My equipment played an important role in the lives of the Hungarian people, and in return, many government officials offered me assistance and protection once the war broke out. This secured my safety while the Hungarians remained in control, but once the Germans arrived that protected status would soon end.

"I wanted to continue my business during the war, but I realized it would be impossible for me as a Jew. I solved the problem by asking Gyula, an old classmate and good friend of mine from school in Mezotur, to become a partner because he was Christian. So in the spring of 1944 I had the business listed in his name ... this was the only way I could be part of my own company, and the only way my 'Jewish' company could survive.

"The business was saved, but as the Nazis became more powerful, I became more vulnerable personally. In October 1944, the first time I was taken by the Nazis, I was dragged off to a forced labor camp. The living conditions were horrific. We were kept outdoors day and night and received very little food. Some of the men were infected with lice. I became very ill with dysentery.

"I was taken to Tiszasuly, to a small hospital for Jewish forced-labor servicemen. As luck would have it, one of the people working there was a soldier whom I knew from Budapest. He had been a sportsman and a diver, and during the early forties he had very bad financial problems. I had helped him financially through that difficult period so he could pursue his dreams. When he saw me at the hospital, very sick and in need of assistance, he saw an opportunity to return the favor. He attended to me, cooking special food so I could get rid of the diarrhea and regain my strength.

"As soon as I was feeling well enough, he helped me escape from the hospital. He instructed me to hide at the town's train station and wait for a train leaving for Budapest. I trusted him; he was a good man. I would follow his advice. When the Budapest bound train started to move, I jumped onto it. I arrived back in Budapest that night, on the 23rd of October, but my homecoming was short lived. On October 28th, the Nazis captured me again, dragging me to the dreaded Brick Factory in Obuda, which served as a gathering and sorting facility. From there thousands of men were forced to march daily toward the Austrian border, where trains were waiting to transport them as slave labor force for the Nazis ... or to their last stop: the death camps.

"I was determined to survive, and again, I escaped and managed to return to Budapest. This time freedom lasted only three days. By now it was the end of November. Rifle-carrying Nazi hoodlums combed the streets, rounding up Jews, and I was captured for the third time. I was thrown into a freight car with many others at the Jozsefvarosi Freight Station, and we were shipped like cattle to the Austrian border. When the train stopped at Felsorakos station, I escaped once more. I was able to run away unnoticed because I was dressed as a villager, not as a labor camp worker. I wore shoes instead of boots, and a shirt and coat instead of a thick pullover. Whenever I returned to Budapest, I was sure to stay dressed that way to better blend in. Other men would have given up by this point—and many did. But each time I was captured, my will to live grew stronger.

"When the train finally pulled away from the station, I began to quietly walk the streets searching for a safe path back home. Along my walk, I met a chauffeur driver awaiting his passenger. From our talk I learned he was the chauffeur for an important Nazi official visiting the town, and I became conscious of every word I said! Did he know I was lying, or not? I inquired if they could drive me back to Budapest. After asking permission from the officer, to avert suspicion, I asked the chauffeur if I could join them in the car for the drive. Since I appeared to be a farmer, it was not a problem for the officer, but for me it was. When I saw the Nazi uniform, I panicked for a moment and prayed my nervousness didn't show. By then I was so weary, it didn't matter, I was just glad to have the ride.

"I was dropped off in a small village near Budapest. I still had some money with me, and while in the village I decided to buy a side of pork and carry it back to Budapest. This would be the only way to have some decent food to eat. In the city there was little food, particularly for Jews. I befriended a villager, bought the meat from him, and divided it into small sacks, then set off for Budapest. By now it was the middle of December 1944. Everybody was living in the ghetto.

"I didn't know where to find you and Mother. I didn't know whom to turn to for information. I returned to the apartment building where you and Mother lived with Grandma and Grandpa. I met one of the gentile neighbors who remained in the building and gave her most of the meat. She was so appreciative, in return she happily told me of your whereabouts.

"She told me that you were living in the ghetto, in a building right next to the entrance gate where she had seen you and Mother. She had gone several times, perhaps out of curiosity, and she had seen Mother from the outside. When I left her she promised she would try to look for the two of you again. She did go as promised and spotted the two of you inside the gate, and gave mother a tiny package of food. I was so happy that someone could let Mother know I was back in Budapest, because we were unable to make contact with each other until after the war.

"In the meantime, I didn't want to risk being caught and deported again. I concentrated on staying hidden. Wherever that would be, I felt better to at least be in the same city as the two of you. I went to my manufacturing plant, now run by my partner, and we came up with an idea. The workers fabricated a metal box like a small trunk, barely big enough for one man to fit in. We hoped a metal box would not be noticed if left in the industrial area next to the plant. We found a good location for the box, and placed it in a vacant lot. This was adjacent to a cemetery, and I paid one of the gravediggers to bring me food every night. I remained locked in this tiny box, in the freezing cold, almost paralyzed for a whole month. I didn't see the sky again until liberation on January 18, 1945."

I put the papers down, astounded at what I had just read. My mind overflowed with thoughts. *How did he breathe? Did he have a blanket? How did he stay warm? Was there something to sit on? How did he sleep?* With all these questions running through my head, I could not wait to pick up Mother, and get some answers.

My car must have driven itself on autopilot to Mother's apartment. I am so engrossed in my thoughts; I barely remember the drive. I am glad she is in front of her building waiting for me. She quickly gets into the car; I can hardly wait to hear her answers to my questions.

I know he had some type of a blanket, but how much good it did I don't know. He used it both as a bed, and as a cover. I know the box was small, not even long enough for him to stretch out or turn on his side. I think he stood up to stretch only when the man came with the food and opened the box. As for breathing, I think they punched some holes but they didn't want to make them too big, or it might look suspicious. As for the rest of your questions, unfortunately I don't know the answers. I guess I didn't ask those myself, and like you, I will always wonder. But, there is one very important thing I want you to remember—and make sure you tell Kyle's class this: despite the hatred around us, there were still many brave and decent people trying to do the right thing. Thanks to them, our family survived this awful war. Because of their bravery, many people are alive today to tell their story.

Although your father's partner helped us survive the war years, his wife had a different mission. The only information that was circulated was Nazi propaganda, and many people believed that everything stated in the newspapers or on the radio was true. A few months before we were captured and taken to the ghetto, the partner's wife, Agnes, came to Grandma and Grandpa's apartment, supposedly to help. She warned me that the Nazis would soon find us, and take us away for good, but your father, who was in a labor camp, would probably return. She suggested that we give her some of your Dad's clothes so he would have them when he came back.

I was outraged at her assumption! But, I had enough sense not to show her my anger and mistrust. Instead, I told her that I had already given everything away. What I had suspected turned out to be true: this woman was an informer who was hoping to benefit from our predicament, and get some of Dad's clothes. She left the apartment, but within hours four men appeared at the door. Two of them wore Hungarian Arrow Cross uniforms, one wore a police officer's uniform, and another was in civilian clothing. The men searched through the house, to see if I had told the woman the truth. I was very fearful, as many people had been deported or killed for lesser crimes. I had no way of knowing what else they were really looking for, and what the consequences could be. During the search, they did find a suitcase full of important personal belongings—jewelry, papers, and money. They seized the suitcase and took it with them. It seemed they were satisfied with what they had found, because they left without harming us. We were relieved and safe—that is, for the time being.

However, this scary episode spawned an amazing turn of events. It turned out that the man who was dressed as a civilian was a detective, and from the papers they took that day, he was able to track us down a few months after liberation. He claimed that he helped us during the raid by persuading the Nazis to leave us alone after they found the suitcase. He told us he came back because now he needed our help. He said that his wife had left him, and he was dismissed as a detective. After having helped so many people, including us, he now needed our help in return. Your father didn't think twice and gave him a job on the spot. He worked for us for almost three years, and it felt good to finally be able to help someone else."

CHAPTER 7
MOTHER AND I

In 1942, your father was called in for the compulsory Hungarian military service. At that time he was the supplier of firefighting equipment to the government, and the expert, so they used him to their benefit. They protected him so he could continue to work for the good of the regime. He was assigned to work in the central distribution warehouse, where he was given special privileges not granted to other men, such as letting him wear civilian clothes and visit home on a regular basis. During one of his visits in early 1944, he withdrew a large sum of money from the bank and left it with me so at least I wouldn't have that worry, knowing that he would not be with me when you were born. Nobody knew what the future held, but we sensed future political upheaval and even more severe food shortages. News traveled slowly, but the rumblings about anti-Jewish treatment in Austria filtered into Hungary. His foresight of a deteriorating Hungary proved accurate.

Left alone without any assistance during the last few weeks of my pregnancy, I felt frightened and insecure.

Helping Jews was not allowed, so I was forced to move in with my parents.

It was Monday, March 13, 1944. My labor pains began during the night, but we waited to go to the hospital until the next afternoon. My father and two sisters took me there. This was a milestone in Dad and my life but he was not able to share it with me. He was allowed to come home for only one day after your birth.

My doctor, Dr. Semmelweiss, was the grandson of the world famous Hungarian physician, Dr. Ignatz Semmelweiss, who discovered the importance of physicians' disinfecting their hands before treating patients. The young doctor followed in his grandfather's footsteps as a researcher and handled very few patients. He was a close friend of your father's cousin, so as a personal favor was willing to accept me as a new patient. He knew that we were Jewish, but he also knew that your father was away and he wanted to help. Despite the political climate, and the fact that he was a Christian, he treated me with great concern and kindness. The young Dr. Semmelweiss's small research institute was located in the inner courtyard of Budapest's main government hospital; it was very small, with only ten beds.

In those days, new mothers were kept in the hospital about seven to ten days after delivery, so I wasn't scheduled to be released until Monday, the 20th of March.

While in the hospital, my parents called every morning to inquire about the previous night and our new baby. Strangely, the day before my release, I did not hear from them at all. I wondered why, but dismissed my worries, concluding that there must be a good reason. But I became more concerned when the nurses did not come into my room that morning, as they always did.

When I looked out into the corridor I saw a lot of commotion. At first I was not alarmed, but when things became more frantic, I asked one of the nurses what was going on. Nervous and quite shaken, she said that early that Sunday morning, Germany had invaded Hungary, and that the Germans had immediately seized the big hospital complex. It was March 19, 1944 ... and I had just brought a new baby into the world.

This was why I didn't get a call from my parents that morning. Now I was very worried about my release from the hospital—knowing that anti-Semitic forces had filled the streets, and gun-toting enemy soldiers were marching through the city! My fear intensified as the time of my release grew near. Then, like an angel, Dr. Semmelweiss flew into my room and said, "I have ordered an ambulance to take you home, and arranged for 'infectious disease' signs to be placed on the sides of the ambulance, so no one will stop or inspect it on your drive home." Dr. Semmelweiss also instructed me to have someone other than a family member accompany us home, someone who did not have any connection to the family—and more importantly, someone who was not Jewish.

Following his advice, I asked one of our employees to accompany you and I on the ride home. Due to the infectious disease sign on the car, nobody bothered us. I am so grateful to my doctor. We had a safe ride home from Buda to the Pest side of the Danube, where your grandparents lived.

Budapest was divided by the Danube River into Buda, which was hilly, and Pest, which was flat. On the Buda side there were mainly single-family houses, whereas on the Pest side people lived in apartment buildings. In those buildings the heating materials for each *unit were stored in large basements. The supplies had to be brought upstairs by the owners as needed. As the war was brewing, supplies were diminishing, and the basement storage areas were converted into bomb shelters. Since the space was originally used for storage, it had bare walls, cement floors, no windows or ventilation, poor lighting, and no heating. To make the area somewhat bearable, people put in sufficient lights and some benches. This was done prior to the Nazi invasion, when the political atmosphere was merely turbulent, with a blazing inferno yet to come. People tried to prepare for the uncertain times ahead—but who could have known the extent of what was to come?*

When the war reached Hungary in full force, everybody suffered...but the people who suffered most were the Jews. When the Germans invaded in March 1944, Miklos Horthy was the Hungarian leader. When he later tried to disengage from Nazi Germany, he was deposed. The following October, a Hungarian anti-Semitic fascist militia: the vicious, Hungarian Arrow-Cross Party, took over the government, with Ferenc Szalasi as the new leader. He was given free rein to increase the violence and control over the Jews. The regime constantly issued new discrimination laws, making living conditions increasingly unbearable for Jews. Szalasi was in power until January 1945, when the time of liberation finally came. Soon after, and to the joy of many, he was caught and hung.

By April 1944, everything was blamed on the Jews. We were singled out as the enemy. For identification, we had to wear a yellow star at all times—to identify us as Jews. The size, color, and placement were specifically defined: a 10x10cm, (about 4" by 4") canary yellow, six-

pointed star, which had to be worn directly above the heart. Whenever I took you for a stroll in the afternoon, not only did I have to wear a yellow star, but I also had to place one on the stroller.

All Jewish designated apartment buildings were marked with a large six-pointed yellow star on the front door.

Entrance to building, marked with yellow star

One day, while I was pushing you in the buggy, a woman stopped and said, "This child is so beautiful, she should live a long life—even if she is Jewish!" Under normal circumstances it would have been lovely to hear a compliment, but in those days, when everyone was afraid, this comment made me very nervous. I couldn't see whether the woman was wearing a yellow star or not. So I could not determine whether it was a compliment made with hope from one Jew to another, or a disparaging and racist remark. That was the last time I took you for a walk; comments like that made me afraid and many people felt these same dark emotions.

Fortunately, my parents already lived in one of these Jewish designated buildings, so we were able to remain there. However, many other people were forced to move in with us. Each room in the apartment became home to a different family and everyone had to share the single kitchen and bathroom. Living in such close quarters put everyone in a fragile mental state. The situation became worse, as it became almost impossible to get food. Mothers had no milk to feed their children, and babies—you included—cried constantly from hunger. Everyone's nerves were frazzled, deteriorating due to hunger, worry, and exhaustion. Fear pervaded every moment of every day.

CHAPTER 8

CHANGE OF POWER

The Arrow-Cross Party enforced their laws viciously, and disregarded all prior documents that provided the so-called foreign protection. To make sure everyone obeyed, they terrorized Jews wherever they could, and began rounding up people from the yellow star designated houses. By the end of October, the Nazis had gathered 35,000 people, including boys under fourteen and men over eighty who had not been taken before. Those Jews who were already in the compulsory military service were removed from their units and placed in specially designated forced labor battalions and treated as slave laborers under very harsh conditions.

On October 23, 1944, several young Hungarian Nazis with loaded rifles appeared in our apartment, and ordered all the women to go to KISOK Field, a large stadium. When I told them I could not leave because I had a baby, they coldly ordered me to leave the baby with someone else. I had no choice. I had to leave you with two older women living in our building. I didn't know if

I would ever see you again. On the way to the soccer stadium, all I could think about was how to escape.

It was far; we had to walk about an hour. When we arrived, we found the soccer field jammed with most of the Jewish female population of Budapest. It would have been your feeding time, so standing there my breasts were getting very full and my blouse was wet from leaking milk. I couldn't move. We were forbidden to speak. We all stood very still and prayed.

Suddenly, a man dressed in Nazi uniform appeared at my side, after pushing his way past my Mother and sisters. He grabbed me, turned me around, and started to push me away. This happened so fast, without a word being said, I did not know whether he was planning to hurt me or kill me. I started to shake from panic. All I could think of was how I could get away and get back to you. What if they took my life and I never saw you again? The man was pushing me from behind and I had no idea where we were headed. When we got to the gate, he quickly opened it and shoved me outside. When I turned around he was gone; disappeared, leaving me all alone. No one else was outside. My heart was racing; I was petrified. I took a deep breath and thought very fast. I ran and hid behind a tree, tore off my yellow star, and without looking back, began to run away from the stadium as fast as I could. Thank God, the streets were empty so I could run unnoticed.

My main concern was you, but leaving my own mother and sisters behind filled me with guilt and anxiety. Everything had happened so fast. I had no time to think. But now I was worried about what was going to happen to them. I did realize that this bizarre incident was the difference between possible death and survival.

I had torn off the yellow star because the curfew for Jews had long since passed. If anybody had seen me, I would have been reported immediately. If I were to be captured now, I would have been sent to a concentration camp, or killed. Without my star I felt freer. No one could recognize a Jew from anyone else.

I planned to run fast, but I soon became exhausted. I found a building entrance, where I stopped for a minute and realized that running or even walking home was not an option. I found a few coins in my pocket and boarded a streetcar. Somehow, I arrived home safely— just before dark.

When I got home, you were crying because it was long past your feeding time. The women who took care of you gave you only water, since there was nothing else. When I saw you, it was like giving birth again. I almost collapsed from relief, realizing what could have happened to you had I not escaped. It was a very difficult moment and one that is hard to forget.

To this day, more than fifty-five years later, the image of the Nazi who rescued me remains clear in my mind. I still wonder who he was, whether he was a Jew dressed in Nazi uniform, or a single decent person among so many evil people. Or perhaps he was a father; showing mercy because he knew what leaking breasts meant. Whoever he was, I am eternally grateful to him and we still think of him as our guardian angel. The thought of having left you alone, hungry and frightened still haunts me. Through all this horror, the blessings were a few incredible humanitarians who risked their lives to save many others.

Though my life was spared, my mother and two sisters were taken from the soccer field to a brick factory

*nearby, where the Nazis assembled Jews prior to their
deportation. My brother, Imre, and my sister's husband,
Karoly, who was a gentile, went to look for my mother
and sisters later that day. They were hoping to find them
and save them with the schutzpass, the safe pass document. When they arrived, the building was empty. They
had already been taken.*

CHAPTER 9
"SCHUTZPASS"

During the Nazi reign of terror, many Jews in several countries were mercilessly put to death. Before World War II, there were approximately 800,000 Jews throughout Hungary. According to estimates in 2000, there were only between 80,000 and 100,000 Jews. We Hungarian Jews at least had two God-sent diplomats who desperately tried to help us survive the slaughter of the Nazi regime.

Raoul Wallenberg, the Swedish diplomat, and Carl Lutz, the Swiss Consul, both performed incredibly heroic acts, risking their own lives to save others. They became world renowned for their humanitarian efforts during those years of hate and evil. While Raoul Wallenberg was specifically sent to Hungary by the Swedish Foreign Ministry to help Hungary's Jews, his counterpart, the lesser-known Carl Lutz, a Swiss diplomat, acted on his own, without his country's orders or consent.

From 1942 to 1945 Lutz was in charge of the foreign interest section in the Swiss Legation in Budapest, representing many countries including the U.S. and United

Kingdom, which were at war with Hungary. He took a personal interest in helping the persecuted Jews. One of his first steps was to recognize as American Citizens persons who could produce letters by American friends or relatives, confirming their efforts to get them visas into the U.S. Then, starting in May 1944, Lutz provided documents to other people who held any type of foreign papers, certifying them as part of a Swiss collective passport for immigration purposes. These documents, which created the impression that their holders were Swiss nationals, formed the basis for the 'safe conduct passport'—called Schutspass—that were later issued by Lutz and the Swedish Raoul Wallenberg to all Jews.

Lutz first issued 7,800 safe conduct documents, the Hungarian government limit, but in reality, distributed many times that number. These documents identified their owners as citizens of Switzerland or Sweden, and thus theoretically immune from Hungarian laws. Carl Lutz also provided thousands of additional blank documents together with original stamps and signatures to the young underground Zionist group, Hasomer Hacair. The Zionist members forged and distributed them to the helpless Jews. These forgeries were perfect and could pass for the real thing. Lutz also established safe houses in Budapest, and with his wife, Gertrud, rescued Jews from concentration camps, deportation centers, and death marches.

Raoul Wallenberg was secretary of the Swedish legation in Budapest from 1944 to 1945. In addition to issuing tens of thousands of false diplomatic papers, he also organized the collection and dissemination of food, medicine, and medical assistance. Wallenberg also saved thousands of lives, including mine and members of my immediate family. We often wonder what would have happened to us without their intervention.

So many documents were issued that the Nazi's plans for deportation became boggled and confusing. The shutzpasses—both real and forged—had no actual value according to international law, yet for a precious time they saved many lives. We can never be thankful enough to Wallenberg and Lutz for their unselfish bravery.

My brother, Imre, worked as a 'gofer' at both the Swedish and Swiss diplomatic offices, and was able to obtain safe passes from both countries for our family. Fortunately, I was always able to save myself by using either the Swiss or Swedish papers. It was helpful to have more than one, because sometimes the Nazis took the one we showed them and tore it up in anger.

The schutzpass granted us some security. When the Nazis detained us, they allowed us to remain in our building, or at least be directed to another 'protected house.' While moving from house to house kept us alive, the living conditions were almost unbearable. There was very little food, and my baby was sick. With twenty-five to thirty people jammed into each small room, sleeping was out of the question. There were not enough beds or even enough room. We all had to lie on the floor at night, very close to one another, pushed against other's bodies and hearing their breathing. Even though it was summer, on the basement floor it was miserably cold. With so many people thrown together in unsanitary con- ditions and lying on cold cement floors, it's no wonder you were always sick. You suffered continually from bouts of pneumonia.

While I was constantly worrying about you, I won- dered too where my mother and sisters could be? Were *they getting any food? Were they even alive? I always wondered whether they would understand my leaving them. I was filled with guilt until the day I saw them alive.*

At that time, you were four months old, and we were only allowed to go outside from nine to eleven in the morning and two to four in the afternoon. Anyone caught on the streets at any other time was captured, and either sent to a concentration camp or executed on the spot.

During those four hours, we had to shop for food. It was difficult. We not only had to go to different shops for each type of food, but all food was in short supply. We also had to stand in long lines to purchase whatever was available. Sometimes we would wait for more than an hour just for bread...then get to the front of the line just as the store announced there was no more left.

Those who did venture out to get supplies, often returned empty-handed, having been rejected because they were Jewish, or because of food shortages. We were hungry, but often were afraid to go outside because of the frequent air raids and heavy bombings.

Non-Jews, on the other hand, did not have to stand in line, they were first to get served and food seldom ran out for them. We tried to resolve our food needs by paying one of our gentile neighbors to shop for us. There were many people willing to help, but it also helped them financially. Fortunately, I still had some of the money your father left with me. At least I was able to get the bare essentials. I was glad to pay the neighbors for their help, and was grateful for their efforts. Without their help we would have starved.

By the middle of 1944, living in the Protected Houses while looking after a baby was extremely difficult. By this time, there were daily bombings by the Allied Forces. The moment the siren sounded, we had to rush down to the shelters below. People were so concerned for their own lives, they paid no attention to anyone else-especially you and I- since we were not regular residents of the building. I quickly had to wrap you in a blanket, put you in a basket, and carry you down to the basement shelter with the help of a family member, all the while fighting the stampede of people.

The siren alerts during bathing were even more disturbing. I had to dress you in a hurry, grab the needed things, and run. We never knew how long we would have to stay down there or what the next moment would bring.

For over four months, from July until the opening of the ghetto at the end of November, we were ordered from one Protected House to another, always hoping the next building would be better. Yet, with every move, there was more misery, less food, less shelter, less space, and fewer basic living necessities.

After a while, even the buildings designated as safe no longer offered safety; the Hungarian Nazis ignored all the 'official' papers, invaded houses at will and gathered up whomever they wished. Those who were young and in good physical condition were gathered for sorting and marched off to concentration camps for slave labor. Others were taken to the banks of the Danube River and executed. This reality hit us hardest when it happened to some people in our building. We heard their bodies were thrown into the river like sacks of garbage.

There were several apartment complexes occupied by the Hungarian Nazis. These addresses became notorious and generated fear of being arrested and taken there. The upstairs was used as offices, and in the basements people were tortured and executed.

Conditions grew worse by the day. By the end of November 1944, what little mercy there had been ended, and we were moved to the ghetto. Surviving in those trying times was a matter of tenacity, sheer willpower, and the good fortune of still having your health. Above all it was thanks to the helpful acts of a few compassionate, courageous people.

CHAPTER 10
LIFE IN THE GHETTO

By the end of November 1944, brainwashed, merciless Nazis and men with Arrow-Cross armbands raided Swiss and Swedish protected houses. They gathered those who were left, mostly women and children, and forced them out onto the streets.

The designated Ghetto of Budapest opened on November 29, 1944. According to historical records from the Hungarian Jewish Archives, there were 63,000 people in the ghetto by then, which covered many square blocks of the city. It had four entrances surrounding the Dohany Synagogue in the middle of the city. So many people were crammed into this dirty patch of land. Family members who were in a different part of the ghetto didn't know of one another's whereabouts the entire time we were imprisoned there. At first the Nazis designated only certain streets and buildings, but later they built a wall with solid iron gates closing off streets at the boundary lines. On December 10, 1944, the gates were locked from the outside, and police and military guards were posted to stand watch. We lived *like this from November 29 1944 to January 18, 1945, liberation day.*

All we could think about was having enough food to eat and staying alive. Since I myself was often starving, I did not produce enough milk to feed you. It was so cold that I never knew whether you were crying from the cold, hunger, or both. I felt helpless and powerless to alleviate your suffering. I held you in my arms all the time, trying to relieve some of your pain and discomfort. Often your crying disturbed other people around us who were also cold and hungry. Nerves were frayed, and people were extremely sensitive. The last thing they wanted to hear was a screaming baby reminding them of their own suffering.

Food became even more difficult to get than before. In some of the ghetto buildings there were original residents who had some food stored in their apartments. Some of these people were willing to cook and provide food for others in exchange for money or valuables.

A central kitchen, located away from the ghetto at the Budapest Jewish Community Center, supplied a meager amount of food. Although as little as it was, it probably saved our lives. The bombings were so constant that the men who were sent for food were afraid to leave the shelters. But eventually people had to risk their lives to save themselves from starvation. It was often days before they could return to the building, and many people who left to find food never came back. They were either killed in the bombings or captured by Nazi soldiers and sent to concentration camps.

When we first arrived at the ghetto, we were fortunate to find a bed to sleep in, up against a wall. On one particular night, you and I were in our room when a tremendous bomb hit the building next to ours, almost leveling it. It was a horrible experience; our whole building shook, and the amount of noise, smoke, dust, and screaming, frightened people overwhelmed us. The sound of falling bricks and broken glass was deafening. As you and I huddled on the bed, hugging each other, the wall beside us suddenly began to crumble; we watched as our 'safety wall' came down around us. Our bed was left intact, but now sitting in the open air; the room was totally exposed to the outside. One wrong step, and we could have fallen down from the third floor.

I remember vividly that terrifying moment: picking you up and carrying you away from all the smoke, debris, and freezing cold air. Now, where were we to go? We had to stay down in the bomb shelter. The bombings were so frequent that we practically lived in the shelter, which had only bare walls with no facilities for washing or bathing. Since there was no heat, the water was often so cold that it froze. Sometimes weeks went by without washing or bathing. One day, when it was a little warmer from the collective body heat, I tried to give you a sponge bath. My good intentions went sour, however, when the next day you became very ill with a high fever.

Yet, in every bad situation there were fleeting moments of great good. Our family physician lived in our building and his wife went upstairs to their apartment to look for some medication. You were constantly crying, but after we got some of the medicine into you, you began to improve some. Recovery was a slow process, but at least we kept you from getting worse. But you barely recovered from one episode before you became ill with something else. During the first nine months of your life you were always sick. Constantly *worried about your health, I kept praying and hoping for conditions to change, or at the very least, prayed for milder weather.*

Down in the cellars, the awful days went by slowly, until suddenly, on the morning of January 16, 1945, rumors started to surface from people who had ventured outside the building. We began to hear the sound of Russians yelling in the distance. It seemed the Russian army was fighting nearby and they were rapidly approaching. We prayed hard for their success. The next morning at dawn, a Russian soldier appeared at the ghetto gates, and told us that we would be free within twenty-four hours.

CHAPTER 11
LIBERATION

The liberation of Hungary from the Nazis was not an overnight process. The Nazis put up a strong resistance. The Russians had to go from building to building, street to street, and town to town. Budapest was a large city, and there were many bitter street-fights. It was slow and bloody. At first, I was afraid to even go out on the street because I didn't know what I would find. Still hearing sporadic gunshots I didn't want to risk my life or yours taking you out, but I also didn't want to leave you in the apartment with anyone.

For a few days I stayed in the building and when I didn't hear any more shots fired and people came back who reassured me that it would be safe to go out, we left. We were worried—just because an area was liberated, it did not mean that we could move around freely. It took some time until the whole city areas were secured. Luckily, the Russians moved fast, the chaos did not last very long. Within three days, the city was freed—the Germans and Hungarian Nazis were gone. Three months later, on April 4, 1945, the whole nation was *declared free from German occupation. It was a time of great joy.*

As liberation from the Germans became a reality, the old laws and restrictions were lifted, political fears diminished, and our thoughts turned to family. We wondered if our loved ones had survived and if so, in what condition. We hoped and dreamed of seeing them again.

After the armed guards left and the ghetto doors finally opened, it took days before many of us found the courage to venture outside of the ghetto. Most of us wanted to go back to where we used to live. I was impatient. By then I was very concerned about your health, and figured that I could take better care of you away from there. I didn't know if Grandma's old apartment building was standing or even if it was safe. I took a chance and left sooner than most others. Luckily, I found the building intact.

Not only was this a blessing, but Grandpa had also arrived shortly before us. Neither of us had known about the other's whereabouts, although we were both living in the ghetto. By sheer coincidence, my brother, Imre, arrived at the apartment at the same time. We had a thankful, tearful reunion. You were still very ill, once again with pneumonia, and my joy was overshadowed with worry and concern. But we managed to get medication, food, and shelter, and fortunately, over time you improved. I was grateful and amazed that you, a one-year-old child, could survive so much sickness under such horrendous conditions.

Even though we were now free to move around, I did not leave the apartment until you felt better and I felt safe. We spent most of the time cleaning up, finding supplies, and searching for food and heating materials. We had to fix all the broken windows. It was the middle of a cold winter. It was a time to begin preparing for the future.

We were grateful to live without the constant fear of bombs exploding near us. We no longer had to walk the streets wearing the yellow star of "shame." It took time to adjust to being free, and not being afraid that we might be imprisoned or killed simply for being Jewish. We were now able to enjoy our newly regained freedom.

However, for many families liberation was bittersweet. Everybody, Jews and Christians alike, had been separated from loved ones for years-and many soon discovered that some of their family members had died.

Entire families were destroyed, along with property, homes, and spirits. It took a long time before people could begin to put their lives back together. Parts of the city and streets were filled with debris from collapsed structures, and other buildings were either bullet-ridden or beyond repair. Some buildings were only partially ruined, but people were afraid to walk inside for fear that they might collapse.

As we settled in, we lived with the hope that our family members would return from the camps or wherever they were hiding. It was a time of great uncertainty, but also a time filled with hope. Your father waited a few days—he didn't want to take any chances. He finally left his hiding place in the metal box, and after a few days arrived at Grandma's apartment in the hope of finding us. He hadn't known we were there. It was an amazing reunion. We could hardly believe the three of us were finally together again, but the anxious wait for my mother and two sisters and the rest of our families continued.

Now we couldn't wait to move back into our old apartment, but there was a problem; during our absence, other people had moved in. It took months before they left, and before they did, they stripped the apartment to its bare walls.

When a former neighbor who had lost her husband and whose home had been taken over by Russians needed help, I felt compelled to offer her and her child a roof over their heads. They had nowhere to go so they moved in with us. Again, living with another family was difficult, but it was important to share, and we could not turn away someone in need. They lived with us for a few months, until the middle of July 1945, when we heard the sad news that the family who had once lived on the floor above us had all perished in Auschwitz. So the woman and her child moved into their upstairs apartment.

As life slowly returned to the city, people tried to put their lives together, but the shortages continued. Basic necessities and food were very difficult to find. Your father was always resourceful and very creative. There were no trains, gasoline, or trucks, so he found a horse-drawn cart and together with his brother, traveled to the country. Whatever little money they had left from before the war, they took on their first trip to purchase food. The peasants were eager to sell their products. They went from village to village and brought back enough to feed us and some extra to sell as a way of making money.

While in the country, they also investigated how they could profit from their efforts in addition to feeding our family. They had learned that the locals were making soap and needed lye for the process. On his return to Budapest, your father made a business contact and he was able to buy some of this chemical. The country folks were thrilled with their newfound source, and on your father's return trip to the region they bought a great deal of food in exchange for the lye. They also brought back soap, so your father and uncle profited greatly from their country visits.

During this time we waited anxiously every day, hoping and anticipating that Grandma and my two sisters would return. They had not been heard from since that horrible day at the soccer stadium. My father and brother lived in Grandpa's apartment. Since the men were living alone, I cooked and took food to them every day, even though we had to walk for almost an hour to get there. I placed the food in the bottom of your baby carriage and we walked. During those daily walks I would cry, thinking and worrying about my mother and sisters. It was so painful to see women of similar ages because I always hoped it would be them. I refused to give up hope for their return.

Finally, after three interminably long months, your grandmother and two aunts appeared. By that time, most of Germany and Poland had been liberated, including the infamous concentration and labor camps. Later we learned that my mother and two sisters had been interned at Ravensbruck and Bergen-Belsen concentration camps in Germany. It was a miracle that they had survived.

Their return journey proved a great hardship to their already weakened bodies. Trains were not yet operating. They walked by day and took refuge in bombed-out or deserted buildings at night, always cold and hungry. Many of the people who survived the camps could not endure the return trip in their weakened condition, and *tragically died along the way. Hope and anticipation kept Grandma, Kato, and Ica alive.*

Reaching the outskirts of Budapest was hard enough, but with transportation not completely restored, they tried to run most of the way toward the apartment, wanting to get there as fast as possible. But when they got close, they began to slow down, and at some point even stopped—consumed with fear: would they find anybody alive?

Some distance from the apartment, by some miracle a former neighbor recognized them and gave them the good news that the rest of the immediate family was alive and anxiously awaiting their return. They burst into tears of joy, and again, began running toward the apartment. Now, completely exhausted, they collapsed a short distance from our building. A little later, gathering all their strength, they were at our front door! Seeing them again was such a tremendous relief; the tears of joy flowed from everyone's eyes. It took some time before the reality that all of us were alive sunk in.

I was fortunate; all of my immediate family had survived. Your father was not so blessed. He had a very small family, and half of them did not return. His sister, Maritza, and her five-year-old son, Peter, were burned in the gas chambers at Auschwitz. His older brother's wife, Manci, lost the child she delivered in Auschwitz.

The story of Manci's child was a very sad one. She was already pregnant when she was taken away from her hometown of Balassagyarmat in July of 1944. When they handed out prison clothes, she got a very large size and was thus able to hide her pregnancy. To her great fortune, she was thrown together in the same barrack with a woman physician she knew from her hometown.

The two became inseparable, and when Manci explained that she was pregnant, the inmate doctor offered to deliver her baby under one condition: if she would not utter a sound. Manci promised to do so even though she knew there would be no anesthetic. When the time came, Manci went into labor, and as promised, she muffled her cries. I don't even like to talk about it, it is such an unbelievable story. Following the delivery, the doctor wrapped the baby girl in paper to suffocate her and immediately disposed of her in the trash. The child could not utter a sound or the birth would have been discovered, and Manci, the baby, and perhaps the whole barrack would have been killed."

"Mother, I've never heard any of this before. This is truly an amazing story, and it's hard to believe anyone could live through such an ordeal. How did you find out all these details?"

Many years later, while discussing the war, after I had shared some of my most demeaning experiences, Manci related her tragic story. This was the first and only time she talked about it. I saw how difficult it was for her at first, but she managed to talk about her pain and about her baby's torturous death. She spoke haltingly through her tears. As she described her pain during the secret labor in the concentration camp, she grabbed her stomach as she relived the agonizing cramps. During the long, hard labor all she could think about was how fast she could give birth and stop the excruciating suffering. She recalled how she had to keep her mouth covered, stifling her screams despite the pain. Her emotional wound opened up and words were pouring out as she described her ordeal.

She wondered a lot about her lost child. Would she have been tall or short? Slim or chubby? Who would she have resembled? And most of all, how different would her and her husband's lives have been with their little girl? She could not help but sob. She had seen her baby girl for only a second. She knew that she would have to be killed right after her first breath. She realized it was the only way to spare her and everybody else's life there. These memories still haunt her every day of her life.

For years, Manci could not look at children, particularly those who were the same age as her daughter would have been. She forced herself to push the thoughts out of her mind and could never talk about her ordeal again, even with her husband, Pista. He also kept it all inside, refusing to talk about it to anybody. Because of the delivery she endured, she was not able to become pregnant ever again. They never had another child.

CHAPTER 12
AFTER THE WAR

The Nazis were gone. The war had ended and we were declared free in April 1945. While it was wonderful, it was a strange and unnerving time for everybody. The bitter reality, the hardships, the taste of freedom, and high hopes for the future were mingled with individual feelings of sadness, ill health, broken lives, and horrible memories. As we listened to news over the re-established radio broadcasts, we learned that all of Europe was filled with the same joy over the elimination of tyranny. Hope filled the air in every country, as people tried to restart their shattered, torn apart lives.

Hungary didn't waste time developing a new era of healing wounds, finding freedom, and building a new future. By 1946, life was more stable, and while many of us had lost family, we were thankful that our closest loved ones had all survived.

The seemingly endless opportunities in Hungary gave us new vigor. This was a time for everyone to build a new life and we all moved forward with much hope; feeling that after what we had gone through, nothing

Left, clockwise: early 1946;
late 1946; March 1947; with Nellie, mother
and grandma Riza, 1946

would be too difficult to handle. New businesses sprang up and thrived, and your father began to rebuild his own business. By 1949 he had re-established himself as a successful business owner.

The Germans had stolen everything from your father's plant, leaving it completely empty. But with his *fine reputation and knowledge, starting his business again was not as difficult as it could have been. He reacquainted himself with his old contacts, while new ones sought him out to purchase his merchandise. Having the customer base was essential, but manufacturing and servicing were problematic due to the lack of supplies. We had to search for the sources. His contacts were able to supply him with the equipment he needed, but getting raw materials was more difficult and in very short supply.*

I always helped in the business. We seemed to have the perfect partnership. While Dad generally made the initial contact with people, I always nurtured the relationships. I worked behind the scenes; helped in the office finalizing the contracts and oversaw the smooth running of the business. I also played a major role at trade shows, which was an important part of our business. Our talents complemented one another. During a medical checkup at a hospital, I had met a woman, Margit, who was going to have the same thyroid surgery I had had several years earlier. With that as common ground, our friendship developed into a close one. During one of our conversations I discovered that Margit's husband was the head of a company that manufactured all of the chemicals we needed. Through her, we made a deal and found new supplies, and raw materials became more available. Slowly, but surely, our manufacturing business once again flourished.

Servicing the extinguishers once they were sold took continuous care and attention, which brought in a constant flow of additional business. This helped us grow much faster than expected.

Your father was not only a hard worker and a successful businessman, but he was also a considerate employer. In addition to their official salaries, he gave our employees bonuses, which provided them with a far better lifestyle than the average worker. His employees always wanted to please him; they were very dedicated and loyal to your father. They appreciated his generosity.

Before the war our company had became one of the official transporters of military supplies. As a result of this connection, every important official within the government knew your father. Government offices were centralized in Budapest and controlled by only a few people. During the Nazi occupation, the Hungarian government withdrew all previous orders and businesses severed connections because we were Jewish. But your dear father was always so generous to his contacts that his relationships with many government officials continued practically uninterrupted.

With renewed government and non-government contacts, all the official departments of the city and country again purchased Dad's products. Once again, all the public transportation vehicles were equipped with his fire extinguishers. Your father always had brilliant timing, and knowing that times had changed, it was necessary to change the business name. "NOVARA" represented the old world. He wanted a name that would represent the 'new world'—our new world. He changed the name to "UNIVERSAL." He felt this would represent him globally and make him well known in other parts of the world.

CHAPTER 13
IDYLLIC YEARS

The years between 1946 and 1949 were wonderful, stimulating, and culturally enriching...and we hoped they would provide a solid foundation for your future.

We lived in one of the most desirable neighborhoods in Budapest, called Lipotvaros, in Wahrmann Street. To this day, it remains one of the nicest areas, nestled close to the beautiful Danube River. The area was filled with architecturally beautiful apartment buildings in the Classical, Baroque, Gothic, Renaissance, Art Nouveau, and Hungarian Romantic styles. Our home was on the third floor of a four-story modern building. It was beautifully furnished and the lovely parquet floor was covered with handmade Persian rugs. A Bosendorfer grand, the Rolls Royce of pianos, stood in the hall. You were too young to have lessons, but you loved sitting there and playing with the keys. I played the piano with you, and you used to sit with me, patiently listening to the melodies.

The buildings were surrounded by large landscaped areas and parks like St. Istvan Park, filled with flowers

Winter, 1947

With my father and friends,
Jutka and Andras, winter, 1947

and greenery. A tranquil place where you and I spent
many happy hours of fun, pushing you on the swings or
sitting and playing in the sand. Most people lived in
apartments so going to the park was a daily ritual. We
ate our main meal at lunchtime, usually at home, but we
always enjoyed picnic snacks shared with your little
friends in the park.

Another of your favorite places was the tennis com-
plex. This was a large square block of several red clay

Left: With friends, Jutka and Andras

Bottom Left: March, 1948

Bottom Right: Summer, 1948

tennis courts, which during the winter months were con-
verted into an ice skating rink. During the good weather
months you spent a lot of time at the courts with your
father, who played regularly.

I was too little to catch the balls, but I loved running around
while Daddy played tennis. I played with the balls and got in the
way of the players. I got red clay stains all over my white clothes.
Mommy would get upset with me because the stains were diffi-

cult to wash out of my clothes. Daddy tried to teach me tennis. At first it was difficult—the racket was too big and heavy for me to hold. People told me all the time, "The racket is bigger than you are."

Businesses were booming, private enterprise was flourishing, and people cherished their newfound freedom. Everybody worked a lot but they were making money and enjoying the fruits of their labor. We all hoped this would be our future.

We loved to entertain and spent a lot of time with friends; sometimes we got together just to talk, other times we played cards. Remember, there was no television then. We all wanted to share good times together, to make up for the lost time. I always enjoyed serving beautifully and set the tables with gorgeous linen. You loved to help, but I always had to warn you, "Be careful not to pull on it or everything will fall and break." Do you remember? I also used to remind you, "When you go to someone else's house, don't touch or break anything."

In Hungary there were no caterers; we lovingly prepared the food at home. I prided myself on serving a sumptuous buffet, filled with food that was delicious as well as a feast for the eyes. It wasn't customary to have a sit-down dinner for guests. At that time we ate our main meal at lunchtime, so the evening meal was usually a light supper. We served it buffet-style—it was beautiful, colorful, and very tasty.

Supper for most people consisted of open-faced sandwiches, made from various breads, cold cuts, and vegetables. This was very time consuming, because they were not just simple little sandwiches, but elegant creations. The open-faced sandwiches were made by cutting a baguette on the diagonal into thin slices, topping them with flavored spreads, then covering them with cold cuts, all in an artistic pattern. Cold cuts were very popular and there was a wide variety. You used to love to nibble on them as we were making them. One of the favorite ingredients was a very popular spread called "korozott," a cream cheese mixture made with lots of paprika, mustard, and chives. It had a delicious, slightly tart, piquant flavor, which everybody loved. This was not only tasty, but also beautiful to look at; it was a colorful, light red from the paprika. Vegetables were also sliced thin and formed in a design to fit the bread. These little sandwiches were then decorated using a pastry bag and tips, filled with toppings of various colors and flavors made from sour cream or cream cheese, and colored light red from paprika, or pale green from finely chopped chives. They were small, so people could sample many varieties. Our friends all served similarly at their homes when it was their turn, but they loved to come to us. They often said, "We love everything you prepare. When can we come for supper again?"

Desserts were not only a delicious ending but also a very important part of the meal. They represented our sweet life, a life of freedom. I loved to bake and prepare fancy desserts, which I learned from a friend who owned a specialty bakery. It gave me so much pleasure that I even had our kitchen built with all the professional equipment. You loved to be in the kitchen so much that we built part of it for your size and height. We even had a marble top for your table just like mine.

I liked watching and helping with the sandwiches but I really loved helping with desserts. I stood at my own table, mixing and rolling dough. I spent many happy hours in the kitchen with Mommy and our cook. I couldn't wait for Mommy to make the delicious and beautiful marzipan fruits. She served them alone or sometimes as cake decorations. Of course, I always sampled everything. Many cakes started with a mixture of eggs and sugar, then beaten egg whites. I loved this part and tasted often, even before the rest of the ingredients were added. I loved to lick the bowl, especially when it was chocolate. Mommy let me do just about everything except put the pans in the oven. I burned myself once and she said, "Until you grow up I will have to do that for you." The oven was part of a big gas stove and the door was heavy.

For me the hardest part of baking was using the pastry bag. It was difficult to fill and hold. The bag was big and my hands were small. I used to squeeze too hard and instead of going on the bread or cakes, it would spill out all over the table. It usually made a big mess. If it was chocolaty I had a chance to lick it, but other times it didn't taste so good. I practiced a lot and finally I learned to use the bag.

Cooking and baking were like my playtime. I had a lot of fun. Mommy always told me, "The food has to look as beautiful as it tastes." I learned to do it right. I cut pastries using a ruler, to make sure that every piece was exactly the same size. People would tease me, but I wanted my pastries to look like the ones Mommy made.

Many times I made a boo-boo, or like once I wasn't careful, and I pulled the tablecloth with all the glasses on it and everything broke into many pieces. Cleaning up the crystal was a problem and a big job. They told me to get far away. Mommy yelled at me, and the next time I wasn't allowed to go near the table after it was set. I was very upset. She told me to be very careful in the future, and if I promised to, I could help her again.

Another time I was busy making dough and I added too

much flour. With a deep breath I blew some of it away. My dark hair became white and my face was covered with flour. I almost choked on the flying flour. Mommy rushed to pick me up, and tried to blow off the flour so I wouldn't breathe in any of it. Cleaning up was a chore, but at least I didn't get yelled at. She did say to be very careful and never blow on it again.

Cooking and baking were not as easy as they are today. Shopping had to be done daily, because there were no refrigerators. The iceman came to our street daily with his cart and filled our icebox. There were no supermarkets. Every item had to be bought in a different shop and prepared and cooked daily. There was a bakery for bread, a dairy shop for all the milk products and eggs, the butcher for meats, and a specialty shop for cold cuts and delicacies.

Although Aunt Rosa did not live in, she was with us most of the time and was in charge of the household; shopping for food, planning our meals, and coordinating other part-time help. There were no washing machines; everything had to be done by hand. One person came in to wash the clothes, and another to iron them. Someone else came to do the heavy work, like window washing and cleaning the rugs, every few months.

Not too many people had cars in those days. Public transportation was excellent and the population was satisfied with it. We were among the lucky ones. Neither Dad nor I drove, we had a chauffeur, Bela, who didn't live in either, but spent a lot of time with us. Owning a car was quite a luxury in the 30's and 40's, but fortunately, we could afford it. We had a beautiful touring car, similar to today's limousine. It was your favorite place, and all of your little friends loved it as well.

I loved to cook and bake, but I loved going to school too; it gave me a chance to be with lots of children my age. At my nursery school we spoke only English. We not only learned to read and write, but we were also taught manners, table etiquette, and social graces. My parents taught me to eat properly with a knife and fork, but the school made sure we did it well. We sat at small tables and chairs. We did a lot of coloring and cutting paper dolls. There were lots of toys to play with and there was a big playground. When it wasn't raining, we always played outside. School was in the mornings and then Bela and Mommy would pick me up at lunchtime.

Some afternoons we went to the park, or I did things with Mommy, but many times she stayed home to prepare food for a party in the evening. Sometimes I stayed home to cook and bake with her, or else I spent the afternoons with Daddy. It was always a big decision. Should I stay home with Mommy or go with Daddy? He worked in the mornings, and was usually free in the afternoons to spend time with me. Every day he went to the famous coffee house, Savoy, where he got together with his friends. They talked a lot, smoked cigarettes or cigars, and played cards. They drank espresso and ate cake. Daddy always ordered me my favorite hot chocolate and a piece of cake. I loved all the cakes, and had a chance to eat a different one each time. I loved sitting on Daddy's lap watching the grownups play. Some days one of his friends also brought his daughter. She and I took our dolls and we had lots of fun playing with them together. I felt very special. Not too many fathers took their daughters to the Savoy coffeehouse. I was well known and treated as special by all his friends, and all the waiters made me feel like a princess.

Daddy loved chocolate. His taste for dark chocolate rubbed off on me. There was a chocolate shop nearby, where every day we had a special treat, "macskanyelv," which means "cat's

tongue." It was a very thin piece of tongue-shaped dark chocolate, and I couldn't wait to bite into it.

> *You liked to do all sorts of things even going to the*
> *factory with Daddy. There were lots of people working*
> *and they always had a special treat for you. Dad and I*
> *exhibited our line of fire extinguishers at many trade*
> *shows and we would take you with us. Wherever we*
> *went, people knew Daddy and respected him. I remem-*
> *ber you often asked, 'How come everybody knows him?'*

I loved watching Mommy dress every day in beautiful
clothes and jewelry. It was exciting when she put on her perfume
and let me have some. I also loved to dress up. All my clothes
were made for me; not only dresses and coats but even pajamas
and hats. I couldn't wait to go to Orban Neni, the special children's dressmaker. She loved having me around, and often asked
me to model. I remember many of my outfits. I really loved one
of them, a dress, coat, and hat outfit in navy blue wool. The coat
lining and collar, the dress's bow, and the hat's pom-pom were
all made of white, navy, and red plaid taffeta. I wore this outfit
in my parents' favorite photograph.

I loved being outdoors, and couldn't wait for summer, which
my parents and I spent every year at a favorite resort, called
Csillaghegy. We used to go there by car, but there was also a
train, which took about half an hour. We spent the whole summer season at the resort where we had an apartment. Many of
my parents' friends also had apartments there and all the children had fun together.

Csillaghegy had three large public swimming pools, each one
special. One was a very deep, Olympic-sized pool for the good
swimmers, another for the average swimmer, and the third had
an artificial wave-making machine in a shallow pool. This was

an exciting experience. It felt like the waves in an ocean but the water was not salty. They turned it on once every hour and both children and adults loved it.

After swimming, we used to sit on the balcony eating ice cream and playing cards. I could count and read the cards so I could join in with the older kids. We played canasta, which was a new game in Hungary, and we were one of the first ones to learn it. We also played a lot of rummy, but canasta was more special. There was one older kid named Robert, Robi for short, who was more willing to play with me than some of the others. Some of them were eight, nine, ten years older, and they didn't want a little girl around them. Robi was always nice to me and always let me win.

You were a happy child, and since you were an only child we wanted you to have interaction with other children, but we also wanted you to benefit from school in other ways. We decided to send you to an English nursery school, so you would learn to speak English. You also spent a lot of time with us and other adults and whenever we talked about all kinds of things, we never sent you out of the room. You often heard our political discussions; sometimes you didn't understand the issues and asked us to explain. We gave you brief answers and always asked you to keep it to yourself; it was for our family only.

With the change in the political climate, conditions once again began to deteriorate, and at some point, we realized we had to leave Hungary. We had to be even more careful about what we said and whom we spoke to. We didn't want you to know the extent of the suffering that existed in the world, and what problems were brewing on the political front. One of the most difficult things to explain was that we could not speak freely; we had to use what was commonly called "flower language." This was a form of code, prearranged with relatives or contacts. For example, since our name was Fekete (which means black), whenever correspondence or conversation involved us, that word was used but in the form of a color. Or if a date had to be arranged, they would say, on that particular day someone is expected to give birth. Although we tried to shelter you, we did give you explanations, but were careful to tell you only what we felt was important for a child to know. Your father and I recognized the problems facing Hungary, and we felt the only solution for a better future was to leave at an opportune time. Unfortunately, there was no opportune time in the near future. Despite this we risked it and tried to escape anyway, but like a nightmare that won't end, we were once again caught.

CHAPTER 14
COMMUNISM AND BRAINWASHING

"IF YOU'RE A COMMUNIST, does that mean you can't be rich or have fancy things?" Kyle asked.

"Not exactly, Kyle. The Communists claimed that it was a one-class society where everybody is equal. But in reality the leaders had privileges, not allowed for the general population. This in effect made them rich and powerful while the masses had little. This is like the saying, "Everybody is equal, but some are more equal than others." Legally they didn't have more, but in reality they did: they had cars and as much food as they wanted without having to stand in line for it. They had telephones, which at that time was a rare commodity. They were also allowed to travel outside of Hungary.

From a historical standpoint, Communism developed and changed over a long period of time, starting in the late 1800's. It began as a possible solution to caring and providing for the basic needs of people, but then it became a struggle for individual political power amongst the leaders. Then later it became harsh and rigid as a result of Stalin abusing his great power. I am sure you learned in geography that the map of Europe is different today than it was as recently as before 1989. With the exception of Yugoslavia, where Tito, the leader, was more moderate, in Eastern Europe, countries like Albania, Romania, Czechoslovakia, Hungary, and Poland were ruled by the harsh Soviet-dominated Communists. Germany was divided into East and West, and when the impenetrable wall went up families were torn apart from one moment to the next. The Berlin Wall was erected in 1961 dividing the city of Berlin; in some places one side of the street became East and was completely cut off from the world. Many families could not see each other from 1961 to 1989. In 1989, when the Berlin Wall fell and Communism collapsed in Europe, many countries, formerly part of the Soviet Union declared independence, and now they are separate countries as they were before the war. Other forms of Communism still exist in several countries, but they are not united by a common border, as they were in Europe.

When Hitler rose to power in 1933, he saw the Soviet Union as a prime area for long-term expansion of the German "master race." While in August 1939, Nazi Germany and the Soviet Union signed an economic and a non-aggression pact, Hitler used it as a temporary maneuver. Germany first invaded Poland, and then despite their agreement, he invaded the Soviet Union in June 1941. The Soviet armies were overwhelmed; cut off from supplies and reinforcements. Thus they were forced to surrender and retreat. Hitler expected a rapid Soviet collapse, but he had not considered the strength of the country rallying to beat the enemy, and that the harsh winter conditions created greater demand for supplies. The Soviet army had a definite advantage because their non-precision equipment performed better in freezing weather conditions, and the West supplied large numbers of vehicles and ammunition. In December 1941, the Soviet Union launched a major counterattack, driving the Germans out of Moscow.

In the summer of 1942, Germany regained the offensive and mounted a massive attack toward the city of Stalingrad (now Volgograd) and the oil fields of the Caucasus. The Soviet Army not only resisted but also surprisingly defeated and cleared the Germans out of the city. This was the battle that became the turning point in the war, and signaled the beginning of the Soviets' long retreat westward across many nations, including Hungary.

In June 1941 Hungary entered World War II as a German ally, following their promise of territorial rewards and a market for Hungarian agricultural goods. But by 1942, the Hungarian government felt that the current regime had become far too subservient to Germany, and Admiral Horthy, the Regent of Hungary, appointed a new Prime Minister to extricate Hungary from its alliance with Nazi Germany. In response to that, Hitler invaded and occupied Hungary in March 1944 and set up a new government. Despite the German invasion, Horthy fought to retain independence, but in October 1944 his regime was overthrown, and a new oppressive government came to power. This evil regime was in power only a short time because the Russian Army steadily advanced, and as part of a January 1945 offensive the Soviet troops entered and liberated Hungary.

Since one of the Nazis' aims was to create an Arian race by eliminating Jews, for us the liberation from Nazi occupation was a godsend. What we didn't realize at the time was that the Soviets wanted to take over political control of Hungary, and establish a major foothold in their quest for Communist rule in that part of Europe.

To reach their goal, the underground Communist Party was renamed the Hungarian Workers' Party, and given an important place in the new coalition government. The Soviet-controlled Communist Party then tried to overthrow the country immediately after the war ended, but was unsuccessful. While the Hungarian people were unhappy with Fascism, they were not convinced that Communism was the way to go. In 1946, only a small group supported the Communist Party, and only about 17% of the population voted for them in that first free election. As a result, Communist supporters, along with the help of the Communists in control of the Soviet Union, began an intense campaign to win the next election.

To achieve this goal, they focused on the Communists' heroism for liberating us from the Fascists and Nazis. To build a power base, they formed political alliances with trade unions, as well as the Social Democratic Party and the National Peasant Party. This increased their voting power and gave them control of several key offices. One of these, the Chief Justice in the Ministry of the Interior, became a powerful tool to change laws and silence opponents. By 1947, they had legally seized control of the Hungarian government. The multiparty system was abolished and the Communist leaders began the transition from Capitalism to Socialism, and their actions were not merciful. They dealt with opposition by arresting undesirables on false charges, and by holding single-slate elections.

In 1948, the Communists won the election. Their methods during the election had been questionable, but people were afraid of the consequences for speaking up against them. Once the Communists gained power, a new "Soviet style" constitution was ratified and the Hungarian People's Republic was proclaimed in August 1949. Postwar cooperation between the Soviet Union and the West by now had collapsed, and Stalin's doctrines were forcefully imposed in all political, economic, and social systems. Stalin supporters became the "new elite," gaining privileges not available to the general population.

Government controlled newspapers and radio stations became the only source of information. Radio Free Europe,

Voice of America, the BBC, and all broadcasts from other countries were intentionally scrambled and jammed. The borders were now closed; entering Hungary from the West was almost impossible, and Hungarian citizens could not leave. Only official representatives of Hungary were allowed outside the country, and even they were accompanied by appointed chaperones, to prevent defections.

Everyone was issued an identification booklet, which had to be carried at all times. Those found on the streets without their booklet were interrogated, abused, or sometimes even taken to Russia and placed in labor camps from which many never returned.

Those who defied the regime by speaking aloud or organizing opposition soon regretted it when the Party's secret police unleashed its full power. In fact, to prevent such dissension, the Party would periodically make "examples" of certain people by having them sent to prison, or publicly executed.

"You're kidding Zsuzsi!" Kyle interrupted. "Just speaking up was a crime? I'm really speechless; it's hard to believe that people were so controlled. Thank God we live in a democracy and we can express ourselves freely. I also can't believe that people couldn't leave the country, traveling is such a big part of our lives. Why haven't we learned some of this in history?"

"I don't know, but I am so glad you recognize the hardships we had to live through. Fear was our constant companion during all those years. An expression called *csengofrasz* developed, which translates to *fear of the doorbell*. When the doorbell rang after 10 p.m., we knew it was trouble. We learned that officials would most often come at that late hour, and usually it was the secret police. Even today, the sound of a doorbell late at night makes my heart skip a beat.

Many people wanted to leave the country, but legal methods were no longer an option. Those who took their chances by trying to escape found that failure held extreme consequences. To deter escapes, the Communists not only punished those who tried to leave, but also went after their family members who remained behind.

"Can you imagine it, Kyle? If you wanted to escape you knew that your father, mother, or children would be tortured or even killed for your desire to taste freedom. As a result, a lot less people tried to escape because of the threat of terror imposed on their loved ones.

"Equality for all" became the crux of the Communist campaign. But, rather than helping people build better lives for themselves, the political leaders chose to distribute this "equality" by redistributing existing wealth and power. The Party mistrusted those who had possessions, because nobody was supposed to have more than the masses. They soon seized and nationalized factories, homes, and land from the wealthy. This process started with big businesses, followed by the takeover of smaller ones, and finally included the seizure of most privately owned property-regardless of its value. Individuals or families were ejected from their homes, businesses, and farmlands, and most of their personal belongings were confiscated.

The rich landowners, who did not actually farm the land themselves, were called "kulaks." Under Party order, they were forced to leave their property altogether, or to share their homes with several other displaced families. If the government allowed these "kulak" families to farm some of their own land, they demanded a level of production that was usually impossible to achieve. If the farmers could not provide the goods required, they were punished. Can you imagine, at times, some of them had to buy produce from other farmers just to satisfy their quota? Eventually, most were forced to give up private ownership and join a government-run collective farm where the requirements were less stringent.

The process of "nationalizing" businesses was a devastating and humiliating procedure for the owners. Unannounced, two or three government officials would walk into a privately owned establishment, and order the owner and his family to collect their personal belongings. They were forced to leave the premises immediately without warning and instructed never to return. These officials would then seal the entrance, and the business now became the property of the government. It was a tragedy for those who had worked hard to establish and build their businesses; suddenly taken away without compensation.

The nationalization of my parents' business occurred immediately after our attempted escape. All our holdings were automatically confiscated and became government property, including our car, vacation home, vineyard, and a large apartment building.

The Communist propaganda was relentless and convincing to many. Workers did not make much money, but were tricked into thinking they were part owners of the factories. In reality, everybody was working for the government. However, no one made sufficient money, except for the top officials who made plenty and enjoyed special privileges.

The basic salary could no longer provide a decent living. People started to look out for their own interests, and corruption soon became rampant. Aside from working their regular jobs, people established secret side businesses, stealing from the collectives and/or using the facilities for their own personal use. They helped themselves to the materials and equipment without permission; it was the only place where it was available.

People who did manage to make extra money had to be very careful where they kept it and even more importantly, how they used it. According to the Party, it was inappropriate to spend too much and live too well. In fact, people were not supposed to have any "extra" money; so private citizens had no need for banks. Only the government was allowed to use the banking system for import-export purposes. If people had extra money, they knew to keep it under a mattress.

And now, imagine all this going on, and having no access to news of the outside world! We either heard false government-contrived information, or no news at all. We quickly learned not to trust anything we were told. All information regarding government action or debate in the Parliament was withheld. We could not even go near the Parliament building, let alone witness any official proceedings."

~

Again we lived in constant fear; our lives controlled by written or unwritten restrictions. Whenever we went out at night, we had to remember to return home before 11 p.m., when the doors to our apartment building would be locked. We could come and go, but we were afraid to come home after-hours, because the custodian would have to open the door, and he could report us to the authorities, for his own gain.

I had a terrible scare one afternoon after purchasing, would you believe, chestnut puree. It is a sweet, mousse-like delicacy and a favorite among Hungarians. Friends were coming over for coffee and dessert, and I planned to serve chestnut puree. I had the shopkeeper put it in my lovely crystal bowl so it would be ready for serving. It is made from cooked, peeled, and mashed chestnuts, sugar, rum, and vanilla. To serve the puree, a layer of whipped cream is spread on the bottom of the dish, followed by a layer of the chestnut mixture pushed thru a potato ricer, resulting in little thin strands of chestnut—

like spaghetti—that looks something like Raggedy Ann's curly strands of hair. After a generous layer of chestnut, the dish is then topped with mounds of whipped cream. It is really delicious.

Upon arriving back home, I found the elevator in our building had been turned off. As I started to walk up the stairs, in my great hurry I accidentally dropped the bowl, breaking it into a million pieces! Normally this would have been only a simple aggravation, but under those circumstances it was a major issue. I ran up to our apartment and brought back down rags to clean up the mess, before anyone could find out that I had purchased a large amount of such an expensive dessert!

There were those who would have gladly reported it to the authorities to win 'brownie points' which might appear in their personal file kept by the government. The government could have accused us of living luxuriously and hoarding money, a major crime, punishable by imprisonment, torture, and public show trials to set an example.

Your father's entrepreneurial effort had paid off, but we had to be careful not to show that we had plenty of money. At this time he was working for the film industry, now a government-controlled propaganda machine. But he somehow managed to conduct the business as a private enterprise. He fared better than the average person, but officially we couldn't have more than others. Often we could not purchase what we wanted to for fear of being considered decadent. One could be severely punished for much less.

We lived in a bizarre polarity world; there was life within our family: open and loving...and then there was *our life beyond the walls of our apartment, which was filled with dangers around every corner. There were government agents spying and reporting on people everywhere-hoping to benefit their own pocketbooks or save their lives. We became very insular and spoke only to our close family members about our predicament. No outsider could be trusted. The Communists made sure no one resisted the prescribed mode of life.*

Workers and children were forced to attend regular weekly or monthly propaganda seminars. At these brainwashing sessions local Party leaders reinforced the virtues of the Party and its benefits for everyone. Roll call was taken each time, and those who were not in attendance had notations made in their government files. These negative remarks were carefully kept, and later used against us in all phases of our lives.

The same propaganda was fed to us in theaters and movies, which had to depict some kind of heroism or successful accomplishment of a Party goal. We also had to participate in frequent marches carrying flags and yelling slogans. Attendance was also enforced at these events, such as the annual May Day celebration on May 1st, and we were forced to carry placards denouncing Western imperialism, especially American policies. Sometimes, the government supplied eggs and ink bottles to throw at buildings such as the American Embassy, which represented a free, independent society. We suffered emotional trauma because it was exactly opposite to our philosophy.

Communist indoctrination began at a very early age. Children were taught Russian ideology and new beliefs to insure the perpetuation and success of Communism.

One of the youth organizations was called Pioneers, modeled after those in Russia. Schoolchildren had to wear a uniform of a white shirt and red kerchief. Regardless of how you felt, you were expected to partic- ipate in various daily activities, including propaganda lectures. The hidden agenda in these lectures was the serious attempt to urge children like yourself to report anyone-even your own parents—if you heard them speaking against the regime.

Unfortunately, many children did report parents or other family members. They were young and did not understand the predicament their parents were in and the tragic consequences of their actions. These relatives were interrogated, persecuted, and sent to labor camps or even executed. Can you imagine how these children felt when they learned what they had done? These chil- dren became the favored property of the government. Many were rewarded with money or educational oppor- tunities at Russian universities, where of course they were totally immersed in Communist philosophy. By starting the brainwashing early, the Party believed that the children would grow up to be true Communists with unquestionable loyalty.

At home we always discussed opposing viewpoints. We spoke to you on a level you could understand about the political climate and our own personal circum- stances. But we instructed you not to talk to anyone out- side the family about how we lived, the things we did, and especially about our political views. We explained that there were people who would use this information to insure a better life for themselves—sell their souls and put their families in jeopardy. Very early on, you learned the importance of having righteous principles, keeping secrets, and knowing that it was sometimes essential to lie. We knew that we could trust you.

One of the biggest problems facing the Communists was the housing shortage. Most of the leaders of the new Communist Party had to move from the country to Budapest, the capital, where they needed homes. Housing was in short supply, and to solve this, the government devised a method of 'displacement and appropriation.' They simply got rid of the undesirable people, like former Capitalists, and took possession of their apartments. First they falsely accused people of committing crimes against the State, and then without a hearing or investigation, these people were persecuted. Some of them just suddenly disappeared and were never heard from again.

While the majority of people suffered, the new leaders were getting rich and growing fond of the luxuries of their new lifestyle."

CHAPTER 15
ESCAPE FROM HUNGARY

By 1949 we had seen the writing on the wall. With new laws in place, the conditions could only grow worse. We knew we had to leave Hungary to avoid the next persecution, and to raise you in freedom. Ica and Imre had successfully escaped to Vienna in March of that year, and kept begging us to join them.

But we were realistic and knew that leaving would be difficult, especially for a man as prominent in business as your father. We would need more than luck to pull it off. Despite the obvious risks, in July 1949, we finally decided to plan our escape. We knew our lives would change drastically and that we would have to give up everything. However, we hoped the loss would be temporary, and that we could create a better life and a better future for you in a new country. We hurried to finalize our plans to leave.

Knowing that money would play an important role in our escape, we arranged to send money out of the country before we left. It was illegal to do this, but since we had an established Swiss bank account prior to the war, we managed to channel money through intermediaries and business connections.

This was not a simple task. The process involved a difficult and circuitous route. Money and other assets being sent to the West had to first be "laundered" by channeling it through numerous hands. Through trusted friends, we were able to find and hire one of the conductors on the Alberg-Orient Express train, which passed through Budapest from Turkey to Paris, to smuggle some of our possessions out of the country.

The conductor himself never came in contact with us directly. An older lady acted as liaison. At each designated meeting with us, she picked up a bag of our valuables, money, and jewelry, but of course, there were no receipts or inventory of any kind. We had no choice but to go on faith, so there was a lot of hoping and praying until notification of the transfer was received months later.

The next step was long and even more complicated. After the war, Vienna was a divided city under American, British, French, and Russian control. The Russian sector was Communist-ruled, while the other countries represented the free world. The Alberg-Orient Express train always arrived in Vienna in the Russian sector. Movement to and from the Russian sector was strictly controlled, and always under scrutiny. After its arrival, several different people handled the money. One person with a special permit had to take it from the Russian to the British sector, and another person had to convert it to Austrian currency and then take it to a local bank. At this point, some of it was sent to Switzerland, while another part of it stayed in Vienna. Since this was all very risky, there was a big price attached to each step.

Every time the money and valuables changed hands, the total value was reduced by some twenty-five to thirty percent. But the price was not important, for we knew by then, that the cost of freedom did not come cheap.

We could have, and should have, left with Ica and Imre in early 1949, but your father wanted to complete a business deal, an export shipment, and regrettably, he decided to wait. Looking back we realized what a grave mistake that was. To start the wheels turning, by various means we were eventually able to make contact with Ica and Imre in Vienna, but communicating was very dangerous. Our every action was scrutinized, telephone conversations were monitored, and we never knew who was watching and listening nearby. We were afraid to hand over a letter to another person for fear the exchange would provoke suspicion. Since your father conducted an export business, he was in a better position than most to make contact with anybody outside of Hungary. When we communicated with Ica and Imre it was through a code language. For example, if we wrote, "Please send six yellow roses to Judy on her birthday, July 20th," it meant that on July 20th Judy took six pieces of gold jewelry. Another line of communication was through those who traveled to the West legally. Fortunately, we had connections with artists and newspaper reporters, who were the only people allowed out of the country at that time. The Communists emphasized the importance of international competitions, and the newspaper representatives reported on the success of the sports figures. Hungarians were outstanding gymnasts, soccer players, and ice skaters. They always had to travel in groups and were never left alone without a chaperone. One of your father's closest friends, Laszlo Lukacs, was a highly regarded sports writer with free access to the West, and acted as liaison to Ica and Imre in Vienna.

"Next to every big gate there is always a small door" is a common expression in Hungary, which roughly translates to finding alternate solutions. It refers to those who will do anything to find a solution to a difficult problem—even if it means doing something illegal. Although it was forbidden, enterprising people made a business out of assisting Hungarians to escape. This involved a so-called "broker"—usually from Budapest), who made the arrangements—and a "farmer," a local man from a nearby village who handled the border crossing as a guide.

When we had finally made all the preparations to leave, Ica made arrangements with a local farmer near the Austro-Hungarian border to take us across. This was similar to the plan Ica and Imre had followed for their successful escape a few months earlier. The "farmer" was familiar with the guards and the general layout of the land. One person was to escort us from the train station, then hand us over to another, who would take us close to the border in a horse-drawn buggy. From there, we would cross over into Austria by foot, guided by a villager.

Using a guide was vital because the Hungarian Army had placed landmines along the border to eliminate escape attempts. The landmines, together with watch-towers, patrolmen, police dogs, and barbed-wire fences created a dangerous no-man's land. It was Winston Churchill who dubbed this forbidden zone The Iron Curtain.

Darkness and unmarked roads made any escape attempt even more dangerous.

Children were often sedated, because sometimes people would be caught when their children's cries were heard by the nearby border patrol. The border itself was not a straight line, and people often crossed over into Austria at one point only to later find themselves back on Hungarian soil and under arrest. The worst was when greedy villagers would take people's money, and then lead them straight into the hands of the guards.

We not only had to worry about the crossing, but the handling of our departure from Budapest. As a diversionary tactic, your father and Bela went to the country several months earlier and purchased a pig, which they left there for future slaughter. The date of our escape was planned for the time when the pig would be ready for slaughter. We planned to send Bela and Aunt Rosa to the country to handle it, so Dad and I would be free to make last-minute arrangements without their presence.

On December 13, 1949, we left our home very early in the morning. At the Budapest train station your father bought seven train tickets: one each for you, Dad, and I, two for my parents, and two for my sister, Kato, and her daughter, Kati.

You were excited, and kept asking where we were going. "We are going to a resort for a few days," we said. You must have felt the tension in the air because you kept asking over and over again. We left Budapest and disembarked the train late at night near Sopron, a town only about half an hour to the Austro-Hungarian border. We met our crossing guide and, after boarding his horse-drawn buggy, we headed toward the border. We trotted along the bumpy road for about ten minutes when we were halted by the cigarette-smoking guard who asked, "Where are you going?"

When we left home that morning, we left a note instructing Bela and Aunt Rosa to look for a letter on the piano under the lace cloth. The letter explained that we had left the country, and to take whatever they could for themselves, before official word of our escape got out. Aunt Rosa and Bela did as they were told and took as many of our belongings as possible. Fortunately, they did this early in the day, because by evening, when we were captured, the AVH became aware of the situation and immediately sealed off our apartment. No one but officials could enter from then on.

CHAPTER 16

COMMUNIST DEPORTATION

MOTHER, ROBERT, AND I are at our daughter Michelle's house, sitting around in the den discussing politics and events of the past week. We received a CD from Hungary with copies of documents and old newspaper clippings that we wanted to share with the kids. In the midst of conversation, Kyle's six-year-old sister, Nicole, calls out, "Come on Rozsi, let's play! Bring the ball and come outside to practice with me. Please, please ..." Rozsi, which translates to 'Rose' in Hungarian, is what Nicole and Kyle call their great grandmother. Nicole grabs the ball and Rozsi's hand and they go outside to the front of the house. Kyle is skateboarding outside with his new toy and one of the neighborhood boys. The front door is open, and soon we hear Rozsi shouting to Nicole; "Don't do that! You have to be very careful. Watch the boys! Don't go there alone ... I'll go with you!" Kyle, who's heard these comments many times, knows it annoys Nicole. He says, "Rozsi, why are you so protective of Nicole and following her around all the time? Why don't you leave her be?"

"You know Kyle," Rozsi says, "That's a good question. Come in the house, let's sit down and I'll try to explain."

The answer is not so simple. When Zsuzsi was a baby I was forced to leave her with strangers and I didn't know if I would ever see her again. Then, a few years later, when she was five years old, the guards kidnapped her from me, and at that time I made a promise to myself never to let her out of my sight or leave her with any stranger. I didn't ever want anything like that to happen again. Then, only one year later, I was faced with another frightening, unknown predicament. The Government ordered our deportation from Budapest, but Zsuzsi's name didn't appear on the document. I was frantic and didn't know where to begin to rectify it. I called my dear friend, Manci, who suggested we leave Zsuzsi behind with her. Without hesitation, I thanked her but said 'no way.' Not knowing what our future would hold, I felt it was most important for the three of us to stay together. I decided not to do anything about it until we were picked up the next morning.

Kyle, I understand what you are thinking, I realize we are in Los Angeles now and things are quite different, but I can never forget those horrible days in Hungary. And with all the terrible things we see in the news even here, my fears are still very much alive. You know, I cannot wait for the weekend when I get the chance to be with you and Nicole. Zsuzsi is grown, and now it is my great grandchildren I worry about.

When they come into the house we stop our discussion, and we all listen as Rozsi tries her best to explain her feelings to Kyle. Sitting around the table, suddenly Kyle turns to me and asks,

"Zsuzsi...Rozsi said that once she was forced to leave you as a baby, and another time you were kidnapped. What was she talking about? Can you tell me when those things happened?"

I nod and say, "I think it is more important for you to hear the Nazi era experiences and our suffering at the hands of the Communists firsthand from Rozsi. I will also tell you what I remember as a child, but in addition, I will show you actual rare documents Robert and I were able to acquire. They describe the seemingly casual but highly thought out directives which caused months and years of suffering to us and many others, whose only crime was being former Capitalists or aristocrats. One piece in particular, the correspondence between the Prime Minister, Rakosi, and the First Secretary of the Communist Party, Gero, outlined their plans, which were to be carried out by their most trusted deputies."

(Translated from the original Hungarian documents)

HIGHLY CONFIDENTIAL:
Comrade Rakosi:
    Attached is the committee's recommendation for the deportation process from Budapest.
    Having read their recommendation, it is my opinion that the committee wants to create too much attention, which would be politically harmful. I believe there is no reason to rush into deporting 12-18,000 people in a hurry, within one week, from Budapest. We have to do it slower and quietly. There is a drawback if we do it slowly, as those who expect to become victims sooner or later will sell their valuables and furnishings under the table, or hide them with friends. I believe this we could handle. However, the slow, method-

ical process will have the advantage of
fewer mistakes, easier placement of the
people in the country for both accommodations and job assignments, and it will not
look like a massive late-night brutal
method of transportation … I believe we
should carry out 100-150 deportations per
week and continue until the fall.
Accordingly, we only need to use the ministries very little, since we have
already assigned them a larger workload
than they can handle.
    —1951 April 27. Gero Erno

Kyle listens intently and takes a sip from his drink. He
shakes his head, eyes wide open, "How could they do such
things? How many people did they do that to?"

MINUTES
    Recorded May 5, 1951, 12 noon, with
regard to the elimination of undesirable
persons from Budapest.
    Present: Rakosi, Gero, …
    The committee regarding the elimina-
tion of undesirable people from Budapest
recommends the following procedure:
    The elimination procedure will be car-
ried out by the Ministry of Interior with
the complete assistance of the AVH…
    The first week they will be taken to
Szolnok district.
    The removal and elimination will be
done through police channels, and within

24 hours of notices being sent.

The deportees' personal belongings will become property of the State and sold off at the National Antique Shop.

We have to work out whether to put several families in one box car or only one. Perhaps a passenger car can be attached to the train.

We have to make sure that there will be no gathering of any kind at the train stops on the way.

Only the local police to inform them of their assigned housing, and they can only leave with the permission of the local authorities.

The displaced people's apartments will be assigned to 30% military officers, 40% industrial workers, and 30% Party officials and ministerial employees. The actual apartment assignments must be worked out with comrade Pongracz, according to the above breakdown.

—Rakosi, First secretary

REPORT

Regarding the displacement of undesirable people from Budapest.

The transport begins at 4 a.m. and is done by truck, making two rounds of pickups. On arrival at the new location the transfer from train station to houses depends on local conditions, either by truck or horse-drawn cart.

This week, the first group on May 22 went to Kotelek, the second to …

According to the experiment so far, the displacement was orderly. We recommend increasing the displacement to 200-225 families, the truck making three rounds. By beginning at 3am, the transfer and boarding can be complete by 10am.

—Budapest, May 26, 1951 Hazi

～

One of Kyle's friends comes in and yells, "Come on, Kyle. Where are you?" Kyle dismisses him, waving his hand. "I'll be there in a minute. I can't go right now." He is so engrossed in hearing my mother's stories; he doesn't want to miss a word.

When Zsuzsi's dad returned from prison in December 1950, we began to live a relatively normal life, but under even greater pressures from the Communist regime. No matter how carefully and quietly we lived our lives; we were watched and scrutinized at every turn. The government kept its eye on "troublemakers" like us, even sifting through the trash to see what was being bought, eaten, and discarded. This information could then be used as grounds for interrogating and eventually punishing dissidents. Threats, beatings, and the disappearance of many ordinary, innocent people increased. The Secret Police were everywhere and the omnipotence of the AVH and their power to terrorize was pervasive.

When the regime decided to act on the recommendations in the above documents, our political profile fell into the "UNDESIRABLE" category. In fact, we were among the first forty-seven families to be rounded up and taken to a Communist internment camp on May 22, 1951. In a strange sense, it was better to have been selected on the very first day because we didn't know what was going on or how bad things were going to get. Our ignorance helped us maintain hope.

We were rounded up early in the morning and shipped to a tiny village of about 1,000 people named Kotelek. It was a three to four hour train ride from Budapest to Szolnok, then another half-hour horse-and-buggy ride on a very bumpy road. Among the other families were many aristocrats, several high-ranking military officers, and political figures from the previous regime, as well as a former Prime Minister. Though we were in the "best possible" company, we were the only Jewish family taken that day.

Kyle sits in disbelief. Robert, Michelle, and Steve are deep in conversation at the other end of the den, when Kyle calls out,

"Dad, Mich, did you know all this? Did Zsuzsi and Rozsi tell you all about it?"

Steve responds, "I'm sorry I don't know what you are talking about. We weren't listening to your discussion, but let's hear about it now!"

"Zsuzsi and Rozsi are telling me what happened to them in Hungary and I can hardly believe it! I never heard anything like this before. I think you should listen. Zsuzsi, when you come and speak to my class, please talk about this. Tell me some more ... you know I love history and I'm really interested. I am so glad to have the chance to learn this from you firsthand."

"No problem," I say. "Rozsi and I will try to explain to you what we went through and how it all happened." Kyle stands up, gets a drink from the refrigerator, and brings it back to the table. He sits down, leans forward, and gripping his drink he says, "Go for it."

"When it all started, I was seven and alone in our apartment for a few minutes at around 8 a.m. Rozsi ran down to the corner bakery for fresh breakfast rolls, when I heard a knock on the door. I thought it might be the custodian of the building, so I looked through the frosted glass. I saw two unfamiliar men. I didn't open the door because I was instructed never to open it for strangers. The men announced that they were from the AVH. They had to speak to my mother. They sounded very stern and angry. I told them that she had gone to the corner bakery and would be back very soon. I did not know what AVH meant; I just knew I was scared. I was trembling and couldn't wait for Mommy to return. They said they would slip a piece of paper under the door and go downstairs to wait for her."

∽

```
MINISTRY OF INTERIOR
   03371 number …
FINAL DECISION
```

```
              I.
```

FEKETE GYORGY … original profession … TECHNICAL EQUIPMENT WHOLESALER

BUDAPEST … XIII … district … FURST SANDOR … street … 9 … the undersigned resident and living in the same household … MRS FEKETE GYORGY and child Fekete Zsuzsanna Marianna … (handwritten in later) … according to the … 8130/1939 K.B number order and the 760/1939 number order …

I ORDER TO EXPEL IMMEDIATELY FROM THE TERRITORY OF BUDAPEST AND I DESIGNATE AS PLACE OF RESIDENCE … SZOLNOK … district …

… KOTELEK … town … In case you want to settle in another district (at a relative's or friend's), after occupying the present ordered location you must submit a request for a new residence to the appropriate district. You have to submit an affidavit from the person inviting you and the appropriate district County council that they are willing to accept you.

Complaint against this final decision can be submitted only to the Budapest Police Headquarters. In spite of any complaint, this order is final and non-postponable.

II.

By this order of the government … 1/a 6.000/1940 number … your home, which is the result of this expulsion must be transferred in writing within 24 hours.

—BUDAPEST, 1951 MAY 18 …

Stamp of the Interior Ministry …

… Signature

Additional information on reverse

∽

When I returned a few minutes later, the uniformed officials greeted me with a very curt announcement: "Gather your immediate personal belongings, leave the rest, and be ready to be picked up at 4 a.m. tomorrow." No explanation; just a note that said the rest of the information and full instructions for the deportation procedure were clearly outlined on the paper they had left under the door. When I got upstairs, Zsuzsi tried to tell me frantically that two men were looking for me, and she was relieved to hear that I had spoken to them.

I was stunned. There was no warning. For a minute I couldn't even think straight. I went upstairs in a hurry and telephoned my husband, George, who was equally shocked. Our first thought was that somebody had reported us for some crime, which we did not commit. George, Zsuzsi's father couldn't leave his work at that moment, but while I took her to school he made some phone calls. We tried to understand the situation by contacting the office that had originated the orders, but no matter whom we contacted, nobody had information about what was happening. The events on the first day of the deportations came as a complete surprise to everyone—both lower level officials and of course the general public. None of our contacts could offer us any assistance either because they were totally unaware of this new law, as were even those at the ministerial level. We were in the first group of high profile deportees, and the process was so new that our search for answers proved fruitless.

That beautiful, bright sunny day soon turned into gloom and doom; a day filled with questions, but no answers. Realizing we could not waste any time we began to pack, not knowing where we were being taken, for how long, or if we could ever come back. Eventually, we gathered our resources and decided to take only what we felt was most important and most precious. Imagine if you had to leave on a few hour's notice, what would you take with you? It was very difficult to think clearly, but we did our best.

The regime was already notorious for "taking care" of all undesirables. People simply disappeared without explanation. We were scared that this would happen to us. There were rumors that men ended up in labor camps or prisons in Siberia, which nobody left alive.

We even contacted Karoly, my sister Kato's former husband, who had become a high-ranking official in the government over the past few years, in hopes of discovering more details about the order through him. He didn't know anything about this ruling either or its consequences.

However, he promised to try to find out more information and do everything in his power to help. That afternoon he stopped by the house, accompanied by another official who told us that if we cooperated with him and were willing to work with him—meaning if we were willing to tell him everything we knew about everyone we knew—then this would not be a permanent sentence for us. He kept repeating that if we cooperated with them we would be set free. Your father arrived home just as this man was making his offer.

We were suspicious of his approach and did not trust his promises, so we refused his offer. "No," we said. We would take our chances. At the time, it seemed better not to strike deals with such people. We didn't want to harm those we knew by revealing their anti-Communist sentiments or actions; but basically, we could not be certain that they would release us even if we did. We figured that they would most likely have used us as propaganda tools against others to benefit their cause. The thought also occurred to us that while they might set us free one day, they might return and arrest us the following day with another false accusation.

All that day we were tense and frantic. Not knowing where we were going or for how long, we took both summer and winter clothes, in limited amounts. I had trouble deciding what clothes to take for Zsuzsi, but amongst other things, eventually I chose some newly finished summer dresses that would fit well. Looking back, I made some ridiculous choices; they didn't take us anywhere that would require wearing a pretty taffeta outfit. We also took some practical items like pots and pans and a folding bed, which turned out to be one of the best decisions we made.

It was a long day and a very long night filled with fear. We didn't sleep at all and we had little time to offer Zsuzsi any comfort. Do you remember Zsuzsi that we asked you to pack your own belongings? We thought it would keep you busy. As a seven-year-old, you did not know what would be important; all we could say was, "Take very little."

Listening to all this for the first time, Michelle, with a quizzical look on her face interjects, "Mom, as a little girl the same age as Nicole how did you choose what to take?"

"I packed my favorite doll and grabbed a small tablecloth that I was almost finished embroidering. I loved to draw and had many beautiful sets of colored pencils, but now I had to choose the one I liked best. I picked a flat box of all the colors, which was almost new. I needed the sharpener and grabbed a bunch of paper. All the toys and games I loved I had to leave. Whatever else I wanted, Mommy said was not necessary or too big. I started to cry but there was little they could do. Mommy and Daddy looked at each other as they tried to comfort me, and said that when we got to our new place there should be a toy store and we would buy new things."

Final decision document, my name handwritten in, May 1957

CHAPTER 17

LIFE IN THE COUNTRY

We didn't sleep at all that night. It was dark outside at 4 a.m. on May 22, 1951. We heard a truck with a very loud motor stop on the street. There were very few vehicles on the street in Budapest at that time.

A uniformed man knocked on our door. Without any formalities he simply said, "Let's go." We were ordered onto the truck with our meager belongings. The other people in the building knew something was going on, but didn't dare come out. We saw many faces watching us, hiding behind the curtains.

We were driven to a train station, where other families were gathered, waiting at the poorly lit platform. The government had worked swiftly before sunrise. After a quick headcount, we were put aboard a train with hard wooden seats, heading for the town of Szolnok, a three to four hour journey. From the train station, all of us were taken by a horse-drawn wagon to Kotelek.

Upon our arrival, a uniformed official addressed our group of about eighty people. He explained that they would treat us well, despite our unacceptable behavior toward the Communists. We all looked at each other. We didn't know what he meant. We all stood still and spoke in hushed, worried tones.

As I listened to the roll call, I realized that we seemed to be the only Jewish family. Hearing the names of the other deportees, there were former royalty and important former ministers and officials. There were a prince, princess, counts, countesses, barons, baronesses, and other honorable so-and-sos, and only a few names sounded typically Hungarian. We were one of only three families without a title.

You know, Kyle, I don't know if you are aware but Hungary was a kingdom way back in time. The first King was crowned in the year 1000, and the political landscape had changed many times as a result of Royal neighbors waging wars and conquering territories. However, their descendants remained major landowners and retained their titles. Until the roll call, we didn't know who the other people were in the group. The list sounded like the Who's Who of the former Austro-Hungarian Empire. Many of the names were familiar to us from history and here suddenly we were meeting their descendants. One of the women, for instance, had a brother whose face actually appeared on a Hungarian coin. Also among the deportees was the Countess Eszterhazi, whose family history is played out in the much-loved musical The Sound of Music.

Kyle interrupted with a rogue smile, "Zsuzsi were you one of the princesses?"

She has always been our princess, Rozsi replied.

And as I was saying: with every name accounted for on the list, one of the policemen counted our group. A minute later he counted again, and then several more times. Getting up at 4 a.m., riding on the uncomfortable wooden seats on the train, followed by a horrific bumpy ride on a wagon normally not used for humans, then standing in the sun without food, we were all agitated. The policemen also looked annoyed. We didn't know what was going on. Nobody said a word, but we were scared. After a huddle, two more policemen counted the group separately, but still they weren't satisfied. One of them in his frustration finally announced that there was one more person than on the list. When I heard this, I yelled out that possibly my daughter was the additional person, because her name was handwritten onto the document just moments before we left Budapest. They immediately looked at their papers, and after realizing their mistake corrected the paperwork very quickly.

I was already angry and frustrated, but this made it even worse. I stepped forward and yelled that there must be another mistake. We were Jewish and we had already suffered before. Surprised at the interruption, the official paused, and then replied that if there had been a mistake, there was nothing he could do about it. As it turned out, my outburst created a major problem for us. Although we were all in the same predicament, the old Christian families still considered themselves better than Jews. From then on, the rest of the group saw us as outsiders and even potential spies. The following week another Jewish family, the Bauers, arrived, and we felt somewhat less isolated and singled out. Mr. Bauer, a former banker, was considered an equally prominent Capitalist, and as such, he automatically became an enemy of the regime.

After the roll call hassle, every family was assigned to a room in one of the houses in the village. The government had appropriated several houses in the village and outlying farmlands, ordering their owners to take in deportees. Originally, one family occupied these two or three room homes, but now a different family occupied each room.

The house to which we were assigned had two rooms and an entry hall, which was typical of the village houses. Formerly owned by Kulaks, well-to-do farm and landowners, whose houses were larger than the average village houses, and the land around them was used for farming.

Prior to this we had never been to the country except to visit summer resorts, which catered to vacationers. We had no idea how difficult life was in other parts of the country; I didn't know how blessed we were, until we arrived there. Our situation was made all the more difficult and uncomfortable because the villagers had no knowledge of city life, and therefore did not really understand our plight. They couldn't understand why we found it so hard to adjust.

In the beginning, we were not welcome in our assigned house. The former owners, Lajos and Maria Lovasz, felt that we were intruders who made their lives cramped and difficult. They resented us deportees. At first they didn't understand that we were victims as well. It took a while for them to realize that we had nothing to do with the government taking away their homes, and that our homes were also taken from us. As we shared our stories with them they understood our genuine fears and our terrible predicament. Slowly, their feelings toward us changed as they realized that we were actually good people who were just as powerless as they were in all of this. We were all suffering as victims of the government's abuse.

"Living in the United States, it's hard for you to understand, but there was no running water in the houses in those villages. We had to get water from a well outside. To take a bath we had to boil the water and then add cold water to cool it down. There were no bathtubs either. We filled a small basin and used a washcloth.

We had to wash ourselves fast and dress quickly. It was cold and we worried about getting sick. We had to be very careful not to get the floor wet since it was made from straw, cow dung, and water, and emitted a very foul odor when wet. I thought a lot about the beautiful parquet floor and rugs we had had in Budapest.

The toilet was also outside. We learned what we could or could not do. I was not allowed to drink anything after 5 o'clock in the evening so I wouldn't have to go to the bathroom at night. But I had to plan ahead just in case I had to go. We kept candles and matches nearby so we could find them easily in the dark, because there was no electricity either.

Life in the country at the time was hard work and little fun. My parents and I were together in the evenings, but there was nothing to do but sit and talk, often in the dark. We talked a lot and they would try to shield me from their true feelings. Once in a while, I had seen Rozsi cry in secret. When I saw that, I broke down and cried with her. I knew how hard this was on my parents. I saw them changing. They slowly began to accept having to live this way. I'd hear them say that at least this was better than being confined in prison. With their loving care and constant support, I too learned to adjust to the misery. I had to leave my memories of Budapest behind and get used to what we had now."

To live as country folk was a drastic change from life in the city. In the city we had employees to handle everyday tasks, but now we were forced to do hard manual labor for our own survival and existence. We had to work the land, and endure the extreme weather and cramped living conditions.

None of our previous business and social connections could prevent our deportation, but at least they were able to get us a work exemption. All the deportees were forced to till the land, but fortunately, our permit exempted Zsuzsi's dad and I from having to do backbreaking farm work for someone else. We did only what we needed for our own needs. I still had to do all the housework, cooking, and baking. He took care of bringing the water from the well, which was a huge job. He had to gather containers and carry them to the well, then pull up the water and fill them, then carry the heavy pails back to the house. He always looked for ways to make our lives easier.

My husband, George, was mechanical, so he helped the farmer with his equipment. Maintenance was essential because new equipment and tools were not available. This helped Lovasz, the kulak, and in return he was helpful if we needed him.

Even in the country there were differences in lifestyle from village to village, depending on the distance from the bigger towns. The greater the distance the more primitive the conditions became. Indoor-outdoor plumbing, hard-surfaced roads, electricity, public transportation, doctors, and hospitals were not readily available, and often nonexistent. Entertainment, arts, cultural activities, and education didn't exist.

Our village had no electricity, and it was very difficult to find sufficient candles. During winter especially, it was quite dark inside even during the day and we needed candlelight just to get around. Reading or any other activity after dark was totally out of the question. We went to bed early to conserve candles, and also, once darkness set in there was absolutely nothing to do. Just like the farmers, we rose early each morning for a day's hard work. Our body clocks had to adjust to the local ways.

We were not locked up in prison, but the authorities kept a very tight control on us. Conditions were prison-like, in that we could not go anywhere, except within this tiny village, without permission. They checked on us twice a day. Every morning and every night the police appeared with large German shepherds, making sure we didn't disappear. Those visits were not always at the same time, so we didn't know when to expect them and that left us feeling nervous and belittled.

Policemen would approach the house quietly. Then, without warning, they would enter and unleash their large German shepherd dogs. The dogs didn't actually bite us, but their growling was scary. They constantly checked up on us and when they found that we actually had food, they questioned us as to how we got the money for it. They didn't like our answers, and definitely did not like that we had some foods that were unfamiliar to them. We learned to live with the indignities we suffered at the hands of the local police.

We were forced together in the same house with another deportee, Laszlo Gyengo, a former high-ranking military officer, and his family. He was an angry, bitter, difficult man—even in good times, but sharing the house made his behavior far more intense.

The original owners, Lajos Lovasz, and his wife, Maria, were moved from the main house to their "summer" house. The summerhouse contained the kitchen, and was connected to the barn about a hundred feet away. The rest of us were assigned to the main house, called the "winter" house, which had a furnace used for heating and baking. The kulak's son and daughter-in-law had one room, Gyengo with his wife, Illy, daughter, Magdi, and son, Peter, another, and we ended up not even with a room but the entry hall. Thank God we had brought our folding bed with us from Budapest, because all three of us could fit on it; at least we had something to lie on.

Living and sleeping in the entry hall had plenty of drawbacks. Whenever anyone wanted to access the wood-burning heater or oven, they had to do it from our space. We would burn dried cornhusks, since wood was not available and it was terribly dirty. The dust and soot from the oven covered our room and it was nearly impossible to breathe or keep clean. It was your father's job to gather the cornhusks, and after the corn was harvested, he left the stalks to dry. Then he cut down and collected them, grappling with the wheelbarrow. It was very difficult for him to manage all this and it had to be done several times a week. To make matters worse, the heat generated from our space came out into the other rooms, so we did not even have the benefit of being warm.

Getting food was also a problem; there were no butchers or bakers in our small village. Like the other deportees, we quickly learned to farm the land so we had something to eat. We planted vegetables, raised chickens, helped the farmers milk cows and make butter. Fruits *and vegetable were only available when they could grow, so we preserved them for the winter months.*

Learning to fend for ourselves might have been an adventure, had it been our choice, but we were resentful because it had been forced upon us and there was no end in sight. Thankfully, some local farmers taught us what to do and before long we could handle small farming ourselves. Work is all we had and all we did. Necessary chores took up most of the day, and, in fact, we never had enough daylight hours to accomplish all our work.

Washing was a big job because first we had to heat the water, and then scrub the clothes well since we didn't have sufficient soap. Without running water, rinsing was even more difficult because we had to empty the tub several times. Wringing out the heavy items and hanging everything outside to dry was sometimes worse than the washing itself. Ironing was another ordeal, because in those days everything was made of natural fibers and had to be ironed, even our cotton underwear. We had only one set of linens, so we had to work frantically to have them ready for use that same evening. The iron itself was hard to handle; it was incredibly heavy, made of iron, and needed special coals for heating. It was a major effort.

"Gosh, this sounds like an episode of *Survivor*, except it's your real story," Kyle exclaims. "I'm so glad I have the chance to hear it from you firsthand."

Baking was also a major job. Illy Gyengo and I baked for everybody in the house. We made a lot of bread, which was our staple food on the farm. Baking was done in the same stone oven that heated the other family's room. The heat and long work hours were exhausting and brought up some of the emotions I'd kept pushed down inside. Zsuzsi and I often cried while baking. As soon as she saw me cry, she would break down and cry as well. At times I couldn't hide my feelings. I tried to explain that this was not the kind of life George and I had planned for her, and how we somehow felt responsible—even though we had done nothing wrong. We kept hoping it would be over soon.

Cooking was something of a juggling act. All three families had to cook at the same time to save fuel. Wood was not available and cornhusks were in short supply; it was tedious to gather, dry, and chop, so we tried to economize and be efficient with what we had. It was a small kitchen, originally intended to serve only one family. We ended up having one-dish meals, because there was not enough room for more than one pot per family. In fact, we did not have many cooking resources in the kitchen at all. Each of the three families had only one shelf for storing pots and pans, dishtowels, and other utensils. Having a few of our own items made the kitchen the most comfortable room in the house, despite all the cooking.

Unlike her husband, Illy Gyengo was easy to be around and very accommodating. There was never an argument among the women in the kitchen. One day Illy mentioned to me that it would be nice to make plum jam, but there were no plums available near us. Plum jam sounded like a good idea—used frequently in Hungarian cooking and baking. It would allow us to dream about better days and the wonderful food we used to enjoy. It seemed like we were always wishing for things we did not have, and there were an awful lot of those.

Lovasz overheard the conversation. He had a horse-drawn buggy and offered to get the plums from a nearby village. He wanted to bring enough back so that he could make some extra money. Your father thought the two of them could make more money if they did it together. Without asking for permission, from the local police, he decided to accompany Lovasz. The trip was successful and undetected. In your father's usual way, they brought back a whole buggy full of plums. Making jam involved long hours of cooking and then preserving the cooked fruit in jars. Immediately, we all got to work, first washing the fruit and removing the pits. Everyone helped except Gyengo.

We did not have sophisticated equipment in the kitchen, but preserving was a way of life in the country. Fruits and vegetables were seasonal, and by preserving them they were available throughout the year. We had to bring in a huge amount of dried corn for fuel, collect as many jars as we could, and boil water to sterilize them. We worked in shifts, and it took more than 24 hours to finish, since someone had to watch and stir the mixture all night long. As soon as the jam was ready, it had to be bottled. For the finishing we sprinkled a preservative on top, then covered the jars with cellophane and tied a string around the neck of the bottle. We then placed the jars in a basket covered with a blanket to keep them warm to complete the preserving process.

We cooked enough plum jam that day to last a year. At the end we were able to sell some of it to neighbors and barter with the villagers for some meat, which was very scarce.

During the winter months, there were periods when, day after day, our main midday meal consisted of noth-

ing else but bean soup and bread. We grew to dislike it after a while, but at least we didn't go hungry. We were so tired of eating the same things every day, there were times when we would rather not eat what was available.

Because we were being punished for our 'crime' the authorities discouraged visitations from relatives, but sometimes looked the other way. We depended a lot on the kindness of others, but at the same time, we had to be very cautious with visitors. Grandpa and Kato managed to come and see us every two or three months from Budapest and always brought supplies. This was not easy for them; trains didn't run regularly and they had to be careful visiting us "enemies of the people." They always brought us either money or food products with which we were able to barter for other things we needed. They brought coffee, chocolate, some baked goods, and meat, which we couldn't get on the farm. It was wonderful to get regular soap and real toilet paper instead of the newspaper shreds we had to use. For the village people this was normal, but not for us. In winter, though, Grandpa was unable to visit and we missed having the extra food. By now, late 1951, Ica and Imre were living in Australia, and regularly sent money or food packages through a government-approved international network. We received most of them, but not all. The local officials most likely appropriated the foreign foods for themselves.

Before one particular visit, my sister, Kato, instructed her three-year-old daughter, Kati, to be quiet on the train and not mention who they were going to visit. A friendly little girl, she talked to everyone on the train and, despite her mother's instructions, told people in her childlike way: "I am not supposed to tell anybody where we are going because we must keep it a secret. We are going to visit my aunt and uncle and cousin." While Kati's chatter may have been innocent enough, it could have resulted in grave consequences for us all—perhaps even cost us our lives. Fortunately, nothing happened, but after this incident, Kato came to visit us alone.

While we worked and adjusted to this alien lifestyle, the children attended the local school during the school year. Hungary's educational system was centrally controlled, so to a large extent, it did not matter where in the country a child attended school. He or she received, more or less, the same education. We tried to give Zsuzsi some continuity: we hoped that attending school with other children would help, and also allow her to keep up with schoolwork.

"I had always been a good student. When we brought our test results home, I always received a better grade than either of the Gyengo children. Magdi and Peter had no problem with that, but their father didn't like it at all. He was already rude to my family because we were Jewish, but getting better grades than his children made it even worse. I would come home excited with a good grade and he greeted me with, "Here comes the ruination of my life - that dirty Jew."

I asked my parents what he meant. They just reassured me that he was angry at being forced to live here. This helped a little, but I never got used to his torment.

At the end of the school year, the annual student achievements were announced. Having become the top student in my school, I was given the honor of carrying the school flag and leading the rest of the students in a ceremonial procession. Laszlo Gyengo watched me lead the other children of the village, which included his own Magdi and Peter. When I saw his face, he looked so mean I almost began to cry. At the end of the parade Magdi and Peter went to their parents and I ran to mine. They hugged and kissed me, and then Daddy took me aside. He lifted me into his arms and put me on his shoulders. He was so proud. He kept telling me what a good job I had done, and not to worry when Gyengo told me mean things. He reassured me that Gyengo was only jealous and a very unhappy man who hid behind his anger. We waited to celebrate until we were alone. Both Mommy and Daddy tried to cheer me up, telling me how proud and thrilled they were. Daddy said, "The best thing to do is just to keep up the good work." Mommy said, "Gyengo will not change. If you can be smarter than he, and don't show him how much it bothers you he might stop saying those things."

Many times it was difficult for me to hide my feelings of despair and sadness. We had little privacy, but Dad and I wanted to shield you from our feelings. He and I had many differences and disagreements. Your father was always the optimist. He felt that things would improve before too long. I was the pessimist, but deep down we were both aware that things could easily go the other way, and get even worse. There was always the possibility of being sent to Siberia, or to any unknown place for hard labor, or, worse yet, to prison to be tortured, and perhaps never to return alive. We lived in constant fear, never knowing how long the present torment would last, or whether something more horrible would follow. It was our strong faith and hope for a better tomorrow that kept us going. We were helpless, but not hopeless.

Uncertainty and primitive, harsh conditions shaped our lives. Being thrown together with members of former aristocratic families did make life a little more toler-

able because we understood each other. The majority of the aristocrats had had servants before their deportation. They had no idea how to cook or take care of their most basic needs. And, since many of them were older, they had an even harder time than most; they were helpless and disoriented. Rich people were often not practical, and not knowing how to care for themselves, they did not choose wisely what to bring with them. On the other hand, they were able to barter with the peasants some of the beautiful items they had brought from home for food. Like us, they had no idea where they were being taken. They brought beautiful linens, towels, jewelry and furs, which were useless, but at least some of them managed to sell them to the villagers in exchange for supplies, food, or money. With that, they were able to purchase goods and assistance from the village people, who helped teach them the skills needed to survive in a primitive environment.

"It's amazing how hardship can force people to change. I certainly would not have liked to be one of them. I'd probably be bitter and lost," Steve says.

They were. They barely survived. Luckily, on holidays, they received care packages from relatives in the United States or Australia through the same government approved international network that Ica used. This organization, IKKA, facilitated delivery of food packages or money to relatives or friends behind the Iron Curtain. These were prepaid in the West, and the sizes and contents varied according to their monetary value. It's a good thing that the aristocrats had a food supply, because they never had visitors.

Illy and I, both thirty-two years old, were the youngest and most adaptable of the women. We were practical and knew how to cook. To make those aristo-crats' life just a little more bearable, the two of us visited them and offered our help two or three times a week.

While they were not aloof and did not behave unpleasantly to us, their speech was more formal than ours. In Hungarian, as in most European languages, there is a formal and an informal manner of speech. Normally, friends and family use the informal, but the aristocracy always used the formal style, even amongst family members. To us, it felt very distant, but eventually we developed a pleasant, warm friendship with them.

One day when visiting, I found one of the aristo-cratic ladies ironing the floor of her room. Maintaining the floor was always a problem, but this woman had come up with an ideal method for repairing it. She wet the floor and smoothed it with the iron. When I saw her down on the floor, I burst out laughing and crying at the same time. I was struck with the irony of the situation; I never would have imagined witnessing an aristocratic woman ironing her own mud floor. The woman responded, "There is no reason to cry. After all, only the cream of the crop of the population is here, while the nobodies have been left back home in Budapest." I could not resist saying I would gladly exchange the privilege of being here with the cream of the crop with being a nobody still living in Budapest. We laughed and cried together.

Just as this woman and I, a Christian aristocrat and a Jew, were able to find common ground, I found myself on the same side with Gyengo when it came to dealing with the authorities. Whenever there were issues involv-

ing all of us, we banded together to create a stronger voice. Gyengo and I were the two most outspoken deportees, and we supported each other. No matter how difficult it was I had to put up with him and put aside my feelings. When it came to dealing with the police and other authority figures of the Communist Regime, we knew where his alliances lay.

Early one morning in 1951, about five months after our arrival in Kotelek, a policeman appeared at our door to inform us that we were to report at 8 a.m. the next morning to help the farmers harvest crops. I asked him if he knew who the Minister of the Interior was. He was surprised at my question, but when he answered 'yes,' I pulled out our deportation orders, showing him the back, where a notation was made stating that I had to work "only by choice."

The policeman wanted to force Gyengo and Illy to go, but following my lead, they refused. This was a dangerous choice for all of us, since it was always hazardous to attract attention to oneself. They tortured us mentally whenever they could and used their dogs to upset Zsuzsi.

"For me, the morning was the worst part of every day. Usually I was still asleep when the dogs would awaken me. My parents would get out of bed immediately, but as I peeked out from under the cover the dogs' cold noses and bad breath greeted me. Their tongues literally attacked me, sniffing and licking me in the face. I tried to get away from their slobbering by turning my face from side to side. The bad breath and dog odor was so vile I always felt sick to my stomach. The only way I could avoid their fast tongues was by getting out of bed. Even then, they didn't leave me alone. They probably sensed that I was afraid of them; it was very intimidating having them there. I couldn't wait for them to leave. I wanted to go back to sleep. Usually it was only a little after 5 a.m., and still dark. The first day this happened, Daddy could see me trembling, and he realized my aversion and disgust toward the dogs. He sat me down in his lap, and tried to explain that it was important not to fight them off because they might bite, especially since they were trained to attack. If I didn't fight them, they might leave me alone. I had never had a dog of my own, so I did not know how to behave toward them. This was my first experience and it was scary."

The police certainly loved to torment us wherever or whenever they could. On one occasion, a countess was washing her hair and failed to hear the policemen entering her house. As she stood there helpless, the policemen watched while the dogs licked her naked body. Another time, Kato had brought us some meat, which we tied into a bundle with some string. There was no refrigerator and the nights were cold, so we hung the meat outside on a nail overnight, until we could cook it the next day. That night, when the police paid their usual visit, they let their dogs eat it.

The policemen also amused themselves by playing pranks on us. One day they ordered one of the men who had a beard to cut it off, and then, the very next day, they demanded he appear with his beard. Another time, they delivered a note that designated a mentally ill young woman as the "best mannered person" in the village, and appointed her to the position of advisor for manners and behavior. Since the family knew this was not possible, they asked me if I would like to do it, giving me the order letter. The police found out that I had the letter, and immediately came to demand its return. I denied knowing anything about it or having received it. Fortunately, there were no repercussions from the incident because it was not an official procedure. The policemen themselves could have gotten into trouble with their superiors, so they just let it go.

After about a year of these episodes, Gyengo and I decided it was time to do something about these terror attacks on the villagers. We sat down and wrote a very strong letter to the government office detailing many of the incidents that had occurred. Surprisingly, after about six months a committee from the government office came to the village, and both of us were summoned to appear before them. While the committee reassured us that these incidents would not be repeated, they also sternly warned us not to forget who we were. In the eyes of the law, we were "society's rejects," against the new "people's democracy," and were considered a serious threat to the success of the regime. As such, they were not required to resolve any complaints in our favor. In order to drive their point home, the committee issued an edict requiring both our families to relocate to a farm about ten kilometers from the village. This was our punishment for speaking up; another way of making our lives even more miserable.

1952 with Magdi and Peter Gyengo on the farm

CHAPTER 18
REMOTE FARM

On the appointed day, an official horse-drawn buggy transferred us and hauled all of our belongings with the chickens in a crate. The farm we were moved to, like every other business in Hungary, had been nationalized and was now under government control. They displaced the owners from their houses there as well, and reassigned the deportees similarly to the way it was done in the villages.

This farmhouse was bigger than in the village, but there were quite a few of us. The single women were forced to stay together in one room. Two of the rooms were already occupied by other deportees: four former aristocrats, a husband and wife in one room and two sisters in the other. He was a count and the ladies were countesses. They were glad to have us join them; they had been sent to the farm directly. The farmer's family was still living in the house when we arrived, but were moved outside to the barn, to make room for the Gyengos and us. The Gyengos were given the larger room and we got a tiny one.

While life in the previous, faraway village had been hard enough for us, being moved to an even more distant farm was worse. We felt that we had been totally cut off from the world. Of course there were no telephones and no communication with even the villagers. Vast fields separated the farms and the distances between houses were greater. We could use horse-and-buggy, which was not readily available to us, or sometimes borrowed bicycles, but there were no paved roads and riding was treacherous. In fact, just getting around was quite difficult and visiting other deportees or keeping in touch was now out of the question. We still had to gather heating materials, fetch water from a well, and farm the land. Of course, there was still no electricity, and the outdoor toilet was even further from the house than before. To make matters worse, we now lived near a rice paddy, which was a breeding place for filthy mosquitoes.

The aristocrats had all been raised with servants so none of them knew how to cook. Prior to our arrival, they paid the farmer to cook for them, or simply ate bread and other items that didn't require cooking. Now they wanted us to alleviate some of their misery by assisting them in their work, especially in the kitchen. Illy and I helped cook for them and tried to show them how to do it for themselves. They did appreciate our help, but it was difficult for them to learn especially in such cramped quarters. In the warmer weather we all ate cold foods so that we wouldn't have to heat the stove. Cured meats and various fresh or pickled vegetables were staples in the Hungarian diet and special favorites in summertime. One of the most popular type of cold foods was cured bacon, which was prepared in various ways.

"There was one of these I liked best. It was a slab of fatty bacon cooked with lots of garlic, then completely covered with paprika on the outside. It was delicious and it was red, my favorite color. Our farmer made many different cold cuts and sausages (kolbasz), and we could buy them. We often ate them with bread, green peppers, and radishes or scallions. There were times when we had white peppers, but not too often. It was a special treat. At night we usually just had bread with butter or lard. On the farm butter was more readily available. My parents had coffee and I had hot chocolate."

When we arrived we were given a piece of land, which we used over and over again. First we had to prepare the earth, turning it and fertilizing it, and plant the seeds. We continued to raise chickens as well as growing our own vegetables. In the village at least we could buy some items like fruit, which we didn't grow, but that was not possible on the farm. If we didn't grow it we couldn't have it. We had to water every day and watch our veggies grow. We had no idea how long it might be before they were ready to eat. Like everything else in our lives, all we could do was wait patiently.

Raising chickens was quite an experience. Every morning they appeared under our window, usually while it was still dark, clucking and scratching, and we would have to get up and throw them food. The ducks and geese, on the other hand, had to be fed by hand with corn so they would produce more meat and a large liver. We had to brace the ducks and geese between our legs, hold their necks in one hand, and push down the corn with the other. While I fed the ducks and geese, you and your father stood by, fanning away the mosquitoes and other bugs. While forcing the corn down the ducks and geese, Dad and I often compared it to the way Communism had been forced down our throats. We always hoped that our plight would end better than theirs.

It was difficult to sleep peacefully. The nights were filled with the noise of rats and field mice. We had to get up at some ungodly hour and light candles so we could chase them away. Our room seemed to be where the rats and mice huddled in large numbers. I was very squeamish, so you and your father had to be the mouse catchers. We didn't know what to do. We asked the farmers how they handled it. We had to devise a way to get rid of them since there were no traps. They suggested we place some cut-up bacon as bait, and cover it with clay flowerpots, leaving space for them to go under. We placed a rock to elevate one side of the pot and when the rodents went for the bait, the pot would fall down on them. Sometimes we had to catch them by hand. You, as a little girl, were not afraid, and were even fast enough to catch them by their tails. With those you caught, your father placed the pot over the rat to cover it, and by morning they were dead from suffocation. I'll never forget what a life we were forced to live. We prayed that the Communists wouldn't do to us what we had to do just to survive.

As I look around there is tension in the room. Everyone is affected by the mental images Mother is painting. Suddenly Kyle speaks up,

"Zsuzsi, did you ever catch Mickey Mouse?"

The tension having been broken, we all laugh and Mother continues. As before, most of the time she directs her conversation to Kyle, Michelle, and Steve, but at other times to me:

Since there were no schools nearby, my formal training as a teacher came in handy. I finished my teachers' college education before I was married, but I never practiced until it became a necessity on the farm. I created a curriculum, and without books or props, I became the teacher for Magdi, Peter, and you. Gyengo was delighted for a change, and I was happy to do it. When it came to helping each other or helping his children, he was always very cooperative. It was important for you children not only to learn, but also to have something pleasant to do, so that the seemingly endless days passed a little more quickly.

In addition to schoolwork, I would try very hard to make everyone's life as pleasant as possible, when I could. Whenever there was a little time, I would bake fancy stuff and offer some to the other deportees and the farmers. Some of the pastries were new to the peasants; they had never tasted or even seen them before. They all loved it, and it helped me to cope with the harsh reality around me. You often helped me, and it gave you something fun to do too. Other than this, unfortunately, there were not too many activity choices available for deportees. After all we were there to be punished. For you children there were very few toys on the farm, so we had to create activities. Cooking and baking was like your playtime. Indeed, our new life taught all of us to be resourceful. Many a time when I baked, we didn't have the necessary ingredients available, so we learned to use substitutes. Our improvisations became the source of many new recipes, which may very well be the reason I seldom follow recipes, but rather create my own versions. Despite the lack of some ingredients, we made delicious desserts that tasted as good as they looked.

"I spent many happy moments in the kitchen. I loved the aroma of bread and cakes baking. I loved their yummy taste even more. Mommy taught me to make many of them. One of my favorites was a breakfast roll. We used sweet yeast dough, spread with vanilla-flavored butter, rolled into a long log, and cut into slices, then baked. During baking we basted them with vanilla-flavored milk, which gave them a delicious flavor and created a glaze, making the rolls look gorgeous and shiny. I couldn't wait to eat them.

My other favorite was *palacsinta*, the Hungarian version of crepes. They could be filled with many different fillings, sweet or savory. Most of the time they were filled with jam or a mixture of farmer's cheese, egg, sugar, lemon rind, and raisins. *Palacsinta* could also be filled with a mixture of cocoa and sugar, or cinnamon and sugar. I loved every variety. And I enjoyed making them as much as eating them. They needed only a few simple ingredients, which we always had.

One day I was showing one of the countesses how to make *palacsinta*, and everyone gathered around to watch. Mommy was very proud of me and let me do everything myself. I was too little to reach the stove so I stood on a chair. While cooking I slipped off the chair and spilled hot oil all over my hand. It was extremely painful, and we had nothing to put on it to reduce the terrible burning. The nearest doctor was ten kilometers away. Fortunately, the farmer offered his horse-and-buggy and drove us to town. One of the aristocrat ladies and Illy came with us to fan my hand during the ride to help ease the pain. The doctor gave us creams to reduce the pain and help with the healing. He was very kind. He was a kulak's son and understood what we were going through. The pain eased by the next day and the wound healed after a week. After that, whenever I made *palacsinta* someone stood by the chair and held my legs to make sure that I would not fall off. I learned my lesson though, and I became more careful."

That was one of the many memorable incidents. And I remember vividly another time when I was making chicken soup. We cut up the meat and vegetables and filled the pot with water. Watching the soup to make sure it would not spill all over the stove, we noticed something swimming on the top. Looking closer, I saw that it was a frog. We never figured out how it got in there. Not knowing whether the frog was poisonous or not, I had no choice but to sacrifice the whole meal. Grabbing the pot filled with all of the wonderful, precious soup ingredients, I had to dump the whole thing out onto the ground; we couldn't take a chance. It was just another blow to our already degraded and humiliated condition. To this day, we are not sure whether it was an accident or if someone playing a prank had put the frog into the water container on purpose.

We had to think fast and make something else for dinner with the ingredients that were on hand. We quickly prepared dough for 'langos,' a fried bread similar to Indian flatbread. Langos was made from yeast dough, rolled out quite thin, cut into 3-4 inch square pieces, and fried, then sprinkled with salt and rubbed with fresh garlic. On the farm we learned another way to prepare it. Instead of cutting it into small pieces and frying, we kept it in one large circle like a pizza, and baked it. When baked, we spread lard or goose fat on top and rubbed it with garlic. Both ways it was delicious. Langos was usually served with soup during the hearty midday meal. Sometimes we even ate it in the evening with tea.

"Ooh! Goose fat! Lard! How on earth did you eat that stuff?" Kyle interrupts.

Well, in small villages fifty, sixty years ago they ate what was available. And even today, in villages in many countries they eat differently than what you would do. I've heard this kind of comment many times before, especially in California where we try to eat a healthy diet. But you have to remember, we had no choices, we had to eat and survive.

While we had hoped moving to the farm would provide us with a little more freedom, it turned out to be as restrictive as living in the village. We had thought there would be fewer people around to watch us, but this was not the case. The police and dogs still came every morning to check up on us, and we lived more or less under house arrest, unable to leave the farm without permission. It was the end of 1952 and there was absolutely no sign that our circumstances would change for the better. Instead, the reality of being shipped to Russia was close at hand.

"In the evenings or earlier when darkness set in we stayed in our room. On the farm there was a bed in the room already, and we put up the one we brought from Budapest, so at least I had my own bed. My parents always discussed their daily goings on and talked about the hardships. They were constantly preoccupied with what could happen to us in the future. They felt helpless not hearing any news. We were cut off from everything. Mail, which was extremely slow and infrequent was our only connection to the outside world. I heard them talking so many times about our situation; I couldn't help but join in. I asked them to explain because there were so many things I didn't understand. They did and I learned a lot. Daddy always had hopeful words, even when Mommy was having a tough time. He kept saying, "It cannot last forever, we have to keep going on." He was always dreaming that when we returned to Budapest he would find a way for us to get out of Hungary, and join Ica and Imre in Australia."

Despite our fears that we'd be rebuffed or punished, we submitted a request for a transfer to a town where you could attend school. Much to our surprise and joy, our request was granted and we were allowed to move to a town by the name of Kunszentmarton, about fifty kilometers away. We couldn't believe it! The town had a school and electricity! While we still had to live in the country under government control, there were fewer police visits, and we were not awakened every morning by barking, licking dogs. This was a definite improvement: having electricity and living under more civilized conditions. With no news to go by, we simply hoped and prayed that if we continued to endure, this too would pass.

Our prayers were answered to some degree, when two years after our deportation, in March of 1953, word spread that Stalin had died and this created much turmoil within the hierarchy of the Soviet regime. The various factions, once kept united under Stalin, began arguing over who would succeed him. The designated heir, Georgi Malenkov, became Prime Minister and First Secretary of the Communist Party, but he held the position for only a few days; he was forced out of office by Nikita Krushchev. We were elated to hear the confirmation of the rumor that during the power struggle the dreaded head of the secret police, Laurent Beria, was arrested and executed. In September 1953, six months after Stalin's death, Krushchev was named First Secretary and he began to replace most of the former officials.

When the political infighting in Russia finally settled down later in September, the repercussions of the huge political shifts began to reverberate throughout Hungary and all of the other Socialist countries. One positive change included the granting of amnesty for all deportees. It was like having a huge burden lifted off of our shoulders! We were finally released from house arrest and allowed to return—but only to the periphery of Budapest. We were still not trusted enough to be allowed to return to our previous lifestyle.

CHAPTER 19
RETURN FROM CAPTIVITY

"DO YOU MEAN A SUBURB of Budapest?" Kyle asks.

Kind of, but it was on the outskirts of the city not part of the metropolitan area. At least we were no longer under arrest, and we were close to Budapest. We were gaining back our dignity, but not completely. To have a legal residence, we had to rent an apartment in Budakeszi, but in reality we lived at Grandma and Grandpa's in the city.

No matter the circumstances, we were now determined to give Zsuzsi the best possible education, and wanted her to attend the best school in the city. This required a registered address within Budapest. This was risky, because we already had an official legal address in Budakeszi. We prayed that the information would not filter down to government headquarters, and the snail's pace of bureaucracy would work in our favor. You were accepted at the school at age nine and started fourth grade in late September 1953, almost a month after the school year began.

Of course, we did not spend much time in Budakeszi, we lived secretly at my parents' apartment, even though staying there was a nightmare for all of us; every moment was filled with fear and anxiety. We were still under Communist rule and every time the doorbell rang we hid, often crawling under the beds. We had to be careful even within the building, because any neighbor or visitor could have been an agent, and we never knew who might report us to the authorities.

The most harrowing incident occurred late one night when our doorbell rang. We were gripped with fear because an unexpected visitor at the door that late at night was usually the secret police. Your father and I ran into the bathroom to hide and were about to jump from the 2nd floor window when Grandpa yelled, "Don't worry, it's okay." He had opened the front door and nobody was there. Then he realized it was raining, and perhaps the wires got wet. Thankfully it was only that. It took some time to collect our thoughts and calm down, knowing what might have happened had we attempted to jump from the window.

The government continued to insult and oppress the people with various attempts to control our lives and keep us subjugated. Yet, we did have some minor victories. In September 1954, a year after our return, we received a bill at our legal address in Budakeszi from the government-owned trucking company. To our surprise, the bill was for transporting us to the train station on the first leg of our journey to deportation. Most people probably would have paid this official-looking document because they were afraid to question it, but I decided to call the invoicing company. I told them that if they could provide proof that we ordered the transfer we would gladly pay it. I also said, to my recollection, that the gov-ernment had ordered the truck, so they should receive the bill. Of course, the company could not produce any proof, and we never paid the bill.

∼

I settled into school, I was very excited. It was a wonderful new experience; I made friends with many of my classmates and received many invitations to birthday parties. However, I could not accept those invitations. My parents did not want to take the chance of being asked questions about where I lived. Since the Party encouraged children to spy on people, even their own fam-ily members, we were afraid of drawing attention to ourselves.

I could not have a normal social life at school. We had to find a way to make friends with children who were not living in the same neighborhood. As a little girl I had learned to play ten-nis and now it might be a way to meet new friends. We asked my friend, Andras, and his father if they could get me into their club on Margaret Island.

This 225-acre island on the Danube separates Buda from Pest. In the nineteenth century it was a public park but until 1900 the only access was by boat. In the twentieth century, the construction of the Margaret Bridge made it accessible and the island became a major recreational area and health resort owing to its therapeutic springs. It was a beautiful part of the city. The tennis club was mainly used by military officers and high-rank-ing officials of the Communist Party, most of who came in uni-form. Andras explained that only a small number of members were civilians, who were accepted because they were outstand-ing players. He was twelve years old, and was one of the club's leading players. He was being groomed to represent Hungary at international tennis competitions. He and his family were neither Communists nor part of the military, but he had earned special privileges because of his talent.

He and his family helped me become a member and I began playing tennis at the club every day after school. It was so exciting to meet other children my age and not have to worry about discussing our residences. We all lived in different parts of the city and no one asked where anyone lived. I loved being with them. Daddy helped me to get to the club. He would finish his workday early, and meet me at school every day. He took the first bus with me, then we walked to the next bus stop and he put me on the No. 26 bus to Margaret Island. He waved good-bye and said, "Be careful and call when you get there." I was ten years old, and felt very grown up and proud that my parents trusted me to go at least a portion of the distance by myself. I was very, very careful.

Immediately after arrival at the club, I would call home as promised. I would spend the afternoon practicing and doing my homework. Before leaving, I would call Daddy to meet me at the same bus stop. He was always careful to be there on time. From there we went home together.

All international competitions, including the Davis Cup, were played at this club. I was one of the young players appointed to be ball boys and girls during major competitions. This gave me a chance to mingle with foreigners, who were very few and far between. I also used the chance to practice my English, seizing every possibility of communicating with the players directly. I continued to develop my tennis skills and began to compete. Between practicing and homework, every moment of my life was filled with joyful activities.

I was very good at mathematics and decided to tutor other children. I didn't get paid—nobody had money—but people found ways to show their appreciation. They paid me in delicious cakes; one of my favorites was called *kugelhoff*. Mommy wasn't able to do much baking at this time, so this seemed very special to me.

I was a good student in most subjects, but I had no talent for singing despite my love of music. My report card often reflected a less than perfect score, because of the lower music grades. The grades were from one to five, with five being the best. My report card was consistently all fives except for music, which was a 4. I asked my music teacher what it would take to get a top grade. She said that if I made a school presentation on the life of a composer, perhaps I could improve my grade. I went to work on it immediately. I knew that there would be a festival that year commemorating the life and works of Bela Bartok, the famous Hungarian composer. So I chose to do a project on his life and accomplishments. My presentation was a huge success and from that day on, I never had to worry about my music grade. I had the same music teacher the following year, so I did a similar project for her. I always offered to help her with just about anything to ensure my good grade.

～

It was always difficult to truly feel secure during those years. Our living conditions were risky and unstable. The regime did not tolerate people who previously benefited from society and called them "parasites." According to them, business owners exploited their employees and this caused them to be labeled. All adults had to work and children had to be sent to childcare centers where the brainwashing began. I joined the collective where I had worked before our deportation; the same one where Grandpa and Kato worked manufacturing small leather goods. Your father, through his previous connections, was rehired to work for the two film companies. We worked, but kept a very low profile both at home and at work.

From 1953 to 1956 we lived a very restricted life, but at long last, if we wanted to, were able to participate in the many cultural activities available in Budapest. Since we lived in hiding we had to be careful not to stay out past 11 p.m., so the building custodian who lived on the premises would not see us coming home. We also could never invite anybody to our home; we felt that if we could not return the favor it was better not to get involved.

Due to mismanagement and abuse of the system, the economy was deteriorating and production levels decreased. Even basic necessities were in short supply. We had to stand in line for just about everything, even basic food items like eggs or bread. While we couldn't buy much of anything, at least they were available most of the time.

There was practically no exporting to the West, so hard currency was not available for importing any goods. First-quality manufactured goods were sent to Russia, while rejects or lower-grade products stayed in Hungary. Worse yet, inferior Russian-made products were sent to Hungary in lieu of hard currency payment, and only those were available. The Russians used Hungary for their economic advantage, while we lived day to day, discontented, under the influence of constant restraint.

Stalin's death three years earlier had resulted in many changes, but the political climate shifted more rapidly between March and September 1956, during the uprisings in the other Eastern Bloc countries. There was more and more talk of freedom and a burning desire for change filled the air. Laws and rules were relaxed or overlooked, and comics began to make jokes about the regime and its leaders. Just a few months earlier, that would have meant instant death for everyone involved. A few foreign films were allowed in from Italy and France, some Western literature was published, and newspapers began to print articles about current events and political issues. For the first time in many years, people felt freer to express their feelings, and dissatisfied voices became louder and louder. As a result, slowly, people began to demand even more action and fewer restrictions from the regime. On the other hand, we kept quiet. We were afraid to speak up because of what had happened to us before. That painful experience was still so fresh in our minds.

General unrest grew, and a sense that change was imminent began to fill the air. As the enforcement of rules eased, people regained contact with the intellectual community in the West, and Radio Free Europe was once again accessible. Accurate news came in, raising even more discontent, as well as a fervor for rebellion.

Budapest had always been a cultural center, with numerous theaters and concert halls, two opera houses, the Academy of Music, and an outdoor amphitheater on Margaret Island. However, during the Communist rule, rather than providing an outlet for the expression of emotions and ideas, artistic ventures had served as a forum for promoting Socialism and propaganda. In 1956, for the first time in many years, freedom of expression within the arts came alive again, offering people the strength to fight for a better future. Entertainment was back in the hands of the artists, which spawned a creative boom, as well as a sense of optimism.

We would have liked to be in contact with Aunt Rosa and Bela, but we knew that some people were still afraid to associate with closely watched people like us. We respected their position. In September 1956, a general amnesty was announced which finally gave freedom to all former deportees, allowing us to legally return to Budapest. We quickly found a room to rent in one of the apartments in the same building as Grandma and Grandpa. Living openly in Budapest was a glorious feeling and offered us a glimmer of hope for a free and better life in the future. Although our living accommodations were very meager, at least we did not have to live in hiding, and for the first time in many years we felt like we were finally free.

All during this time we wondered about who was living in our old apartment since we had been taken away in 1951. Could there ever be a possibility of living there again? Did they keep all the furnishings or were they also sold off like after 1949? But we had endured so much that we were afraid to even attempt to go to the apartment and ask questions.

By this time Grandma and Grandpa were in the process of immigrating to Australia, and because there was so much to do for them, we couldn't devote attention to ourselves. We hoped that after they left Hungary, we would be able to follow them. We decided to stay in the rented room.

CHAPTER 20
REVOLUTION

Within a short time after Stalin's death in 1953, revolts broke out in Czechoslovakia, later in Berlin, and then spread throughout East Germany, but were quickly and severely crushed by Russian tanks after only days of bitter street-fighting. But then, in late June 1956, a strike by Polish workers in Poznan was followed by a full-scale uprising and seizure of control of the city.

During this time unrest was brewing in Hungary also. The Writers Union Congress denounced "the regime of tyranny," and many people voiced their outrage more openly and more frequently. Prompted by these events, a group of Hungarian University students organized a large meeting to be held on October 23, 1956, in front of the statue of General Bem, a leader in the fight for freedom one hundred years earlier. The students marched defiantly from the statue to a nearby building, which housed the two government-controlled radio stations. Their plan was to force their way in and broadcast their demands for reform and for the return of Premier Imre Nagy.

The radio station building was protected by many AVH guards. When the students attempted to enter, the police tried to disperse the crowd with tear gas, beatings, and numerous arrests. When the crowd resisted, the police opened fire and killed several people, further angering and inciting the crowd. With this, the Hungarian revolution had begun. That night they tried to tear down a statue of Stalin—but quite ironically they discovered that Stalin's statue, like his beliefs, was too firmly planted in solid foundation. They didn't have the right tools at first, but they would get them and the statue came down!

The "Bloody Revolution," as it came to be known, began as peaceful demonstrations, but quickly turned into violent riots and battles in the street. News of the killings spread with lightning speed to other parts of the city and the country, as workers and freedom fighters began to take over factories, weapons depots, and Soviet tanks. A new multiparty government was formed almost overnight, and hopes for true political change had come alive.

Imre Nagy had been forced to resign several years earlier from the Communist Party for his liberal policies, but was soon reappointed as Prime Minister as the revolt commenced in full force. Considered a national hero, Nagy promised free elections as well as full Soviet withdrawal from Hungary. Newly formed "workers councils" issued an ultimatum that strikes would continue until all Russian troops left the country. Hungary was now the hungry tiger...and on October 30th, the remaining Red Army tanks pulled out. Her people had finally won.

At 5:45 p.m. on October 23rd, 1956, Mom and I were leaving the dressmaker's. We walked out into the street and found ourselves in the midst of a huge commotion. Loud, cheering crowds had gathered on the streets, trucks were filled with excited, screaming young people waving flags and yelling "Freedom! Down with Stalinism and Communism!" We had no idea what was going on, so we raced home to safety. We were scared, and the sight of trucks filled with people made it worse especially because it was dark. All we could think of was the truck in which we had been taken away in the dark, early morning hours in 1951. We held onto each other and tried to push through the crowds to get away from the main road and get home as quickly as possible. When we arrived, Dad had also just gotten home and was talking about what he saw and heard. At first we thought they were only rumors, but soon we learned that the Revolution had indeed begun! We had been dreaming of life beyond Communism, and now we hoped this was our opportunity for true freedom. I often heard my parents reminisce about the good life we had once had, and they hoped this would be a new beginning.

As the Revolutionaries gained control, many of the dreaded AVH officers were rounded up and killed. Many political prisoners were freed. For the first time in about eight years we were able to listen to the BBC and other Western broadcasts. As soon as the country had open communication with the West, Hungary requested assistance. Radio Free Europe and the Voice of America announced that help was on the way and encouraged Hungarians to keep fighting, which would result in the Soviet troops pulling back. In spite of repeated statements promising assistance, the West never came. The

United Nations was tied up with negotiations in the aftermath of the Suez Canal crisis.

During this waiting period, the borders were open and many people did not wait for assistance from the West. They decided to leave Hungary of their own accord—ultimately about 200,000 people left. They did not trust the shaky political conditions, not knowing whether the promised help would arrive or when, and did not want to take any chances by waiting too long. They chose to get out while the going was good.

We couldn't leave. Mom and Dad explained that they had to focus on my grandparents. Grandma and Grandpa had received passports to legally immigrate to Australia, where Ica and Imre acted as their sponsors. They were permitted to leave only because they were elderly and on pensions. The Party no longer considered them as contributing members of society, and their leaving would relieve the country of the burden of having to pay their pensions. But Grandpa was not well and his illness slowed down their departure. Prior to entering Australia he had to be cleared medically, and we had to make sure he was well enough to make the long journey. We made every effort to speed up their departure, but it still took some time. Mom spent every available moment handling their affairs. For those two crucial months, until they left, we could not think of ourselves.

We had been living in the rented room until the Hungarian revolution broke out on October 23, 1956. We then thought about what we should do: try to find another apartment of our own, or wait it out there. We knew that after my grandparents left Hungary, we wanted to follow them, so we decided to stay.

The revolution moved us forward, but our period of hope was short-lived: on Sunday November 4, 1956, at 4pm the Russian tanks returned with a vengeance. Soviet troops suppressed the revolt, Hungary's valiant fight was overpowered, and the thousands of people involved in the struggle for freedom suffered greatly. Thousands of Hungarians died, many were jailed, and many more were caught and taken to the Soviet Union, where they were placed in hard labor or internment camps.

Realizing that help was not forthcoming from the West, people gave up hope of a lasting change. Beginning on November 4th, 1956, an avalanche of Hungarians headed for the Austrian border. According to reports, by noon five thousand had crossed over safely. Within a couple of weeks, a total of 2% of the population, over 200,000 people, fled Hungary for other lands; we only wished we could have been among them. We made preliminary steps and hoped that the conditions would still allow us to cross over to Austria. Kato and Kati were waiting to go with us. We planned to leave as soon as Grandma and Grandpa had left the country.

The Russians tried to increase security along the borders. They succeeded, and by the middle of December such an escape became nearly impossible.

Living conditions became worse than ever. The streets were filled with Russian foot soldiers bearing guns and tanks. We were afraid to go out. People were stopped, arrested, and taken away. Now, again, no one at all was allowed to leave the country. Passports were no longer issued. The laws were tightened, scrutiny increased, and life in Hungary became even more frightening.

With the situation worsening, we realized it may not be simple, but as soon as Grandma and Grandpa left in December, we focused all of our attention to our future freedom.

CHAPTER 21
ATTEMPTED ESCAPES

ON DECEMBER 10TH, 1956, the day after my grandparents finally left Budapest, my parents and aunt decided to try to escape. It was far from an easy decision, for we had paid dearly for our first attempt in 1949. The patrols and personnel build-up had not yet been fully organized at the border, so we felt that there was still the possibility of escaping. Some enterprising country folk near border towns had developed a moneymaking opportunity to escort people across the border to Austria. Dad made arrangements through a contact to help us. Without any delay, on December 13th, 1956, we fled Budapest by train and headed for the border.

Despite our high hopes, once again, our escape attempt failed! We were met at the train station by our prearranged border-crossing peasant with his horse-drawn wagon, similar to the one in 1949. Once we had paid him the agreed amount we began our journey toward the border, just as we had then... However, after only a short ride Hungarian border patrol guards captured us. We were arrested again and taken to jail.

Remembering our previous attempt, we wondered what would happen to us this time. Fortunately, the authorities were not completely organized under the new regime, procedures were not in place, and they were not prepared for enforcement of sentences. They released us after only a few days. We returned to Budapest, but instead of laying low, this experience made us even bolder, and on January 4th, 1957, we made yet another daring attempt to escape Hungary. We prayed that the border was still in a chaotic state and this time we would succeed. This time, our dreams were shattered much too soon. They arrested us at the train station before the train even left Budapest! It seems the spies were once again out in full force. We were taken to prison, and luckily again, they kept us for only a few days. There were so many people attempting to escape that the prisons were filled to capacity.

By now our hopes to escape were fading, and we did not want to press our luck. We decided that we should obtain passports and leave through the front door. While officially passports were not obtainable, perhaps through bribery we might still have a chance. We realized that we needed a foolproof plan this time. We had to find a connection and the money to make it all happen. Your father found a way to get some of our money back from Switzerland. He knew a man who had connections to the West and could make arrangements to retrieve the money. In about ten days magically we received it and then felt more confident about our plan. Your father and I went to the passport office, which of course was jammed with people. We searched for our applications, which had been submitted much earlier, at the same time as your grandparents', but supposedly our file had been lost.

I had an idea, and requested a telegram from Ica in Australia. I had her write that Grandpa was dying, and unless we could get our passports immediately, we would not see him alive. Having come to the passport office with this telegram in hand, I used my intuition to find someone who looked like he or she might be sympathetic to a dying, old man.

Looking around in the crowd I noticed a man sitting behind a desk in the distance. We made eye contact and I approached him. When I got close to him I noticed his uniform and realized he was a high-ranking officer—which was a blessing. I explained our situation, telling him that our documents were missing, and showed him the telegram from Ica. He listened attentively, and then said that if everything I told him were in fact true, he would see to it that we got our passports as soon as possible. He promised to search for our file and notify us when he found it. I did not want to take a chance on that, so I told him that I would go home immediately and bring back duplicates of all the documents. There was no Xerox at that time so we had to use carbon paper. From my business experience I knew the importance of keeping copies of everything. My heart leapt with joy that I had had the foresight to make copies of them...just in case!

While this all seemed promising, we were still afraid that it could be a trap; it was common practice for officials to make promises and even accept bribes, and then report the incident to the authorities. It was impossible to predict exactly what people would do during this *time, and there was always a thin line between a genuine desire to help and harmful intentions.*

When I returned with the documents, it was the end of the day and that official had already left his office. However, his secretary was just leaving for the day, so I decided to follow her. When she entered the Hotel Beke's pastry shop, I noticed her greeting the manager warmly. I happened to know the manager well, and after waiting for the secretary to leave, I spoke to Martha and explained my situation. I asked her if she could and would help by acting as a liaison between the secretary and me, and letting us know the status of our passports. This way, we could have advance knowledge and leave without any delay when they were ready. Martha said she would be glad to help—that is, if I paid her. I asked how much. Before she had a chance to answer, I offered her 10,000 Forints, which was about one year's average salary. She jumped at the generous offer, and a deal was struck. Her instant response led me to believe that her close relationship with the secretary had probably helped others before me. Just like the border crossing created a business opportunity for the peasants, people in the city used their personal connections to supplement their meager income. She assured me that she would do her best to put our case in the hands of the secretary for personal, fast attention. She told me that according to her previous successful attempts, we should receive our passports within a short period of time, but together with our documents we must submit a written declaration that we would leave everything we owned to the government, including my parents' apartment and all of its contents.

It seems money could talk. I could hardly believe it— our passports were issued within two weeks. But then, we had another hurdle to overcome! The passports were just one half of the emigration or exiting process...we also needed exit permits! Those were not issued until the National Bank verified that everything had been recorded and paid for.

Official requirements were generally not clear and the regime created roadblocks wherever possible. There was an awful lot of red tape to freedom. The Hungarians made it very difficult and uncomfortable for anyone to leave the country. The next few days we worked furiously to prepare and complete every step prior to our departure.

My parents asked me to select what I wanted to take. I took all the clothes I had, and some art supplies and needlework materials, so I would have something to work on during the trip. I packed most of my art supplies in my suitcase, and a put a few in my carry-on. I also took one of my most treasured silver pieces: a miniature tea set, a replica of the large one we used to have in our home. It seemed I was forever packing to leave.

We sorted our belongings and tried to figure out what to take. Knowing we were going to start a whole new life, we selected only the most meaningful items. At the top of our list were photographs: the old album that Aunt Rosa and Bela had rescued, and a few basic personal belongings. We gathered a few rugs, some silver items, and your father's stamp collection. We packed everything that didn't require special handling, so we would be ready at very short notice. Other than clothing, everything required a government release and a payment. Every item's value had to be paid either in gold or silver. These formalities took a lot of time and patience, which we did not have. To avoid some of the valuations, we tried to declare jewelry as semi-precious or fake, rather than precious. One ring was passed off as having glass stones, though it actually had diamonds. The stamp collection also had to be checked. It required a special permit, which took a whole day for the bank to issue.

Once everything was evaluated and declared, the payment transactions took place in the offices of the National Bank of Hungary, prior to issuing the exit permits. They would not allow us to leave unless it was done according to the strictly enforced rules. We paid all the money and exchanged all the silver and gold as they requested. The stamp collection was placed in a large envelope and on the face of it was written, "TO BE OPENED ONLY AFTER CROSSING THE BORDER." We wondered why this item was treated differently than the rest, but when we asked, they simply said, "this is how it is done." We had no choice but to accept their meaningless explanation and hope for the best. We had planned to sell the stamps in Vienna so that we could have some money on which to live.

The bakery manager, Martha, held up her end of the bargain, and on Saturday March 16th, 1957, we received advance notice that the exit permits would be issued very soon! We finished packing and scheduled the final customs appointment for luggage examination for the day prior to the train's scheduled departure to Vienna. Thankfully, our luggage was approved and we immediately shipped our belongings ahead of us to Austria.

Under normal circumstances we would never have done this, but, knowing that the Alberg-Orient Express, which traveled between Budapest and Vienna, did not run every day, we decided to take this major risk and hope for the best. Any delay due to our luggage would have been a huge risk, knowing that they could have easily revoked our exit permits at any time. At this point, all we cared about was being ready to leave! We also knew that circumstances could change without notice. When I think back on it, it was incredible that we shipped everything before we even had our papers.

When our exit permits arrived two days later on Monday, we were prepared and able to leave immediately. The next day, Tuesday, March 19th, 1957, we left on the Alberg-Orient Express to Vienna. A glorious day in our lives! The first day on our journey to freedom.

CHAPTER 22
LEAVING HUNGARY

AT LONG LAST, WE WERE LEAVING HUNGARY. We were excited, fearful, and yet full of hope. The train station was practically empty, and dimly lit. The few people on the platform were all workers bundled up in warm clothes doing their jobs. We carried our personal luggage, and walked until we found our passenger car. Mom and Dad were each carrying two bags. Kato carried her bags in one hand and held onto Kati with the other. Kati had a small bag with her favorite teddy bear in it. I had one bag plus my coat.

We finally found the car. We boarded and found our reserved seats. It was a small compartment for all five of us. There were very few people on the train aside from us. We were on the Alberg Express, the Budapest-to-Vienna segment of the Orient Express, going from Istanbul to Paris. Since the communist government forbade citizens of Hungary to travel out of the country, we were the only people who boarded the train in Budapest. It was eerie. The other passengers already on the train were foreigners, traveling through. We were scared, and didn't dare speak to anyone, move, or even look around. The whistle blew at 11 p.m., and the train began to move. Slowly increasing speed, it chugged along, leaving the dimly lit railway station behind.

Having gone through so much before, we could hardly believe we would really make it out of Hungary until it actually happened. Despite the fact that we were sitting on a foreign train, we were still in communist Hungary. I saw the worry and uncertainty in my parents' eyes, and sensed the tension. Being on yet another train, hoping once again to leave Hungary brought back many unpleasant memories. All of our failed escape attempts had started on trains. We held our breath as the train picked up speed in the darkness.

No one spoke, but the silence was deafening. The border checkpoint was ahead of us. Kato read to Kati until she fell asleep. She looked relieved that she wouldn't have to answer all of Kati's questions. No one talked.

At thirteen years of age I had experienced so much, that by now I was well aware of the potential danger. As long as we were on Hungarian soil, anything could happen. They could revoke our exit papers at the last minute, or send us back to prison. My imagination ran wild and I'm sure similar thoughts were on my parents' mind. We knew that at the security checkpoint in Hegyeshalom, the last stop in Hungary, we would have to get off the train with all of our belongings for the final search by Hungarian officials before crossing into Austria. I was worried but didn't say anything to my parents; I didn't want them to know how scared I was.

There was little to do and I wasn't in the mood to draw or read. I didn't even bother opening my bag. Just sitting and not speaking during the three-hour train ride to Vienna made the trip seem even longer. It gave me plenty of time to worry. I stared out the icy window, though there was nothing to see in the darkness. I saw Mom nervously trying to relax. She kept her hands clasped tightly together. Dad, on the other hand, fell asleep immediately. The pressure of the past few days finally took its toll, and now there was nothing left for him to do but rest.

I was far from sleepy. My thoughts began to race. I just sat quietly, hoping that all would go smoothly. I watched my father's face continue to relax as he fell into a deeper sleep. I closed my eyes, but I could not fall asleep. As the train clattered along the tracks, I thought about what lay ahead at the end of this journey. Since we were forbidden to travel or even read about living in another country, I couldn't imagine what our new life would be like. We would need to adapt to an entirely different culture with a new language and customs. It would be a whole new way of life for us.

The train pulled into Hegyeshalom border checkpoint. We were ordered to get off the train and carry our bags with us to the border patrol offices. There were a few foreigners there with only briefcases, so they went through the formalities very quickly. The five of us were the only passengers going through the lengthy procedure. I didn't say a word, but I was worried about getting off and leaving our train. Would they let us re-board? What if the train left without us? I worried that the border patrol would take too long checking us out—perhaps intentionally.

The wait was agonizing. We were afraid to speak unless they asked us a question. We didn't know what to expect. They could pick on anything they didn't like, or behave according to their individual attitude. Then, without warning, one of the border guards called Dad and took him away! A female guard took Mom and me into a cubicle, and my heart leaped into my chest! We remained frozen and silent through a very thorough body check, and then realized they only wanted to make certain that we were not smuggling anything out. The guards said nothing.

Our fear turned to terror in the silence. But then moments later, we had passed this part of the exam.

I stood still, shaking, while they examined my parents' bags. They had to verify that everything we were taking with us appeared on the official list. All the bags had to be checked; the seals broken and the contents examined.

After Mom and Dad were passed, as I turned my bag inside out for the search, the pencil box fell out, along with my papers and embroidery. Then with a loud bang, a paper bag fell out. It was my favorite adorable silver tea set—undeclared! Mom almost fainted. She turned white as a ghost, and her hands began shaking. Dad stood stiffly next to her; both speechless. The officer asked, "What is this?" Looking at my mother, I sensed we were in trouble, but for a second I didn't know what to say. Then, quickly I answered, "It is mine. It's part of my dollhouse, which I had to leave in Budapest. I wanted to keep this one item, it was my favorite piece from it." It really wasn't so. It was always in my parents' breakfront in the living room. I don't know where the thought came from, but somehow the words came out. I figured this sounded believable to the guard. Mom managed to regain her composure, and with Dad's arm firmly around her waist, she said, "She packed her own bag. We didn't know she brought that." The guard said nothing. "She is just a young child carrying her own little treasure." And with that, he let us go.

Whew!! With bags in hand, we walked back to the train as fast as we could. My legs were still shaking, but I would not slow down. We boarded the train in a hurry and kept our mouths shut. We sat down, tense and holding our breath until the engine started. As the train began to move I still sat there without uttering a sound. I didn't know how to apologize for my stupidity ... our whole life teetered on that moment of foolishness! When the train finally crossed into Austrian soil, I burst out saying how sorry I was. When we saw the first Austrian sign, I broke down sobbing. Sitting between Mom and Dad, they hugged and kissed and comforted me. Then all five of us, including Kato and Kati, held hands and thanked God for saving us one more time. Dad kept saying, "This is time for celebration, not for crying. This is the moment we have been waiting for, for almost eight years."

As the train sped toward Vienna, Mom suddenly remarked, "This is truly a memorable day!" Dad nodded and finished the sentence, "Today is March 19th, 1957, and we have just finally left Hungary. A great day, but remember how special a day this is: it's also the thirteenth anniversary of the Nazi invasion."

We looked at each other and knew that we never wanted to return again.

At train station leaving Vienna for Trieste, April 1957

With Kato and Kati, mother and I and friends in Trieste

CHAPTER 23
VIENNA

WE BREATHED A HUGE SIGH OF RELIEF when we crossed over into Austria. It was another hour until we arrived in Vienna, but this part of the train ride was exciting and exhilarating. All our anxieties were behind us, and we were filled with hope and dreams of a better future. Even the uncertainty of a new life in a very distant land could not dampen our spirits once the Hungarian border was behind us.

With the major hurdle behind us, we hadn't even arrived, yet slowly we began to worry about the future. We kept wondering how much of the money we sent out we would still have? We had sent out millions in 1948 and 1949, but how much was there now? We would have to wait until we got to Australia to get our answer. We knew Ica and Imre had sent part of it to our account in Switzerland, and the remainder they took with them to Australia.

As we approached Vienna, the sun came up and the bright light made us forget our dark days in Hungary. When we arrived at about 6am, a pleasant surprise greeted us at the train station. A representative of the HIAS, the Hebrew Immigrant Aid Society, was there to offer us immediate assistance. HIAS was aware of what people faced when they finally reached a free country, and were there to offer help and relief. We were reminded of the humanitarian acts we had witnessed during the war, and here we were, the grateful recipients once again.

Unbeknownst to us, we were already registered with the HIAS. When Ica and Imre arrived in Vienna in 1949 expecting us to follow them soon, they had the HIAS record our names, which had remained in the files all this time. The HIAS representative escorted us to their offices, where he found us hotel accommodations and gave us some money for our daily needs. This touched us deeply, and your father and I immediately decided that the minute we were in a position to do so, we would donate money to this organization. We hoped that our future contribution would help to make other immigrants' lives a little easier, just as the generous donations of strangers had eased our load.

We checked into the hotel. It was very simple, no frills, but to us it felt like paradise. Kato and Kati had their own room and we had ours. We expected to be in Vienna for about two weeks, so we unpacked what we thought would be necessary. We all took showers one by one. That was a real turning point in our lives. We were cleansed of the old and the bad, and now the new and the good was ahead of us. With that feeling of euphoria, we started to walk down the stairs. We hurried to get out onto the street and feel our freedom.

Our first evening in Vienna was such an amazing experience.

For the first time in many years we saw brightly lit streets, even the traffic lights seemed to shine brighter! Store windows were beautifully decorated and filled with attractive merchandise, which were not available in Hungary. Every window was filled with colorful, unique products. Everything seemed to sparkle. We couldn't get enough. Clothing stores were filled with fabulous new clothes, and although we didn't have any money to buy, we enjoyed the sight all the same. People filled the coffee houses and sat at sidewalk cafés sipping hot coffee and tasting delicious, decadent pastries. And soon it would all be there for our taking! We walked the streets till we dropped.

Newsstands were filled with so many magazines. We could hardly believe our eyes; so few were available in Hungary. There were so many fashion magazines; I couldn't wait to look through them. I loved clothes! I loved color! And I loved to draw. Seeing them was an indescribable thrill.

Everything was different. Everything reflected a sense of freedom. People were dressed in such a variety of bright colors— not the gray, bleak tones common in Communist-ruled Hungary. Color, color, everywhere! And another huge difference: no one stood in line for food … and there was plenty of it. At first we just admired the huge displays of magnificent fruits. Then we bought some. We could not get enough bananas and oranges, both of which were new tastes to us. We ate as if eating was going out of style! We soon realized that from this point on, these rare and succulent fruits would be available to us whenever we wanted them. Our hearts were as full as our stomachs.

This was our introduction to the lifestyle of the West. It was our first taste of our new future. It felt good, knowing that people viewed us as tourists, rather than criminals.

We viewed Vienna with anticipation, excitement, and a bit of anxiety. To pay for our expenses, we had planned to sell your father's stamp collection as soon as we arrived. However, when we opened the envelope, to our great disappointment and anger, there were no stamps inside—only shredded newspaper. This was why the Hungarian officials had written, "open only after crossing the border" on the sealed envelope that originally contained the valuable stamps! Our main source of income to pay for our living expenses was gone. Totally gone! They took advantage of and abused anyone leaving, as much as they could. I don't know why we were even surprised. With little money on hand, we now began to wonder how much money was left with Ica and Imre in Australia. Would the HIAS pay for our passage, or we would need to have Ica send that amount right away?

Much to our surprise, it turned out that the HIAS in Vienna had already contacted Ica and Imre in Australia immediately after our arrival. They had made all the travel arrangements, but requested money from Ica to cover everything. We also needed enough money for the rest of our stay in Vienna and train tickets to Trieste, Italy, to catch the boat to Australia. With no money from the stamp collection, we had to further deplete our already shrinking account.

While we were realistic with our money situation, we didn't know when and if we would ever get back to Europe, so we made the most of every moment. Despite being cautious, sometimes we felt guilty spending. We spent little but enjoyed it a lot.

We enjoyed Vienna, but Trieste, a lovely, busy Italian port, offered a more dramatic change from life in Hungary. Austrians tend to be more reserved, serious people, and their lifestyle and foods were very similar to

Hungarians. The Italians, by contrast, were friendly and jovial people who sang in the streets and always appeared to be carefree.

The food in Italy was very different. In the mornings the most wonderful, delicious rolls were baked, both sweet and plain. The wonderful aroma of baked goods in Trieste permeated the air, the scent quite different from any we had experienced before. There were so many breads new to us, and we could hardly wait to gobble up every one of them! Each one was better than the last, and a feast both for the eye and the palate. Breads and baked goods in Hungary were delicious also, but other than the large variety of pastries, the selection was limited. It made your father so happy to run to the nearest bakery every morning. He didn't speak Italian, but by using his hands and feet and putting an "O" at the end of the words, he made himself understood. He fitted in very well. Like the Italians, Dad had always been the singing optimist.

At first, I wasn't a very adventurous eater. But since the baked goods were so delicious, we were eager to sample their most famous Italian food, pasta. Pasta was not completely foreign to us, but the way it was served was new. We had eaten a lot of it in Hungary, because meat was not always available, and pasta was often prepared as a main course. However, Hungarians serve it more on the sweet side, while Italians serve it as a first course with various savory toppings. My parents had me try many of them and I loved most.

In Hungary, we were familiar with only one shape, the flat noodle, like fettuccine, but we soon learned that Italians enjoyed many other shapes and sizes. In fact, during our stay in Italy, we felt like we had an education in pasta preparation, and learned the appropriate toppings for each shape and size. Every day and in various places, pasta seemed to be served differently. According to the people who tried to explain to us, the thickness of the sauce determined the best pasta to use because each sauce would adhere better to specific shapes. Italian cooks were creative in their toppings, and even when they were simple, they were delicious. We had a wonderful time sampling all of these new discoveries. We wished we could learn more and understand better how to make some of the sauces or the delicious sweets. We were surprised that every meal began with a plate of pasta, followed by a meat course. We often wondered how, after a big bowl of pasta, people could enjoy a second course. Life seemed wonderful, and we felt like children let loose in a candy store. Everything was new, satisfying, and fulfilling and, most importantly, there was a calm that we had not felt for many, many years.

We would have liked to be able to communicate with the people, but none of us spoke Italian. After a few days, I picked up a few basic words that helped. I learned "please," "thank you," "hello," "goodbye," and the numbers, which together with my hands helped to make simple conversation. Hearing me talk, my parents often used a phrase to express their pleasure; "You cannot be sold in Italy anymore."

CHAPTER 24

LEAVING FOR AUSTRALIA

After our arrival in Trieste, the HIAS representative in charge of our group contacted everyone and stated that ten of us would need to stay behind for a few weeks and take the next boat. He explained that there were ten other new arrivals that had to leave immediately, and there was not enough room aboard ship for them as well our entire group. Since we all knew that circumstances might change in a matter of weeks, or even days, no one offered to give up his or her spot. So, we resigned ourselves to pulling names out of a hat. Our family and Kato's were among the unfortunate ones to have to board the later ship. We had no choice but to make the best of it; it seemed it was still two steps forward, and one step back.

We had spent two weeks in Vienna, a couple of days in Trieste, and now we traveled by train to Genoa, where HIAS put us up in a hotel for the next month. It was the second week of April 1957. We walked a lot and did as much sightseeing as possible. I managed to pick up a little more Italian, which helped us to get around more easily. In our spare time we played cards to pass the time.

> At the end of April, a little sooner than expected, we boarded the Oceania. The ship carried about 500 people, the majority of whom were either tourists traveling for pleasure, or immigrants freely departing from Western European countries. We were part of a smaller group of immigrants, refugees, who had no experience in international travel, especially for such an extended journey. There were thirty-nine of us Hungarians.
>
> At that time, people in Europe traveled, but mainly by train, since the distances between countries were not so great. Traveling by plane was far more limited and quite expensive in those days. For us, flying would have been even more costly, because we would have had to ship our belongings separately. Traveling by ship was going to be a long journey, but it was more practical. We had never been on a large ocean liner before, but were just glad to finally be on our way.
>
> At first we were told that the voyage would take about six weeks, since we had to go around the southern tip of Africa via the Cape of Good Hope. However, when our voyage was delayed, the rescheduled trip wound up taking only thirty days. Now we would be sailing through the Suez Canal. Beside our concerns and uncertainties, it was exciting to think that we would be experiencing a part of history. At the same time, we had our worries about being the very first ship to cross after the Israel-Arab War.
>
> This particular vessel was a two-class ship, which meant that first and tourist class passengers were separate. We were in tourist class and were not allowed to go

to the first class section, even though we were all dying to see what it was like.

All of the Hungarians were put in large dormitories rather than individual cabins: all the men in one, and the women in another. This made us feel very uncomfortable since we learned that other passengers had their own cabins, even in tourist class. The ship's office explained that this was a more expensive ship than the one for which we had originally paid, and that the amount paid covered only dormitory type of accommodation. We did not have money to request an upgrade, so we were stuck. Another blow... but a small price to pay for our freedom.

Mom decided that we should try to see what we could do to improve our circumstances. I went with her to the Captain and, with the little Italian and English that I knew, described our situation. We explained that we had originally been assigned to travel a month earlier, and were under the impression that each family was to have had an individual cabin. We also appealed to his sense of compassion by explaining that after all we had suffered, a smooth voyage would make a huge difference in our lives. We asked if there was anything he could do. He was very understanding and offered us two available cabins, one for Kato and Kati and the other for Mother and I. There was no cabin for three available, so we happily accepted the double accommodations. When we settled into our new accommodations, we were able to enjoy the ship, the cuisine, and the socializing that we had missed so much.

There were many pleasant experiences during the thirty days aboard ship, but the voyage also brought to mind that being Jewish made me a target in certain parts of the world. Mom had told me stories about the war, bigotry, and the hardships we survived as Jews during the Nazi era, but seeing it for myself was different. When our ship docked in Yemen, I learned firsthand that the people there considered Jews to be the enemy, regardless of their individual circumstances.

We also had another incident, which brought back sad, even frightening feelings experienced during the previous ten years. The Oceania was the first passenger ship to cross the Suez Canal after the 1956 Israeli-Arab war, and the canal was not yet totally cleared of the mines and wreckage of other ships. As we were passing through the canal, headed for the port of Aden in Yemen, our ship hit something and could not proceed. We were stuck. We sat there all day, filled with anxiety. We still had the Communist oppression and the lack of transparency on our minds, and we worried about what might be behind this. Nobody from the ship said anything, except that they were trying to clear it so we could continue. Fortunately, after nine hours of uncertainty, by late afternoon we were able to proceed, but there was never any explanation given.

Whatever the reason, we were greatly relieved, and glad to be heading to Aden. The officers aboard ship knew from the papers we had filled out which of the passengers were Jewish. They specifically instructed us to keep a low profile and warned us that anything could happen—if we left the ship—while we were in port. They could not be responsible for our safety in a foreign land. We were very disappointed. We had thought that once we left Communism behind, we would not feel the threat of racial or religious persecution. But, we were still closer to freedom than we had ever been, so we just stayed onboard. At the end of the day our ship left Yemen. We wished we could have seen the town of Aden. The passengers who chose to get off the ship returned telling us how truly wonderful it was... we could only assume they were right; it sounded like a fascinating place with a very different culture from what we knew.

As we sailed the Indian Ocean, we had another unexpected, unbelievable experience. There was a typhoon only ten knots away from us. The force and effect of the winds created waves, which were so high they crisscrossed the ship from side to side. Most of the passengers became very seasick. The crew set up ropes throughout the ship connecting doors and hallways for everybody to hang onto in order to keep from falling. The ship not only rode up and down on the waves, but it pitched from left to right. It was frightening. Never in my life could I imagine that feeling of helplessness, being somewhere out in the middle of a big ocean, tossed about so wildly. Kato kept a very close watch on Kati, and my parents and I stayed together in the lounge to watch the angry ocean. The whole experience was so new it felt both frightening and exciting. We didn't realize how serious the conditions were.

During the typhoon, they shut down the dining room and we were served simple meals in the lounge, but the majority of people did not eat at all. They were too sick to eat or even be near any food. We were lucky that none of our family got seasick. Mom, Dad, and I, and quite a few other passengers stayed in the lounge far above the cabins, and at times when the waves were somewhat calm, we even ventured outside for some fresh air. When the waves got to be too dangerous, we stayed in the lounge and even slept there. Normally this was unacceptable, but under the circumstances the captain looked the other way—going down to the cabins had become intolerable from the stench of seasickness.

Within a couple of days we were out of the typhoon's reach, and returned to our cabin. But a couple of days later Kati came down with the measles. The ship's doctor diagnosed her quickly, but had no idea how she contracted the disease—we assumed it was from someone aboard the ship, but he didn't say. This put you at risk of contagion as well, and I was very worried being in the middle of the ocean and soon disembarking in a foreign country. To separate you and Kati, I took you to the lounge where we slept during the storm, while Kato and Kati stayed in the cabin. Your father stayed in the large group cabin with the men, but came up in the lounge with us when many of the men in there became ill from the rough seas. We knew the ship did not allow sleeping in the lounge, but that was my only solution for the moment. When one of the officers noticed us, we explained our situation. They offered you and I yet another unoccupied cabin—this time in first class, where we stayed until Kati was well again.

Aside from these difficulties and the general concerns, the majority of the month-long trip across the ocean was a pleasant experience. The Italian passengers were fun loving, and like the Hungarians, enjoyed life to the fullest. We traveled from Genoa across the Mediterranean through the Suez Canal, then south of India on the Indian Ocean, and stopped at the Island of Ceylon (now known as Sri Lanka). We marveled at the beauty of the island: a lush tropical setting, with palm trees everywhere. We spent a lovely day sightseeing and ate lunch at the Mount Lavinia hotel. It was a deluxe resort hotel, where we were pampered and treated like royalty. It was a magical experience sprinkled with lots of anxieties. We felt guilty spending money on such a day, but it was the only one we had freedom to enjoy and experience another culture. We sat on a balcony over-

looking the ocean, sipping exotic drinks, and taking in everything! Waiters and helpers dressed only in sarongs showered us with service. It was strange to us, but all so wonderful! After drinks, we were served a lavish lunch and reminisced about the many nights we had entertained our friends in Hungary. We kept reminding you that although we enjoyed a similar lifestyle when you were a little girl, our life in Australia would not be easy at first. Dad and I were wondering and anticipating throughout the journey, but the unknown was difficult to explain. We were flooded with pleasant memories that filled our minds for the next few days until we arrived in Perth, Western Australia. From Perth we traveled southward along the Australian Coast, and finally arrived in Melbourne.

Prior to our arrival, Dad organized a farewell party aboard ship and invited all of our new friends. We requested a private area in a corner of the lounge. He arranged with the waiters to provide us with trays, napkins, glassware, and serving pieces. We so enjoyed the preparation! We shared some of the various baked goods, salamis, and chocolates we had brought from Europe with our new friends. We had originally thought that the food might be necessary, since we had no idea what the journey would be like. As it turned out, we did not have to dip into those resources, so we figured we would use the food after we arrived in Australia. But to our surprise, as we approached Australia, we learned that it was illegal to take food into the country. So what better way to make use of the good food than to share it with others? One of the other passengers brought sparkling wine and we made a grand toast to our friendship, a safe passage, and our new life ahead.

CHAPTER 25

LIFE IN AUSTRALIA

We could hardly wait to arrive in Australia. It was May 1957. My sister, Ica, and my brother, Imre, had arrived in Melbourne in 1951. In early 1952, Imre had moved to Sydney, but Ica remained in Melbourne with her husband and their two children. When we arrived in Australia, we stayed with my sister and her family, but within a couple of weeks we realized it wasn't working out.

Her husband had a dental laboratory and treated patients in his home office, and we felt we were intruding despite their reassurances to the contrary. They wanted to make us comfortable, but we saw how hard he worked to support Ica and their two children, and we did not want to be a financial burden. In addition, their family was very religious, but ours was not. They kept the Sabbath by not driving or working, and had a kosher kitchen. We did not want to disrespect their ways, so after a couple of weeks, we decided to move to Sydney where my brother, Imre, and your grandparents lived. They were the ones who left in Dec 1956, soon after the uprising. Kato and Kati also decided to come with us, and we all boarded a train headed for Sydney.

Prior to leaving for Australia, Imre had become a master baker in Vienna. Knowing that Sydney had more European immigrants than Melbourne, he decided to try his luck there. He started small, opening a retail store next to the bakery. This was a very smart move because it allowed him to earn money while the locals became familiar with his wonderful bakery products.

Imre made delicious rolls, including the famous Austrian Kaiser roll, which fast became his most popular item. Customers soon wanted to enjoy them at restaurants, and began demanding fancier breads. To satisfy the customers' demands, the restaurants bought baked goods from him, and soon his business grew to be one of the biggest bakeries in Sydney.

A single man, Imre was renting a large apartment and insisted that we move in with him until we became more familiar with the city. There was a shortage of apartments in Sydney, and the only way to get one was to pay "key money," an expensive deposit. After a few weeks, we were able to get a low interest loan with the help of Jewish Family Services, and paid the deposit for three one-bedroom apartments in the same building. One of the three units was for my parents, another for Kato and Kati, and the third one for us. We wanted to keep my parents nearby since Grandpa's health was deteriorating and he was continually in and out of hospital.

Now there was no money left in our account, even though we had sent Ica and Imre so much. We kept wondering where it had all gone, but I accepted Ica and Imre's explanation—after all they were my family, but *your father didn't believe that we could have used up that much money. He questioned exactly how they handled it. Did they use some for themselves? We never found out, but the relationship between him, Ica, and Imre was strained after that. I could never change his mind.*

Our new life in Australia was hard. It meant getting used to a new language, new customs, and new people. Everything was foreign and we spoke only a few words of English. You knew a little more. The first weeks were particularly rough. We had to learn our way around the city, get used to heavy traffic, and adjust to driving on the left side of the street. At first, simply crossing the street was a dangerous experience, because we always looked the wrong way.

New arrivals congregated at cafés in an area of Sydney called Kings Cross. There they would find a little bit of Europe transplanted to Australia. These cafés offered foods and other familiar trappings from the old countries. Coffee, in particular, was very important to Europeans, and Australians were not that familiar with fine coffee. To satisfy the demands of the many immigrants, all the little cafés began serving espresso and cappuccino along with delicious pastries. As the need grew, cafés expanded to serve a variety of national favorite foods. Hungarians, for example, were eager to enjoy gulyas, the typical Hungarian stew, and stuffed cabbage, as well as favorite desserts like strudel, chestnut puree, and palacsinta.

Some Australians didn't like these foreign influences. Prior to the 1950's, there were few immigrants entering Australia, but after the Hungarian uprising in 1956, a large influx of refugees brought foreign attitudes, behav-

iors, and customs, which many Australians were reluctant to accept. In addition, it seemed the Australians resented the immigrants' determination and willingness to work hard to improve their lives, making it difficult to integrate. Wanting to make up for what they had left behind in their own countries, immigrants would work tirelessly to earn enough money to build a new future for themselves. Though their ceaseless efforts, many became quite successful and such success brought with it growing resentment from the Australians.

The situation changed, however, with the onset of American television. Many American programs showed the positive side of immigrants settling into new lives without tyranny, and assimilating into the American way of life. America's acceptance of newcomers helped the Australians to see both sides of the issue, and they began to accept, even appreciate and integrate, some of the European influences into their lives. At the same time, we also began to adjust better to the Australian way of life. Always wanting to feel more comfortable and accepted, immigrants frequently became citizens and changed their names to more common English names. We changed our name from the Hungarian "Fekete" to "Black"—an exact translation. Fekete Gyorgy became George Black, Fekete Rozsi was now Rose Black, and Fekete Zsuzsanna became Susanne Black.

Initially, we gravitated to what felt familiar. Our first apartment was in the residential part of Kings Cross— the Little Europe of Sydney. Without delay, your father and I got jobs with Australian companies. I started to work in a clothing factory and your father in a fire extinguisher manufacturing company. The work was hard because we could not communicate with fellow workers.

Not knowing the language and the local customs, we were not always welcomed by the natives. It was a start, however, and we were thankful to have jobs. Your father had the secret dream of starting his own business again, but at that time he was content just to work and learn the language and local customs. We worked at our respective jobs for approximately eighteen months.

Like my parents, I had some difficulty getting used to our new life. Entering school was a big adjustment for me, and I didn't like anything about it. The school didn't offer, and I didn't have any special assistance with the new language. I had to listen and absorb as much as I could. I attended regular classes and had to use the dictionary to understand the material and assignments. At first my progress was slow, but after a couple of months, suddenly everything began to click, and I became comfortable with the English instructions.

I went to school near Kings Cross with other immigrant children from various countries. Although we shared a European background, it soon became apparent that their families did not have the same educational goals as mine. Many children had learning habits and previous education inferior to mine, and while I was always eager to learn more, it seemed they couldn't care less about school. Most never handed in their homework assignments, didn't ask questions, and their English did not seem to improve. I didn't like that attitude or behavior. After several weeks, I asked my parents if there was any way for me to attend another school. It was decided that I would finish the year at that school and learn English well, so I would be better prepared to transfer to a more difficult school at the start of the following year. The educational system in Australia was similar to Hungary's in that it was intensive, and the curriculum consisted of mainly compulsory subjects with very few electives.

One recommendation sounded promising: an expensive private school called St. Catherine's. It was considered one of the finest schools in Sydney. It was an all girls school run by the Church of England and located in Waverly, a lovely residential section of the city. After investigating the school, your father and I decided that it was worth sacrificing everything in order to send you there.

While we were eager to send you to a fine school, we didn't quite realize the full extent of our commitment. Tuition itself was quite high, but it was just the beginning of the expenses. Extra-curricular activities, such as field trips, cultural events, and sewing and cooking classes, all required lots of supplies adding greatly to the initial expense. But we felt they were essential to your integration into school life and we wanted you to participate.

While the education was wonderful, it was difficult for me to adjust socially. The school was filled with Australian girls who were not fond of non-Australians. My general behavior and formal manners were strange and probably very uncomfortable for them. They did not hide their dislike of me, and frequently made derogatory comments. This, of course, made me feel very isolated and rejected.

I thought it might be easier to make friends with Jewish girls. I felt being Jewish with a similar background would be a common bond, and make meeting new friends easier, so I approached one girl who I thought was Jewish. I asked her if she knew of any clubs that I could join to meet people. She told me that she was not Jewish and had no idea about such Jewish clubs.

A few months later, my uncle, Imre, got married at one of the neighborhood synagogues, and I noticed teenagers gathered in one of the meeting rooms. Looking in, I was surprised to see that same girl from school that had told me she was not Jewish. And there she was, participating in a youth organization get-together. I didn't say anything to her or anyone else about it, but my feelings were badly hurt. I realized that sharing a common religion was not enough to be accepted. Being a foreigner of any kind kept the social doors shut.

Eventually, my relationship with my classmates improved a little and school became more pleasant. But socializing on a personal level was quite another thing. While riding home on the bus the other girls would act as if they didn't know me. One of the teachers of European heritage wanted to host a student get-together so we could all get to know each other in a relaxed social setting. She was very kind, and arranged two or three student gatherings, but the other children never really warmed up to me. I remained an outsider. I would simply have to cope–I had become quite good at that.

Meanwhile, your father and I focused on learning enough English to buy a business of our own. We needed more money, particularly to cover your school expenses. We felt that was the only way to get ahead, so we were determined to make your education a priority. We worked continually to make ends meet.

Serendipitously, a young couple whom we had met aboard ship and kept in touch with happened to be selling their pastry shop. We decided to buy it with all of our savings, which we gathered during the previous months. Again, we wished we had more left from all that we had sent out. Imre, who already had a successful business, signed as a guarantor, and we were able to get a bank loan relatively quickly. Kato, who had met and married a man in Sydney, joined us in the venture, and the four of us became co-owners of the shop. We were now able to put all of our energies into building the business.

Every one of us was willing to work hard, and soon we expanded the pastry shop into a full restaurant. We increased the store hours from 6 a.m. to midnight, but that often extended to 1 or 2 a.m., because we didn't want to lose any business. We prepared, cooked, baked, served, and cleaned, working 15-16 hour shifts. In order to get some rest, and have a bit of quality free time, the two couples worked alternate shifts. This gave us a little bit of a personal life, but we were usually so exhausted we did very little. Just being home as a family was enough. It was very hard work, but we were glad to have the opportunity and grateful to be free. Honest hard work felt more like a blessing than a problem.

No matter how unwelcome we felt in Australia, we still appreciated being there. We didn't want to be Hungarians anymore; we wanted to integrate into the Australian way of life. Becoming citizens was our next common goal. We tried to get our citizenship as quickly as possible in spite of all the hardships, or maybe because of them. We had to be residents for five years before we were eligible. It happened in 1962: a couple of memorable incidents occurred during the swearing-in ceremony on September 26th, my Dad's birthday. One of the government officials noticed his birth date, and wanting to give him a special honor, asked if he would give a short speech. When the official left to return to the podium, Mother asked Dad if he had understood what the man said. He did not. I had to explain to him what they wanted.

Dad was not a shy person, and despite his minimal English, he figured he would be able to fake it somehow. We instructed him to say hello to everyone and to thank everybody for the opportunity to become a citizen. He agreed. The ceremony was lengthy with lots of speeches, and I had to go to the bathroom. As I was returning to my seat, I saw Dad already at the podium, and I suddenly felt anxious and embarrassed. I knew that he did not speak much English, and didn't want him to make a fool of himself. He didn't feel self-conscious at all. "I vant to sank you for zis honor and I am excited to become a citizen," he said. I smiled and was very relieved; and in my heart I hoped his accent would not take away from the meaning. When I saw him bow to the crowd showing his appreciation, my concerns turned to pride and guilt—I felt terrible that I had doubted my father. I should have known that he always found the right thing to say, and in his few words he expressed what he felt.

There was one incident that occurred during the ceremony, before his speech; it had some repercussions later. The officials announced that everyone should place his or her hand on the appropriate Bible according to their religion. I did not hear that announcement because I was interpreting the speeches for your father. When I placed my hand on the Bible in front of me, in my excitement, I didn't even notice it happened to be a Christian Bible. The other Jews around us seemed to have noticed it. Weeks later I went to see a Hungarian doctor, who was also sworn in as a citizen that day. He appeared to behave in a distant manner. Previously, he had always been very kind, so I asked him why he was behaving so strangely. He replied, "You denied your religion at the swearing-in. You did not want others to know that you were Jewish." I was shocked to hear this, and had no idea what he was talking about. When he explained, I told him the truth—that I didn't hear the announcement and I would never deny my beliefs! I just followed everybody else around me, put my hand on the closest book— didn't realize there was a Bible for Christians and another book for Jews.

In December 1961, I was finishing up my school year at St. Catherine's and preparing for graduation. At the graduation ceremony, I was to receive a special honor in recognition of my scholastic achievements. I had come in second in my class and the faculty realized this was a particular accomplishment because I had only been in Australia about one year when I entered school. When my special honor was announced, everyone applauded and some of the parents congratulated me afterwards, but not any of my classmates. I didn't know whether they resented me for being a foreigner who did better than the native born, or because I was Jewish. Of course my parents were proud and thrilled. They felt greatly rewarded for all their sacrifices. We had a big party in our apartment, and invited family and friends to share the honor. Mom and I prepared all the food, which brought back many memories of the times she and I had spent together in the kitchen when I was a child.

After graduation, I had several choices regarding my future. In Australia, students who graduated basic high school could continue for one additional year of advance studies and earn the equivalent of a college degree. This degree was called "matriculation," and would be followed by medical school, law, or other higher education. I chose to complete this additional year. By now I was eighteen, and instead of pursuing medical school and becoming a surgeon, which I always wanted to do, I decided that for the time being I would go to a business college. I attended an intensive six-month course. There I learned secretarial skills such as typing, shorthand, business etiquette, and basic office procedures.

While there, I met a girl named Margaret, who became my closest friend. She was born in Australia, but her parents were from Austria. It was a great relief to finally find such a wonderful friend. And even though she had a serious boyfriend, she never let that interfere with our strong friendship. A few months later, Margaret and Chris got married, and I was part of their wedding.

After graduation I began working as a secretary in a legal office for a group of patent attorneys. I was always interested in scientific and technical work and was very skilled in mathematics. Working in a patent attorney's office offered me access to many interesting technical issues. I remembered how patents had helped my father in his business in Hungary, and this made it all the more interesting.

I also dreamed of traveling and seeing the rest of the world. We now lived as free citizens in a free country, and I knew that traveling to foreign countries was now quite possible. I wanted to experience new cultures, new people … new everything! Given all of my negative social experiences at school, I never felt completely comfortable or at home in Australia. Not being able to fully integrate, I always wanted to travel. But, feeling lonely, I was hoping to find a compatible friend with whom I could travel and discover new places!

Well, fortune smiled on me, because within months of my mentioning it to my parents, they met a couple that had a daughter my age, Eva, and she also wanted to go on an overseas trip. Even better, Eva had relatives living in Los Angeles who were delighted to welcome us into their home! It seemed like the perfect plan: a companion, a home to stay in, and an exciting destination. There was only one catch: my parents weren't thrilled about the idea of my voyaging halfway around the world without them.

Convincing them to let me travel without them was not easy, but at least they were willing to listen. I gave them many reasons regarding my unhappy life in Australia. There were also many other young women who decided to travel after graduating from school. Australians were able to work in England; so many girls went there. My parents always wanted the best for me and worked very hard to provide it. They told me that they had sheltered and protected me all my life, so, of course, the idea of being all on my own far away worried them. Indeed, throughout my teenage years I often asked my mother why they were so protective of me. I knew that they trusted me, so why were they so worried? She always responded, "We feel more secure when you are near us." Now that I was older, they realized they had to give me more freedom. Only once during one of our many discussions did Mother reveal her deep feelings: she was uneasy and concerned when she wasn't sure of my whereabouts, and the thought of those terrible separations flooded her memory and made her ill with worry.

Knowing what it meant to Mother, I appreciated even more my parents' willingness to let me travel on my own, and sought to reassure them by constantly keeping them informed of my comings and goings. Mother lived with deep emotional scars from the two times when she almost lost me, her only child, and now she was letting me go with her blessing. After a lot of discussion, and despite my mother's concerns, Eva and I finally convinced our parents to support our dreams of traveling.

As luck would have it, while preparing for the trip I met a young man and we became very close. Not having dated much, this was such an exciting new experience for me. I felt that I had finally found someone I could relate to and share things with; we understood each other so well. He was quite handsome and came from a very good Hungarian family. They had arrived in Australia in the late 1940's and had created a lovely life for themselves. His father owned a large clothing manufacturing business and his mother helped out in the office. Peter had just become a lawyer and was working in a law firm.

He was just a little boy when he and his parents arrived, but by the time he started school he spoke English like a native and felt quite comfortable in Australia. But he had heard about the ill treatment of foreigners from his parents, and understood my concerns about remaining in Australia forever. All of a sudden, I was put in the position of having to make a major decision: should I stay in Australia so I could eventually marry this young man, or should I follow through with my original plans? Peter was very supportive of whatever my decision would be. As much as I know he wanted me to stay, he didn't try to influence me either way.

It was a very difficult decision, but I felt compelled to stick with my original plan. If things were meant to be, I would return some day and we would be reunited. By then, my parents were very supportive of my decision to go. With all the risks and chances they had taken, they felt that I would regret giving up my dream. Now that my decision had been made, I was finally ready to embark on a grand, new adventure!

CHAPTER 26

LEAVING AUSTRALIA

AUSTRALIA IS CALLED "DOWN UNDER" because it is so far from everywhere. The distance and the time it took to get there fascinated me. Australia was the only Western life I had experienced, and I couldn't wait to see what America was like. Leaving was not only an adventure, but also a turning point for me. Being on my own, far away from my parents, seeing the world as an adult, and not knowing what was ahead for me...it was all so exciting! Eva and I bought passage to Los Angeles on the P&O Shipping Line's *Canberra*. We were to depart Sydney on February 10th, 1963, on a journey that would take twenty-one days. We also purchased passage on the SS France, traveling from New York to France in early October.

The *Canberra* was P&O's newest ship and we were antici-pating an exciting journey. Although I remembered my first experience on a ship from Europe to Australia, I knew that this was going to be very different. This time, I was a young woman who had made my own decision to travel, and I intended to enjoy every aspect of it.

It was also a two-class ship, and despite being in tourist class, our accommodations were quite deluxe compared to the same class on our trip to Australia. Some of the passengers were immigrating to the United States, while the majority were vacationers. Everybody spoke English and joined in the activities and festivities. Everyone wanted to enjoy himself, and there were lots to do—entertainment and food to help us do just that. We found the other passengers pleasant and enjoyed many interesting conversations and experiences.

I'll never forget the day we left Sydney; it was 95 degrees with 100 percent humidity. It was rather uncomfortable and our own excitement added to the heat. As Eva and I stood outside on deck waving goodbye to our families, our clothing stuck to us, and beads of perspiration trickled down our faces. Mine was mixed with tears. This was the first time I had left my parents of my own choice. While I was excited about all the new experiences that lay ahead of me, I was sad for my parents, who were so kind and unselfish in letting me go. It was also hard to leave my best friend, Margaret, and even harder to say goodbye to my wonderful boyfriend, Peter.

I didn't know when I would see Margaret or Peter again. Eva was a new acquaintance, and we had only paired up for the purpose of traveling together. If not for this reason, we might have never met. She was a couple of years older, and that's really all I knew about her. Travel was our common ground. My feelings about leaving Australia were different from Eva's, and it was difficult for me to describe them to her. She was born there. She had no knowledge of what we lived through in Europe, or my sense of alienation in Australia, and I wasn't sure how much of it, if any, I should tell her. I didn't want her to feel bad, and I was afraid of being hurt by her response. If she felt the way the majority of other girls my age had felt about my being a foreigner, I would be upset all over again.

After the ship set sail, Eva and I returned to our cabin. We were both eager to shower and change our clothes. While she showered, I unpacked and then it was my turn. For me, this was a symbolic cleansing and the departure from Australia marked a decisive step into adulthood.

This realization hit me hard, and after showering, I took some time on deck to reflect. I found a quiet spot of solitude where I could gather my thoughts while staring into the distance. The calm ocean offered a peaceful moment of transition. I really needed that. Hungary, with all its hardships, lies, and lack of human rights, the unjust time spent in prison, our deportation, and the separation from my parents were all in the past. I had moved on and built an identity for myself in Australia.

During the years in Australia, I had always tried to manage my life. I enjoyed people and tried to overcome obstacles to leading a happy life. School and my workload were never a problem, but the lack of social life was more difficult. English came naturally to me, and I spoke Hungarian only to my parents. I learned many Australian customs, disliked some, and readily adopted others. As I stood on the deck of the ship, I realized that yet another phase of my life lay ahead of me, and that now more than ever, I must live in the present rather than in the past. This time, however, I was in control. I had said goodbye to my parents, and for the first time the choice was mine. I had left behind a potential husband; I was traveling across the world as a single young woman, in search of my destiny.

As the ship left the harbor, Sydney's pride, the famous Harbor Bridge became smaller, and I thought a great deal about my parents. How much they loved and protected me, and the hardships they had suffered in order to provide a good life in our newly adopted country. From the day I was born, they had sheltered and even spoiled me. For the nineteen years of my life, my parents had been by my side. Now, as Sydney Harbor faded away on the horizon, I suddenly realized I was alone without their security.

I was determined to keep in close contact with my parents and show my appreciation for all of their hard work, and the support they had shown me. I decided that I would write to them every single day and keep them well informed of my activities. Whether it was a letter, a card, or just a note, they would receive something each day from me letting them know how much they meant to me.

Along with my desire to keep my parents informed, I also wanted to feel like a grownup and able to stand on my own two feet. I never let anyone know how scared I truly felt. Imagining myself alone in the great, big world was a frightening thought, but experiencing it was even scarier. Every day there was something new to learn, and while the challenges were often overwhelming, they were also stimulating. I was determined to make my own way. I was definitely growing up.

CHAPTER 27
ARRIVING IN LOS ANGELES

EVA AND I EAGERLY ANTICIPATED our arrival in the United States, and talked about it much of the time. Anna and Hugo Weiss, Eva's distant relatives, greeted us enthusiastically on our arrival. They were incredibly generous from the very first moment, welcoming us with open arms and offering unlimited support. We could not have imagined better hosts. They lived a cultured, but modest life. She was a violinist, interested in classical music, and he co-owned an upscale specialty butcher shop. His customers included major celebrities, and through these contacts he often had small parts in films, or offered technical advice for market and butcher scenes within the movie industry. In fact, just prior to our arrival, he was technical director on *Irma La Douce*, starring Jack Lemmon and Shirley MacLaine.

Anna and Hugo had never had children of their own, so we were showered with love and attention. They searched for interesting lectures, programs, and theatrical performances that would interest us, and encouraged us to familiarize ourselves with the city and its surrounding areas. They even gave us one of their cars to use, which provided the freedom to discover the best the sprawling city of Los Angeles had to offer. Eva knew how to drive and I had to take driving lessons. Within a couple of months I got my license and we took turns driving around the city. Every day was filled with wonderful new experiences, and I often felt like I was the luckiest person in the world.

I was curious to see if I could find any old friends living in Los Angeles. I looked through the telephone book for any familiar names, and was thrilled to find a friend of my parents from Budapest. They had a daughter, Susan, who was three years older than I. I called, and when they heard that I was in Los Angeles without my parents, they could not believe it. They knew my parents well, and said that I was the most protected, sheltered child they had ever known. I was not even allowed to cross the street alone, and now, here I was traveling miles and miles from my parents' protection. This made me realize even more how unselfish my parents had been in letting me go.

We helped out at our adopted home and dreamed of the possibility of staying in Los Angeles permanently. We loved America from the very first moment and our attachment grew stronger each day. Anna and Hugo were very active in the Jewish community, and we attended many functions with them, which gave us the opportunity to meet lots of people. A few weeks after our arrival, we attended a Purim Ball, where much to my surprise, I was selected to be crowned Queen Esther!

I remembered how organizations and synagogues in Sydney held functions for their members, often making them fundraising events. For Purim, it is customary to have one of the youngsters selected to preside over the festivities. While I knew about such events, my parents were not actively religious, and other than the High Holidays, we did not attend synagogue. This was a whole new kind of experience for me and I loved every minute of it. We felt so at home in Los Angeles and I found it more like Budapest than Sydney—which seemed somewhat provincial in comparison. This made the adjustment easy in many ways.

Many Australians came to the U.S. to study and take back ideas. I discovered many little helpful household items that added a lot to the quality of life. I wanted to share some of these with my parents and sent them some normal things used in everyday life in the U.S., but which were unknown or unavailable in Australia. For example, I sent them paper towels with a holder, which they loved. The only problem was that I had to keep sending packages of paper towels to replenish their supply! I also kept them well supplied with decorative paper guest towels and kitchen gadgets. People here laughed at me, but I knew how meaningful it was to my parents, particularly my mother.

Eva and I would have liked to stay and work to make some money, but that, as we quickly found out, was out of the question. Visitors could not work without a special permit or social security number. I tried very hard, even looking for a job at the Australian Consulate, but unfortunately they did not need anyone at the time.

I tried another avenue. After my dream of becoming a surgeon in Australia had faded, I began thinking of studying dress design. I thought perhaps I could find some work in that area. I had always been interested in clothing and dressing well, and loved to sketch outfits. Through our host, I was put in contact with Jean Louis, the famous dress designer, who worked on movies and designed for many celebrities, including Loretta Young. I was very lucky; his firm was willing to hire me as an apprentice! However, I had to decline because I lacked a work permit, and I was unable to get one. I was disappointed about having to turn the job down, but I wouldn't work illegally. I did not want to jeopardize my chances of staying in the United States.

Thanks to my parents, I was not in dire need of money. They sent enough to pay for necessities, and the Weiss's would not accept anything for food and board. This was one of their many generous gestures, all of which made our stay special. Eva and I showed our appreciation by buying many gifts for them. Once we realized that finding work through proper channels was out of the question, we decided to help Hugo in his business, to show our gratitude for their generous hospitality.

Four or five weeks went by and Eva and I began to feel more "American." We enjoyed everything about life in Los Angeles. We tried to lose our strong Australian accents, so we could blend into the scene. We felt welcomed, and we both shared our sense of belonging. For me particularly, this was very meaningful. I felt much more at home in Los Angeles after only a short time, than I had after living in Sydney for several years.

About two months after our arrival, Eva began dating a young American man. They soon announced their decision to get married in May of 1963. The wedding was planned for August, which meant that Eva would not continue on our intended journey to Europe, and I would have to travel alone. Eva asked me to stay and be part of their wedding. While I was very happy for her, I still wanted to continue with my original plans. After reviewing my options, taking into account my dislike of Australia, I decided that I did not want to just return and give up my original traveling plans. I also wanted to make sure that I wouldn't lose the cost of my passage to Europe. The ship was to take us to France, and from there we were going to go to London, where I would be able to work. Since Australia was part of the British Commonwealth, working there was permitted. I discussed it numerous times with my parents over the telephone. I decided to continue as originally planned. The only question was would I do it alone?

CHAPTER 28
LEAVING LOS ANGELES

I DIDN'T FEEL COMFORTABLE TRAVELING BY MYSELF, and my parents definitely would not let me go alone. So we searched for another person who would be able to meet me in America and join me for the rest of the trip. Luckily, Mother had spoken to a friend whose daughter, Jutka, became excited at the idea and subsequently made plans to arrive in America in mid-September.

In the meantime, Eva got married in August and moved into a house with her new husband, while I continued to live with Anna and Hugo. The previous months had gone by very fast, but now time passed very slowly. I still had access to Anna's car, now on my own, but I felt lonely most of the time. Eva and I had done many wonderful things together, and doing things alone was not the same. I had a lot of time on my hands waiting for my new travel companion. During the years since leaving Hungary I had kept up my correspondence with my old friend in Hungary (also named Jutka), but since arriving in Los Angeles I had not written to her. I decided to write to her, because I remembered they had relatives living in the States, but I wasn't sure where.

Jutka was glad to hear from me and in her reply she mentioned her cousin, Robert, and his parents, who had also escaped in 1956 and were now living in Cleveland, Ohio. I thought that it would be nice to visit them once my new travel companion arrived, so I contacted Jutka's aunt and uncle, Gizi and Laci.

Gizi had not seen me in many years. She happily invited us to visit Cleveland and to stay at their home. She also suggested we visit her son, Robert, on our way. He had just graduated from dental school, and entered the U.S. Navy as a lieutenant. He was stationed at the Great Lakes Naval Training Center, about half an hour North of Chicago, prior to being assigned to a specific post. I remembered Robert and thought it would be nice to see someone from my early years in Hungary. The last time I saw him and his family was in the summer of 1949 in Csillaghegy. I was excited at the prospect of seeing a familiar face, and reminiscing about the good old days when we were children.

Our original plans called for traveling by Greyhound bus through the United States. Happily, Cleveland was on the way to New York, so I accepted their invitation and when my new travel companion arrived from Australia, we set out by bus for Chicago and Cleveland.

When I got off the bus in Chicago, I recognized Robert immediately, but he failed to recognize me. I had been a roly-poly little girl of five the last time we met, and now here I was a full-grown woman. I remembered him as the big boy who was always nice to me when I lived in Csillaghegy. He was fourteen then, and now he was twenty-eight. Perhaps he did not change as much as I did. He was almost six feet tall, slim, and his hair was the same wavy red I remembered. As I got off the bus, I wanted to play a little game. I just walked by him, waiting to see if he remembered me. It did not happen, so I decided to walk back and start talking to him. He was surprised and embarrassed that he had not recognized me right away. After a warm embrace, and the introduction to Jutka, he tried to make up for it by showering me with compliments. He said I looked terrific and had grown into a beautiful young woman. We were excited at the prospect of reacquainting after so many years. We would have so much to talk about. We knew many of the same people, not to mention his cousins, Jutka and Andras, in Hungary.

We had timed our arrival for a Friday so that Robert would be able to stay in the city for the weekend. Robert had reserved two hotel rooms—one for the women and one for the men; he had brought along a colleague of his so that we would make a foursome. The skyline of Chicago was breathtaking, and just walking on Michigan Avenue was a thrill. Unlike Los Angeles, Chicago had a lot of beautiful old buildings. The magnificent white Wrigley Building contrasted with the brand new, modern twin Marina Towers. We ate at fun local places, and followed dinner with long walks along the lake. It was such a cosmopolitan city; I felt at home right away! We spent a lot of time at the wonderful Art Institute of Chicago, which had one of the largest collections of impressionist paintings in the world.

My first night there we enjoyed a lovely evening of dinner and an ice-skating show at the Palmer House Hilton. When we returned to our hotel, my girlfriend fell asleep in the room, and Robert and I stayed up reminiscing until 3 a.m. We had a wonderful time. He knew some of what had happened to my family in the recent years, but did not know all the details and was very interested in finding them out. By the end of the weekend, we felt like old friends, and I was sorry to be leaving Chicago so soon.

Robert had been very generous to Jutka and I, especially since she was a complete stranger to him. I wanted to find a nice gift to show him our appreciation. I found out that in the Navy shiny shoes were a requirement, especially for officers. I found a beautiful shoeshine kit with a leather case, had it mono-grammed, and sent it to him prior to our departure. I was hoping it would arrive soon and that we would be able to talk again on the telephone once I arrived at his parents' home in Cleveland.

On Monday morning, Jutka and I took a bus to Cleveland, where we were warmly welcomed by Robert's parents. Shortly after our arrival we were taken around to visit other relatives in Cleveland who had left Hungary in the early '20s. Those were several wonderful days filled with familiar faces and exchanging stories. Gizi and Laci related the saga of their escape. They and Robert had left Budapest on December 3, 1956, and after a train ride to the border they stayed at a farmhouse until 3 a.m. the next morning. During the night, three more families who were going to be helped by this farmer arrived at the house. That night, instead of a horse and buggy ride, they were put in an open-top railroad container, which was used for transporting sugar beets and other farm products. In their car, they laid one layer of sugar beets on the bottom, then Robert, his parents, and the seven other people laid on their sides on top of the beets. They were covered with a wooden plank, which they supported with their head and shoulders. The wooden plank was covered with another deep layer of sugar beets to hide everyone. Their passage took about an hour, but it seemed like forever.

They didn't take anything with them except the clothes on their backs, and Laci carried a briefcase containing gold jewelry, which they hoped to convert into money. When they got close to the border they walked a few hundred meters through cornfields until they reached a small river separating Hungary from Austria. They then had to get onboard an old, rickety wooden boat filled with water. Before getting in, they had to use buckets to empty the boat, and then started on the crossing. They had to keep bailing the water, because there was a hole and it kept filling up. Across the river they saw the Austrian flag. After about a six-minute ride in this rowboat they got out on Austrian soil. Gizi kneeled down and kissed the ground. At that time the border was not guarded yet. They were greatly relieved and overjoyed, but by then they almost collapsed. At this time it was getting light. They still had another two to three kilometer walk to the village, where there was a makeshift office set up to help refugees. The officials gave Robert and his parents two options – waiting to go through the regular channels for entry into the United States, which might take several weeks or even months, or go to Vienna to the American Embassy, which might take less than two weeks. They sold a piece of jewelry in the village to purchase train tickets to Vienna. When they reported at the Embassy there, their names showed up with previous registration numbers. Robert's parents had registered with the American authorities in the late forties when they were thinking of emigrating, and those numbers were still on record. This expedited the processing and by December 28th, 1956, they were able to leave Vienna for the United States. Gizi's sister and her husband drove from Cleveland to New Jersey to meet them, and then they all drove back to Cleveland. All three of them found work right away, and in September 1957, Robert entered Tufts University in Boston to satisfy college requirements first, and then transferred to dental school at Case Western Reserve in Cleveland.

At the end of our first week in Robert's parents' home, they were expecting company for dinner. Gizi was busy in the kitchen when the telephone rang, so I answered it. It was Robert and he thanked me for the beautiful gift, a shoeshine kit in a monogrammed leather case. He raved about the lovely time we had spent together the previous weekend. I completely agreed with him and said that I hoped we would have a chance to meet again in the future. At that point, my plan was to leave Cleveland for New York with Jutka, and catch the boat to Europe as originally scheduled. I had a visitor's visa that was going to expire within a few weeks, so we had to get on with our travel plans.

After a brief chat with Robert, I passed the phone to Gizi and she spoke to him for a while. After their conversation, she took me aside and told me that during their short conversation, Robert had said that he wanted to ask me to marry him, and was going to call back the next morning. I was shocked and speechless! It was strange and a bit funny. The truth is that while we were in Chicago spending time together, I had entertained the idea of Robert as a potential husband, but during our conversations he had mentioned that he had a long-standing girlfriend. He told me that Margaret, who was not Jewish, had just returned from visiting her parents in England where she discussed the probability of marriage to Robert and a conversion to Judaism. Robert did not go into great detail, but I also knew that she was a nurse, so even their professions had a lot in common. She also lived in Cleveland and they had met while both were working in a hospital. His parents knew her and liked her very much.

Nevertheless, our strong connection over the weekend in Chicago was undeniable. After spending two solid days with him, I came to realize how much we had in common. Besides being Jewish, our families knew each other well, and we had both left Hungary hoping for a better life in the West. With these similarities, I felt that we had a good chance to build a life together. He had a good profession, he was gentle, and from our lengthy talks, I felt that he would make a great lifetime companion. I did not dare to dream too much, however, because I did not want to be disappointed. So when Gizi told me the news, I was thrilled.

Next morning's telephone call from Robert to me was fairly short, yet we understood each other perfectly. He, too, felt like I was someone he had known for a long time, someone who shared his values and experiences, and could therefore understand him. We both felt that having so much in common gave us the best chance for a successful marriage. Remember, this was in 1963, and at that time many young couples based their decision to marry on shared values and goals, rather than on sexual attraction. Robert and I were very comfortable about becoming life partners for these reasons.

Even though I had been forewarned by Gizi and tried to prepare myself, once we hung up the telephone, I sat there somewhat stunned, my mind racing in all directions. I wondered what to do about Jutka, who depended on me as a traveling companion and would now be left alone, just like I had been when Eva met someone. What would happen to our plans and my passage to Europe? I hoped I would be able to trade in my ticket for cash. Then thoughts about a pending wedding flooded my mind. I was excited, exhilarated, and scared at the same time. How would I handle all the details in a strange place? And just the thought of getting married! How could I organize it alone, without Mother, who was so far away? Even telephone contact was a problem because of the time difference between Cleveland and Sydney. And what about after the wedding? Where would we live? After all, Robert was in the U.S. Navy and he might be sent somewhere far away on short notice. Where would I stay? What would I do? I had so many questions and very few answers.

When I finally digested it all, I could hardly wait to call my parents, but with the time difference I had to sit and wait as the clock ticked away. I didn't want to wake them up in the middle of their precious sleep. When I finally called, at about 7 a.m. their time, my father answered the phone. I asked him to get

Mother on the extension so I could speak to both of them at the same time. He asked why, but by then Mom had picked up the phone. I blurted out my big news, and I asked them what they thought. I told them that I would accept the proposal only if they agreed to follow me to America, because there was no way I could live here permanently without them. They were stunned. Big changes were happening so fast. It was difficult to sense their reaction because the sound was so muffled, I couldn't hear clearly everything they said. But, a few sentences later I heard them say how happy they were to hear that instead of a stranger, my future husband would be someone they had known. After only a few more questions, they said that of course they would come! They assured me that my happiness was all that mattered to them, and that they would gladly support my decision.

> *Your phone call took us completely by surprise. You had left just six months prior and now so much was happening, and so far away from us. We always hoped you would find a life partner who shared your values and would be there with you under all circumstances. We felt Robert would be the right person and our expectations were fulfilled. When we hung up we were speechless. Although we said we would come to America and join you, we did have some concerns about how we could make such a move. Firstly, we knew it was difficult to get into the United States. There was a quota system and we had no idea if we would meet the criteria. Would we be able to immigrate to the United States? Secondly, would we be able to sell the business to have enough money? In addition to these, your father and I made a long list of questions to ask next time we spoke to you. Where would the wedding be? Could you organize it all alone? Who would we find to work for us in the restau-*

rant while we went to the wedding? We could hardly
wait for our next telephone conversation. When we
finally spoke to you again, these questions were
answered, and we felt much more comfortable. We knew
we would have to work hard to make it all happen, but
this time we were in control of when and where we
moved; and this time it was our choice.

The first weekend after our engagement, Robert came home
to Cleveland, and his main concern was to talk to Margaret.
Before he left his parents' house he told me it was going to be
one of the most difficult conversations he had ever had. He
cared about her feelings and hoped that she would understand.
I wondered how long it would be before he returned from her.
She lived about fifteen minutes from his parents' house, so I figured it would be a couple of hours.

An hour and a half later he was back, drained but relieved.
I noticed his eyes were red. He felt he had handled it in the best
possible way. He didn't go into too many details about their conversation, and I didn't want to pry, but he kept saying that he
was so relieved. We kissed and embraced and I was glad to have
that issue behind us.

Now, I had my own difficult situation to address. I needed
to tell Jutka that she would have to continue the trip without
me. It was very difficult for me as well, because after all, she
came to be my travel companion, and now I was leaving her
alone. I remembered how I felt when Eva told me I had to continue on alone. We talked a lot looking for solutions. I was hoping Jutka would find someone to travel with and keep her plans.
She was disappointed but she also understood. At least it seemed
that way. I was quite relieved when I found out that she had relatives living in Toronto, Canada, and after waiting a few days at
Gizi and Laci's house, she left for Toronto. I felt calmer without

her there, because I felt so guilty about abandoning her. I was able to arrange for the refund of my ticket by submitting an affidavit that I would be getting married. Then preparations for our wedding began.

Our wedding plans had to be made with several major issues in mind. First, Robert had to receive special permission from the Navy to take time off. We also didn't know where he would be sent next, or when, so we had to act swiftly. Great Lakes was only his initial tour of duty, and from there people were sent to various parts of the world, whether they were officers or not. Another issue involved my visa expiration date, which was rapidly approaching. And, finally, we needed to schedule my parents' trip for the wedding. We finally found a date that seemed to work, taking everything into consideration. We set the wedding for December 28th, 1963. While it was a very short period of time in which to plan a proper wedding, we had no choice and were determined to make it happen.

Planning anything in an unfamiliar city is a problem, especially a wedding. In Cleveland it was particularly difficult. Finding a place was the easiest. A member of Robert's family belonged to a lovely reform temple called Fairmont, and we managed to reserve our desired date. Getting my wedding dress made proved a bit more complicated. I had the design for my dream dress in my head, and sketched it for a dressmaker in Cleveland whom my future mother-in-law knew.

Most engaged couples have a courtship; spending time getting to know one another and making plans for their future together...we did not have that pleasure or luxury. Since I was in Cleveland and Robert was at Great Lakes, our short period of courtship was wonderful, but limited. We tried to see each other every weekend, but it was not easy. We often discussed how it would have been if we had married in Hungary. Living there was so restricted and limited, there were very few choices—the deci-

sions were usually easy, either this or that. We felt fortunate living in America and having many decisions to make.

Wedding festivities made the waiting period go by quickly,
but emotionally it was very difficult. I did not have Mother by
my side with whom to share it. I called every few days to keep
her and Dad apprised of all the plans. Despite the distance I
wanted the three of us to share the joys of planning. They gave
their suggestions and I tried to include them in the plans. They
transferred money for me to handle all the arrangements and
have my dress made. My parents could travel to the U.S. only a
little more than a week before the wedding because of work and
other financial obligations. It was a huge effort on their part to
pay for and come to the wedding, but it was very important for
us to share this joyous occasion.

Most of the guests were from Robert's side. Mother invited
her two cousins who lived in Toronto, and both happily
accepted. One couple came with their son and the other with
their daughter. There were altogether nine of us from my side,
but we were glad to be able to share our happiness with family.
Despite the numbers, my parents still paid for the wedding as
was customary.

The days leading up to the big event were filled with all of
the usual emotional turmoil accompanying a wedding. However,
there was also some unexpected tension created by my future in-
laws. They had known my parents for many years, and could
not understand that their financial worth had changed greatly
since the late 1940's. Whenever I tried to explain all we had been
through, they refused to believe me, claiming that I did not look
like the daughter of poor people. My appearance did not scream
"poverty," so they assumed we were still wealthy and just not
willing to contribute more.

I was finally able to convince them that my parents' lifestyle
had been greatly diminished since our escape from Hungary, and

then they turned their anger in another direction. Now, they accused me of being a gold digger! They believed that I was marrying Robert for his future income, and would divorce him later and take whatever I could! Fearing this was my "plan," they urged Robert to call off the wedding. This created a lot of friction between his family and me, but thanks to Robert's strength of conviction, his parents had to step back, and the wedding plans continued. His parents were still convinced of my dishonesty, and the relationship between them and myself was now shattered.

This was a very trying period for me, because I was very hurt by Gizi's comments. Robert was not there and I couldn't always call him. I had no one to talk to about this since I had decided not to tell my parents about this problem until later. I didn't want to upset or hurt them. There was a lot of tension in the house, but I still tried to put on a good face. I had to live with them and I couldn't be disrespectful. I continued helping in the kitchen with cooking and cleaning up and we ate dinner together. Sometimes sitting at the dinner table with them I would lose my appetite. The loneliness and hurt reminded me of my orphanage days when I longed to see my parents. Every evening at home seemed like an eternity. Now, I was older and had to resolve all the issues by myself. This time, though, I knew there would be an end to it soon, and tried to think of the excitement of the wedding and our future. There was only one television and we watched it together. Some evenings I would occupy myself with wedding details just to get out of spending the evening with Gizi and Laci. Saying goodnight to them was always short but polite.

I tried to go to Chicago as often as I could, sometimes to be with Robert and other times to buy the things that were not available in Cleveland. It seemed like a very long time from October to December with this cloud of tension hanging over me. Whenever Robert and I spoke, he was very understanding and supportive. He was the only person to whom I could vent. But I was always very careful about what I said; after all, they were his parents. I always prefaced my comments with, "How would you feel if you were in my shoes?" His response was usually that his parents were just protecting their only son, and they were from a different generation and way of thinking. He asked me to be understanding and tolerant. After all, our being together was the more important thing. I felt that resolving this crisis would become the foundation for our future relationship. I felt bitter toward his parents, and I couldn't wait for my parents' arrival to share with them my true feelings. Many times the memories of Mother and me reuniting after her prison sentence came to my mind. This time again, after almost the same number of months of separation, I had so much to tell her. I could freely express my emotions—we shed so many tears, it would have filled a lake.

Sunday before the wedding, Mom arrived from Sydney. Dad would arrive three days later. Laci and I drove to the airport to meet her. Gizi decided to stay at home in case we needed the space in the car for luggage. The reunion was emotional, much of it tears of joy, but for me mixed with lots of heavy feelings. Mother didn't know any of the problems, so she and Laci reminisced during the ride and it was pleasant. In Laci's presence I couldn't say anything to her. I had to wait till later in the evening when mother and I were alone in our room. She was quite shocked to hear about Gizi's comments and feelings. It created tension between the two mothers. Three days later when my father arrived, the five of us had a long discussion and cleared the air, for the time being. My parents tried to overcome all the animosity and make those few days memorable, and filled with joy. On the surface it seemed to work, but like me they felt very uncomfortable during their whole stay. Although we managed to

Flags on our wedding cake: Australian and American

With our parents on our wedding day, December 1963

make peace with each other as a family, my relationship with them was never as good as it once had been. I forgave them, but I could never completely forget their insult to my character. Once my parents went back to Australia, the distance diminished some of the anger they felt.

Robert's two cousins and their children were part of the wedding, and Judy, the cousin to whom he was closest, served as my matron of honor. The guest list was made up from Robert's classmates from dental school, a couple of his friends, and mainly Gizi and Laci's friends and relatives. On my side, Mom's cousins' presence was very meaningful in the sea of unfamiliar faces. No one except my parents could come from Australia. On my father's side, there was only my Uncle Janos, who at the time lived in Vienna and was unable to travel, and Uncle Pista in Hungary. His coming was also out of the question because it was still not allowed for anyone to travel to the West.

The color scheme for the bridal party was lavender, my favorite color, and the two mothers wore a deeper shade of purple to match. My white chiffon velvet dress turned out beautiful, just as I had hoped, simple but elegant with a medium length train. The ceremony went smoothly, in a traditional manner.

While I listened to Robert's words my mind wondered. I couldn't help but be reminded of Gizi's comments and kept hoping that all would go well, proving her wrong in the long run. I also appreciated my good fortune, that finally my parents and I would have the opportunity to live in the country of our dreams. As soon as the ceremony was over, in spite of my smiles, Robert sensed my distress. He held me close and tight, trying to reassure me. He kept repeating that we were leaving Cleveland within a couple of days and would be far away from his parents. We didn't spend much time discussing this, but enough for me to feel a bit better. A cocktail and dinner reception followed, where I had a chance to meet many of Robert's family's friends. Robert and I shared the love of dancing from the moment we met, and the orchestra provided wonderful music. We tried not to think of anything negative, only the future ahead of us. We enjoyed dancing cheek-to-cheek and I loved being in his arms. I felt triumphant and we were both jubilant. Our wedding cake was decorated with the flags of Australia and America, our new homelands, and our hearts were filled with the joy of freedom and peace.

As it happened, about two weeks before the wedding, Robert received a relocation order from the U.S. Navy and was expected to report to Port Hueneme, California, for his next tour of duty.

One day after our wedding we left for California and my parents returned to Australia. After only a few short weeks— how different our lives had become! Robert and I were married and living in this amazing country without either set of parents nearby. It was particularly hard for me to be without mine, especially so far away. Also, when and if we had the money, we would have the opportunity to travel, not like in Hungary. But at least now we had each other.

CHAPTER 29
LIFE IN THE MILITARY

ADJUSTING TO MARRIED LIFE, new surroundings, naval regulations, and being totally on our own put a lot of pressure on us. We arrived in California on December 29th, 1963, and immediately rented a car to drive to Port Hueneme, an hour-and-a-half North of Los Angeles. After a couple of days in a motel we found a comfortable, one-bedroom apartment in Oxnard, near the Navy base, and moved in the first week of January 1964. We opened all of our wedding gifts and enjoyed having them around us. My parents' gift was the silver flatware set we brought from Hungary, and they also surprised me with the same miniature silver tea set that I had smuggled out.

The tea set brought back lots of memories, and this was the first opportunity I had to share with Robert the details of my life in Hungary and our harrowing escape. During these moments, I quickly realized that material things were not as important to Robert as they were to me. Remembering how he had to leave everything behind when he left Hungary, he didn't want to ever go through that again. He was not interested in collecting and getting attached to things, and then having it all taken away. In contrast, I still loved beautiful things around me, especially the meaningful items from my parents, which were very dear and close to my heart. We also received crystal vases, silver candelabras, a lovely set of china for eight, and a set of stainless steel cutlery. We enjoyed using all of our gifts when having friends over for dinner. I prided myself on setting a beautiful table and creating lovely flower arrangements. We often had people over to play scrabble or monopoly, and enjoy my freshly baked sweets.

I loved to cook and often invited Robert's colleagues for dinner. Whenever I was cooking and preparing, I imagined how thrilled my parents would have been to see me grown up, married, and entertaining. I often remembered the happy moments Mother and I spent together cooking and baking and seeing her entertain in style. She taught me so much, she would have been proud. They would have loved to see us surrounded by beautiful things similar to what they had when I was a little girl. We wished we could have shared this with our parents. We often longed for them, and despite the distance from them, we were determined to make it all work.

Our first big purchase was an old jalopy; a 1954 blue Ford. We knew we would be driving it for only a short time, so we didn't want to spend much on it.

Two months after arriving in Oxnard, Robert received another order deploying him to Guam during the Vietnam War. Deployment meant that his permanent station was in Port Hueneme, but his battalion of approximately 600 men was to be transferred on assignment to Guam and Vietnam. He was the dentist for the Construction Battalion, which was responsible for building the Chu Lai Airfield in Vietnam.

I tried hard not to show my sadness. Though I knew that there was nothing that could be done to change the situation, I was scared to be left on my own again without my husband or family nearby. I had always known there was a good chance this would happen, and now that it had become a reality; I made up my mind to cope with it. The next two months before Robert left, we enjoyed every moment of being together, and tried not to think about our separation. We drove into Los Angeles twice a week and went to the theater, museums, and to the movies.

Several weekends we went away to discover Southern California. Once we went to Las Vegas, Nevada ... what a culture shock that was! We arrived at night, and seeing the city in lights was mesmerizing. Walking into the crowded casinos with the nonstop sounds of the slot machines was an exhilarating and overwhelming experience. The sounds of the slot machines, seeing people sit for hours feeding the machines, whether smiling or cursing, presented an unreal atmosphere. Sometimes I felt like I was living a dream.

Robert left on a ship in late March of 1964, just three months after our wedding. For the first ten days I could not even correspond with him, because the ship had to reach Hawaii before he could receive mail. I was extremely lonely. The challenge was great, but after a few weeks, the hope of being together again flashed a ray of sunshine. My father's positive attitude rubbed off on me and thinking about our reunion helped to overcome my loneliness.

Hoping to cheer myself up, I decided to drive into Los Angeles to see old friends. While driving on the freeway, I got a flat tire. I didn't even know what had happened, I just knew that I could not drive the car. I tried to drive under the bumpy conditions for a short distance to get close to one of the phone boxes on the freeway.

When I stopped and realized what the trouble was, I started to worry. I had never changed a tire, and I had no idea what to do. But, soon I calmed myself and thought to call the AAA for help and they came and took care of everything. I felt proud of myself for handling it, just a bit shaken. I had only been driving for about a year, so even that was a new experience to confront.

When I arrived at Anna and Hugo's house, I felt very relieved. I planned to spend the evening with them, but as soon as I arrived I called Eva, and she said she and Eric also wanted to join us for dinner. It was comforting to spend a lovely evening with all of them. I did not want to drive back to Oxnard alone so late, so I spent the night at Anna and Hugo's house. By morning I was in a much better frame of mind and was ready to drive back to Oxnard.

When I arrived home, it still felt so lonely and depressing to be by myself in our little apartment. I didn't want to feel like that for six more months, so I came up with a plan. I decided to visit my parents in Sydney and stay with them during the six months to a year that Robert would be gone. This would save us the monthly rent and I would have a chance to see my parents. I kept busy planning the trip and putting our affairs in order. I hoped to be able to leave by the end of April.

I had to give notice on our apartment, put all of our belongings into storage, and sell the car. I bought my ticket to Sydney from Pan American, and their routing allowed me a free stopover on Guam. With everything accomplished, I left Los Angeles for Sydney at the end of April … with a very important stopover on Guam!

Officially, only people who were actually stationed on Guam were allowed to live there with their spouses. Robert's battalion was deployed, not stationed there. So, in order for us to be together, Robert rented a room from a Navy family and I stayed there, while he maintained his residence in the Bachelor Officers' Quarters. We tried to lead a low-profile married life, so the superiors in his battalion would not object. Daytime activities and being with other wives was not a problem, but we didn't want to be seen together at night or weekends. However, after a couple of months Robert's Commanding Officer demanded my departure. He felt it was demoralizing for the rest of the group for one member's wife to be there while others were not. We had no choice but to obey the order, and we made arrangements for my departure. To our great amusement and surprise, Pan American, which was the only airline flying into Guam, had just announced a strike. It was impossible for me to leave right away, and I had to stay for an additional six weeks.

The Officers' Club provided many activities for the wives during the day and I continued my participation. We had classes in crafts and cooking, and lectures on many subjects. For me it was most interesting. This was my first experience spending time with other young married women, and I had certainly never lived on a tropical island before! It was a very unusual experience, and a little scary at first seeing geckos climbing the walls! Instead of being afraid of them, I grew to like them, because they ate all the bugs and insects inside the house. Also, it was the first time I saw a light bulb inside a closet kept on twenty-four hours a day to dry out the humidity. I kept myself busy during the day while Robert worked at the dental clinic. We spent every evening together and shared our daily activities. We truly loved our precious time together. When the strike ended six weeks later, in August, I flew on to Sydney to stay with my parents.

It was an emotional and exciting reunion, and this time, I was in Australia as a visitor—there by my own choosing. I was also excited to reconnect with my friend, Margaret, and her husband, Chris, and share with them what life in America was like. To come and go as you please is taken for granted by most Americans, but to me it was everything. To add to my good fortune, having served one year in the Navy, Robert had accrued vacation time, and was able to join me for a week in Sydney. This was a wonderful opportunity for him to meet my family and friends in Australia.

In September of 1964, Robert and I returned to live in Oxnard, for nine more months. It was an agricultural community, surrounded by some of the richest farmland in the world, with lots of strawberry fields and sugar beet factories. In fact, it was known as Sugartown, or the Lima Bean or Strawberry Capital of the United States.

We rented a larger apartment, with one bedroom and a den, which gave us more space. We had acquired many things on Guam, like stereo equipment, an extra set of china, and cameras. When we got together with other couples, we would compare our purchases and the stories that went with them. We really enjoyed those months of growing and readjusting to a stable life. Our social life revolved around dinners at each other's homes, but this was not enough for us. We both loved big cities with all their hustle and bustle, cultural events, and museums. Comparatively, life in Oxnard was rather dull to us. Oxnard was a small town, only sixty miles from Los Angeles, but to us it felt more like living on a mountaintop, far from civilization.

We craved the culture and arts that Los Angeles offered. We frequently drove into the city, and always talked about the possibility of staying there after Robert was discharged from the Navy. But before that dream could become a reality, Robert had to take and pass the California State Board Dental Examination, one of the most difficult dental exams in the country. While in the Navy, Robert registered to take the exam and had to prepare very fast. The exam was scheduled for mid-October, and we returned in mid-September.

At that particular time, the exam was given in San Francisco and Robert needed patients to treat as part of his test. He had no contacts in San Francisco, so he had to select from among his colleagues on the Navy Base a patient who satisfied the prescribed requirements for the exam. Due to bad weather, flights out of Oxnard were cancelled. I would have to drive the patient to San Francisco during the night to arrive for the exam by morning. It was a long eight-hour trip, but we arrived on time. Robert took the written exam, treated the patient, and after three months of anxious waiting, we were informed that he had passed. What an accomplishment! We were ecstatic, because we knew how difficult it was to pass. Every other dentist we knew from out of state had to take the exam at least twice, and he had passed on his first attempt.

In June of 1965, when Robert was discharged, we left the Navy to start the next phase of our lives as civilians. We felt very lucky that we could finally begin to plan an exciting new life in Los Angeles.

CHAPTER 30
CIVILIAN LIFE

BEFORE LEAVING THE NAVY, Robert and I found a small, comfortable apartment in Beverly Hills, and on June 8th, 1965, we moved in. Prior to his discharge we investigated the purchase of a practice. Dental supply companies helped to connect buyers and sellers of practices. We were not very familiar with the demographics of Los Angeles, so when we were offered a small, inactive dental practice in Santa Monica, one of the seaside sections of Los Angeles. We jumped in and bought it. How naïve we were! And we were naïve in many ways. It was an older community and people were not receptive to the newest procedures in dentistry.

After a few months we realized that this was not working, and searched for another practice. By now we were more familiar and also knew other dentists in the area. We found a practice in Beverly Hills where the dentist wanted to retire. The little savings we had, we spent on the first practice, so now we had to have it all financed by the bank. Apart from a handful of patients who followed us, we had to abandon the practice; the lease had expired, the equipment had no resale value, and the new practice was fully equipped. It was a tough lesson because we lost the money we spent buying the first practice. We learned the importance of investigating and evaluating before jumping into decisions. We worked very hard to build up the new practice, and were truly grateful to have the opportunity to create a good life. We often wondered how Robert's classmates in Hungary handled their restricted circumstances.

In the Santa Monica practice, we worked together full time and having so few patients gave us a lot of spare time to strengthen our relationship. In the Beverly Hills office I only worked part time, but I did a lot of work developing the clientele. This was 1966, and dentists were not allowed to advertise. Patients came by word of mouth, through patient recommendations. The growth of the practice depended on us making contacts and developing good relationships with the patients.

A lot of hard work paid off. After the first couple of years, we realized that the majority of patients stayed with us, and with Robert being such a fine dentist, he was able to build a successful practice. We continued living in Beverly Hills in a small apartment, then years later we bought a lovely, spacious house. We were dedicated members of the community; involved in organizations developed to help improve the lives of less fortunate people. We also built wonderful friendships, and of course, we entertained a lot! We would have fabulous dinner parties or friends would often come over for dessert and conversation. We learned to play bridge and through that we developed many new friends.

We lived a stimulating, wonderfully hectic life, but still we longed to have our parents near us to share it with. We talked about having children, particularly since we were both only children. We often reflected on the hardships our parents faced when they were young, and we were so very grateful for our life of freedom. To be young and free like spring...the time when all things are bright, fresh, and in bloom—it was now time to start a family.

I became pregnant, and that period was one of the most trying, yet exhilarating, times of our lives. My parents were so far away that I did not want to worry them with each and every concern; sometimes from a distance things might seem worse than they really were. Instead, we usually told them about situations after the fact. But the thrill and anticipation of having a baby we couldn't keep from them for long. We called them when I entered my fourth month, once we knew all was well. They were ecstatic, but wished they could be with us to share in the excitement. Hearing the news of a grandchild on the way, made them extremely eager to move to Los Angeles. We called them every week to give them progress reports on what we were doing to prepare for the new arrival.

On March 31st, 1966, our daughter, Michelle, was born! Robert and I were totally dependent on each other but we had wonderful, supportive friends. By the time Michelle was six months old, Robert's parents had moved to Los Angeles from Cleveland to be near us. By now, Gizi must have realized I wasn't going to divorce Robert and run off with his money. They moved into an apartment not too far from us and we would see them once or twice a week, although they were much older and not particularly interested in babysitting. Gizi would say to me, "I only knew how to handle boys." Still it was good to have them involved in Michelle's life on any level.

My parents were very eager to come to the United States, and while they planned their immigration, we had much to do to help them. In order to bring them here, I had to become an American citizen. Normally it took a minimum of five years residency to apply for citizenship, but if one were married to an officer in the military, the time requirement was reduced to three years. As soon as I became eligible in December 1966, I submitted all the necessary documents. I loved the United States and was eager to become a citizen. I often wondered...how did I get here? How could this young girl board a train from a desolate Hungarian orphanage, and arrive in Beverly Hills; and now live a free and independent life as a wife and mother? I know now that the will to be free can move mountains.

In preparation for our eventual move, we decided to sell our business so we would have some money and be free to join you in Los Angeles. It was very difficult to sell a restaurant at that time, due to economic conditions in Australia and the general business climate. When we bought the store there were perhaps two or three similar to ours. By the time we wanted to sell, there were over thirty. People were eating out more with the influence of the European lifestyle, and restaurants provided a place for people to socialize.

When we finally managed to sell it, I decided to go to the University to learn English. During the previous years, I didn't have much of an opportunity to study because we worked so hard. We often worked 16-18 hour days, and at the end of the day we had little energy left to study English. After selling the business, I had time to pursue my education and I was excited to attend classes.

When the instructor at the University and the administrative staff discovered I had lived in Australia almost ten years and did not speak English well, they wanted to know why. After I described our past and the difficult circumstances under which our family had immigrated, they respected me so much that they asked if I would work there and manage the University cafeteria.

Although I just wanted to take classes to improve my English, I was very flattered and accepted the offer. I worked there for a year-and-a-half, the time period it took to get our entry visa into the U.S. After that long wait, we finally made the big move from Australia in 1968. Our once dispersed family became whole again.

It was a lovely surprise to have you find an apartment for us before we arrived. It gave us an instant feeling of home and settling in was much easier. Our apartment being close to you gave us a chance to see you and Michelle often. Even before we purchased our car, we were able to walk the seven or eight blocks to you. However, establishing our lives in a new country did not come easily. Our English had improved, so we could adapt to the American customs more easily, but it took a lot of hard work. We never lost our determination to succeed. Hard work never stopped us before, and wouldn't this time either—despite our ages. In 1968, your father was sixty-one years old and I was forty-nine. Once again, Dad established a small fire extinguisher service business, Atomic Fire Protection Company, and managed to build it into a successful venture. He started by asking friends and acquaintances that owned large apartment buildings or factories where there were numerous fire extinguishers for servicing. From there his referrals grew and his business blossomed. He expanded the business with small apartment buildings where he acquired the whole block in some places. He conducted the entire business all by himself; he was truly amazing.

As the years passed, Michelle grew up and became more independent, allowing me a little more free time to pursue some of my own interests. I had always been interested in politics, people, and other cultures, and enjoyed traveling, so I began to think about becoming a travel agent. I thought the career would provide an interesting and fulfilling way to interact with people. It would also offer opportunities to visit many corners of the world. A few months earlier I had met a couple that owned a travel agency, and I decided to call them to see if I could work there. They offered to train me in exchange for helping out in the office. The agency was in Beverly Hills, and everyone there was very knowledgeable, which helped me build a solid foundation in the field.

After working at this agency for about a year, I met a woman whose parents owned an agency nearby. She asked me to join her and become the younger generation of the office, developing and expanding the business. We became partners very soon. Working in a partnership allowed flexibility. I was able to spend a lot of time with Michelle, taking her to extramural activities during her first years of school. As she grew older she needed me less and less, and I was able to spend more time on developing my business. When she left for college eight years later, I left the partnership and opened my own agency.

During her four years at college, we saw Michelle develop into a responsible, young lady, full of the American spirit. After graduation she returned to live at home. Our dream was for her to have a good education, have a fulfilling profession; and of course in time find Mr. Wonderful and settle down near us. Mr. Wonderful did arrive, and Michelle and Steve announced their engagement in March 1993. Their wedding took place in November of the same year, just weeks before our 30th wedding anniversary: it was a very special day for all of us. Unfortunately my father-in-law had passed away several years earlier, just three weeks before Michelle's Bat-mitzvah, but the other three grandparents were still with us. While my mother-in-law was not well enough to attend, my mother and father were able to make it, with Dad in a wheelchair. If not for Mother's efforts to keep him alive long enough to see Michelle get married, my father also would have passed away long before her wedding day. My mother was there in all her glory, beaming from ear to ear.

Michelle's husband, Steve, became the son we never had. He also brought his son, Kyle, from a previous marriage into the family. Kyle became our first grandchild, an adorable six-year-old at the time of Michelle and Steve's marriage. I wanted the time to enjoy our extended family, so in 1994 I sold my agency to join another prestigious office, and continued as an independent agent.

In 1996, we were blessed with a granddaughter who, of course, is the apple of our eye. For Mother, having great-grandchildren was a dream come true. She loved to be with Nicole, and would forego any plans just to spend time with her. As she grew, we took Nicole to the park, swimming lessons, gymnastics, and reveled in her scholastic achievements. It was gratifying for all of us to take four-generation photos of the women in our family. We cherish these captured moments and are eager to record them for the future. My mother is getting older and I treasure every moment with her. She has been a constant inspiration and role model for me, and I hope Michelle and her daughter will appreciate the strength of character she has instilled in all of us.

∼

As I reflect on the events in my life, I realize how few photos we have chronicling my early years, and I find myself taking lots of photos and video recordings to save those moments of joy and accomplishment that made us all so strong. I know what a treasure my one and only photo album is, and it is my hope that Michelle's family will have the pleasure of recording their

With Michelle, early 1990

Family in the park, 1998

1989, My parents, Robert and I, dressed for a celebration

memories, to remember and learn from what we have shared, so it can enrich their lives. The dream of yesterday is the hope of today and the reality of tomorrow.

It is amazing how certain events have a lasting impact on the rest of our lives. Robert and I once had a conversation with someone about underground parking lots and came to the realization that whenever we have the option to remain above ground, we always choose that. Somehow we follow an innate instinct to stay above ground that must stem from the days we spent in bomb shelters, and from being confined in small places by the Nazis and later the Communists.

Similarly, after Michelle left for college, Robert and I wanted to sell our house and move to a condominium. While we were looking, we both eliminated certain buildings without even knowing why. We assumed that we usually liked similar things and that this was just another example of our compatibility. However, I was discussing this with a friend one day, when suddenly I realized the reason: to enter one of the complexes we had rejected, one would have to drive below street level. Instinctively, it had the same feeling as going underground into a bomb shelter. The many months of living in fear and having to run underground during the war resulted in this subconscious fear and loathing.

Despite the scars that many past traumas have left on us, I feel extraordinarily fortunate. Every now and then, I cannot help but think about where I came from and how fortunate I am to be now living here in this wonderful country. Even though there were some traumatic times through my early years in Hungary, that period of my life left an indelible mark on my character, and I will be forever grateful for that.

The loss of our freedom, and the fear and oppression wrought by living under Nazi and Communist regimes left me devastated, yet humble and more appreciative of what I did have. Before the invasion, we had a lot, so consequently we had a lot to lose, and we certainly lost it. Yet at the same time, we never lost our hope or determination. Eventually, we overcame our obstacles and rose above our trials every time. Being persecuted and starting a new life several times over is a true test of our inner strength and ability to rise to the occasion. We are proud that we were able to persevere.

We looked at our experiences as opportunities for growth and strengthening, which helped us to cope in extremely difficult situations. There is a lot of merit to the saying, "Every cloud has its silver lining," and in the belief that conquering difficult circumstances makes you a stronger, wiser, better person. Adversity does build character and I believe that my depth of compassion, generosity, and tolerance stem from my early experiences. I am constantly reminded of my father emphasizing the value and benefit of positive thinking:

The pessimist sees a problem
In every opportunity
While the optimist sees
An opportunity in every problem.

CHAPTER 31
KYLE'S CLASSROOM

TODAY IS MAY 21ST, 2002. As Robert and I are driving to Kyle's school to be there by 9 a.m., I am mentally preparing what I will say to the students. We are discussing issues that would be the most meaningful to fourteen-year-olds. I suddenly realize the date is the anniversary of our deportation in 1951. I want them to know that they are only a year older than I was when we left Hungary; the turning point in my life and the start of my long journey to freedom. I also plan to ask them how they would have responded to the smuggling incident at the border checkpoint.

"Boys and girls, this is Kyle's grandmother," Ms. Anderson says to the class. "You are fortunate to have someone give you her firsthand experiences, not only during the Nazi occupation, but also under Communism." The students sat at their desks, Kyle in the front row to my right side, and I stood in front of them with the blackboard behind me.

I had some concern about how to relate my experiences on a level they could understand. After all, they grew up in this free country. Looking around, each child appeared interested and was focused on me. Kyle sat listening with a pencil in his hand. Not one person spoke or fidgeted. My worries disappeared.

"I am very glad and honored to be here to speak to you today. I would like to introduce to you, standing in the back, my husband, Robert, and our daughter, Michelle, Kyle's mom. I hope you will find my story meaningful. I was born just six days before the Germans invaded and occupied Hungary.

Has anyone heard of or traveled to Hungary? It seems none of you have been there, but at least some have heard about it. Before you came in, to make it easier to understand the history of Germany's spread of power, Robert sketched the map of Europe on the blackboard, showing Hungary's strategic location. I was a baby during the occupation, so the early part of my story is through my mother relating her experiences to me.

"You may have heard other people relating their experiences through books, film, or personal recollection. Everybody has a unique story. Ours began when my mother, her two sisters, and their mother, my grandmother, were marched at gunpoint to a field where the Hungarian Nazis sorted people into groups before shipping them to concentration camps.

Despite her pleas to stay with me, my mom was forced to go and leave me behind. They were forbidden to talk to one another. Suddenly a man in Nazi uniform came up to my mother and pushed her out of the crowd, all the way to the gate. When she was outside he left her and disappeared. She had this split-second chance to come back to me, while her mother and sisters were not as lucky. They were shipped to a concentration camp. She ran toward our apartment, and almost collapsed by the time she got there. She found me screaming but thankful to be together."

∼

I kept looking around to see the youngsters' reactions, particularly Kyle's. He put his pencil down, and put his hands over his eyes; it made me wonder what he was thinking. Ms Anderson warned me that some of the boys were very talkative, but hoped that they would be respectful and listen. I was gratified because they seemed to be attentive; felt they were with me and my story. I could see that it affected all of them. One boy, who was doodling at first, put his pen down and simply listened. There was such quietness in the room; I could feel their empathy.

Kyle and I, 2003

~

"The next few months we lived under very difficult conditions. The Nazis wanted to get rid of us Jews, but thanks to two wonderful humanitarian diplomats our lives were spared. Raoul Wallenberg from Sweden and Carl Lutz from Switzerland distributed fake documents, which protected us and many others for a while by making us citizens of their country—thank God. I want you all to remember that even when most people were doing terrible things, there were also some decent, caring ones. They, and others like them, were called *Righteous Gentiles*, who are now honored at a memorial park in Israel.

"Those fake documents were honored for a while, but later nothing helped. Some people were taken away to die, or like us, were forced to move into the ghetto. The ghetto is not the same as what you may think of in this country. Our ghetto covered a large area of Budapest. They actually built a wall around it, locked the gates, and uniformed Nazis guarded it. We could go outside for only two hours in the morning and two hours in the afternoon. We had very little food and we were near starvation. We lived there for about six weeks in the freezing December winter of 1944. Much of the time we spent down in the bomb shelters, which had cement floors, without heating or warm clothes. Thankfully, six weeks later the Russian Army came into Hungary and defeated the Germans. Liberating Budapest and the country took weeks because the Germans didn't give up easily.

"We were thankful to the Soviet Union for defeating Germany in 1945, but then they wanted to stay and rule our country. Not everybody trusted them, and it took three years before the Communists won the election in 1948. During that three-year period my parents slowly established a new life and we lived well for a few years.

"Under Communism we were never told the truth; we heard only government controlled information, called propaganda. The news was always suppressed; everything was a secret. We were afraid to discuss events with people because we couldn't trust anybody. People were taken away under false accusation or without explanation. Children were brainwashed to report on their family members, even parents, if they heard things at home that sounded different from what they were told at brainwashing sessions.

"Under these difficult conditions, life deteriorated and became difficult. My parents wanted to leave Hungary, but when we tried to escape, the border patrol captured us and imprisoned us. When I was five years old, I was kidnapped from my parents and for a week we didn't know what had happened to each other. You can imagine how scary that was for a five-year-old! While they were in prison, I was taken to an orphanage where every day was pure misery. Instead of keeping us healthy like they had promised, they would inject us with various illnesses and use us for medical experiments. I was lucky that I only developed chicken pox, because a cousin of mine was given polio! She was also five years old at the time. Her family tried to escape sometime before us, but the conditions were not as strict. then, and they were released after a few days, unlike us. About a week later she became very ill, developed a fever accompanied by muscle aches, and began throwing up. The following day, the muscle pain intensified and she became paralyzed. Only after the paralysis did they diagnose her with polio. Fortunately she had a mild case, which did not require an "iron lung;" a machine that helped polio victims to breathe. With her mother's help they started extensive therapy to mobilize her extremities, and after a few weeks she regained mobility. Through her parents' constant diligence and efforts she has lived a normal life, but to this day, she suffers the effects of the crippling disease, having to walk with a cane.

"After I recuperated, a friend of my parents came to get me and I had to stay with an aunt and uncle. After about a year, my parents were released from prison and we were together again.

"By this time, at the end of 1950, no one could any longer own his business. The government took over and controlled every private enterprise. Everybody worked for the government, in what were called collectives.

"We had a beautiful home, but according to the government it was too fancy. The regime wanted regular citizens to have less, but the leaders always had more than the average people. There was a shortage of apartments in Budapest, because many of these new leaders came to live in the city. To give them apartments, they devised a plan to displace people like us and move us to the country. This is what was called the communist deportation.

"There was practically no public outcry because when people found out about it, they were afraid to speak out against the regime or discuss it. They were afraid to reveal their association with so-called dissidents. We ourselves always wondered, but never knew, how many other people were affected and where they were taken, or how long this process would last. Everything was a secret. Our inquiries were never answered, and we only discovered the facts fifty years later, after seeing declassified documents.

"I hope some of my experiences will make you realize how lucky you are to be an American and that you must never take your freedom for granted. By the time I was almost the same age as you are now, I had lived many lives, and even possibly saved my family from death with quick thinking at the border. When we were finally allowed to leave Hungary, at the last security checkpoint we had a major problem with one of my favorite possessions. I didn't realize it should have been declared to the authorities, so they thought I was smuggling it out of the country. I quickly said it was one of my toys, which was not true, but telling a white lie saved our lives. How would you have handled that situation? Remember, I was only thirteen. You can imagine how that experience makes the tea set all the more meaningful. It sits in a special place in my house, in a china cabinet in our living room, and I look at it every day. The pleasure of seeing it fills my heart with joy and gratitude.

"In my lifetime I have lived through Nazism and Communism. I certainly hope there will not be another fanatic group which will control our lives. Soviet-style Communism is behind us, but other styles of Communism still exist in China, North Korea, and Cuba. We must be aware that while China is adapting to western capitalistic lifestyle, militaristic North Korea is a potential threat to the world, and Cuba is only ninety miles from Florida. To illustrate the importance of awareness, I'd like to share with you boys and girls an incident that happened only about three years ago on a trip to Cuba.

"One evening on our way to another hotel with three friends, our taxi driver stopped a few blocks before our destination and asked us to get out of the cab. He explained that the local police followed taxis traveling to American-style hotels and interrogated passengers. Generally speaking, this meant a reprimand, but in essence it was a demand for a portion of the fare from the driver. Having grown up in a similar environment, my husband and I understood, and were willing to comply with the driver's request. Our travel companions, on the other hand, did not appreciate his request and insisted on being driven right up to the hotel. Our driver reluctantly did that, and as soon as we left the cab, we saw the police appear from nowhere. The "holdup" was swift, and sadly routine. Although foreign to my friends, this incident is typical in Communist countries where people in power often abuse their authority for personal gain.

"Because of the political choices made in these countries, the threat of Communism could rear its ugly head again, given the right circumstances. I hope after today you will be better prepared to stand up and fight against future tyranny, by knowing what my family and I went through. I've learned so much over the years and have come to realize that in all bad things there is always something good. Having a good formal education and a lot of information from my parents insured my ability to be aware of and to cope with adversity.

"When you travel you realize how other people live, and the value system of other cultures. What our lifestyle offers may not be commonplace in other countries regarding their living conditions, as well as their politics. You are in a better position to evaluate what is happening in other parts of the world if you experience their culture and environment. Not everybody can live like we do in the U.S., so it's important that we try to understand other cultures and show each other mutual respect.

"The Internet has greatly reduced the scope of the world. Instead of waiting for weeks for news to come to us, we have instant access to it from anywhere in the world. Since September 11th, 2002, we must think differently. We know that there are fanatical groups that want to destroy the things they don't have, and by their religious definitions, can never have. This anger and envy results in the benefit of only a few at the expense of many.

"Thinking of what is going on now, I cannot help but compare my early life with what the terrorists are doing to the world at the present time. They are jealous of our freedoms and our success as a democracy, and that is the fuel behind their hatred. Their philosophy does not allow freedom of expression, and those who disagree publicly are imprisoned or killed. All of you must learn, study, and be well informed to insure your individual rights. You should always stand up for your beliefs. Freedom of speech is the foundation that makes America strong, but you must always make your own decisions about what you hear and read. Be open-minded, but also read between the lines. Listen, learn, respect, ask why, and decide. Knowledge is power. Knowledge is your guide through life. Listen to others, and try to separate right from wrong. But most importantly, we need to always respect each other and our many differences.

"Nobody believed the Nazis came to hurt them, but they ultimately did. Terrorists are people who believe that their way is the only way, as did the Nazis and the Communists. We must maintain the fight for the truth. Biased views distort it.

"It is my sincere desire to inspire you with my family's tenacious journey from oppression to freedom, and to show you my deep appreciation for this country I now call my own: The United States of America.

"And finally, no matter what, always have hope and faith. Take responsibility! There is always a tomorrow. Evil will eventually be defeated by the power of the righteous. Treasure our constitution; it's there to protect you. I hope my experiences will help to instill in you the importance of education, awareness, and tolerance for others."

CHAPTER 32
THE HUNGARIAN BRAIN DRAIN

ALTHOUGH I WAS TIRED FROM STANDING and speaking all day to six eight grade classes, I was also exhilarated! It was almost 4 o'clock by the time we left the school, but before having dinner at Michelle's house, Robert and I reflected upon the value of the day. While I was speaking to the kids, he was watching their reactions and saw that I was getting through to them. We sat over coffee and talked about how my story might have affected them.

It was an amazing experience for me to speak to so many youngsters, all of whom were very interested in what I had to say. As soon as I finished with my presentation, almost every hand went up to ask questions. I was elated with their response and was eager to answer as many as possible in the time allotted. They would have like to ask more but had to rush to the following class. I was also watching Michelle with great interest, and anticipating her reaction. During the breaks between classes she kept asking me questions about what she had just heard. Many things she had not known before.

Ms. Anderson herself was interested in learning more about life in Europe during the 40's and 50's, and greatly appreciated my offer to speak to all the 8th grade classes. I in turn was so pleased that she cared enough to have so many students hear me speak. As it turned out, I was there the whole day, and spoke to a total of about 200 students.

I was exhilarated but needed a little time to relax, so Robert and I stopped for a cappuccino before going to Michelle's house. When we got there, Kyle greeted us with a big hug and kiss.

"What did the kids think, Kyle?"

"They liked it."

"And what did you think?"

"I loved it. I was surprised to hear my classmates ask about the ghetto. I knew the meaning of it during the Nazi era, which is so different from the meaning today, but they didn't. I don't think they realized what people experienced and what they had to do to survive."

"I am so glad you asked me to do this. I think the kids really learned a lot today, and now realize the enormous harm that evil people can do. I also hope that I convinced them of the importance of knowledge, and the power of self and conviction. I often think back to the time when you came into our lives ... it's amazing that nine years later I am telling your classmates all about my life."

As we sat around the dinner table, Michelle asked Nicole if she knew where we had been that day. She said 'yes' because another mother had taken her home from school.

"Do you know what we did there?"

"No, Mommy, what did you do?"

After explaining it to my six-year-old granddaughter, we continued our discussion, which led to the importance of education. I have talked to Kyle often about what it takes to get into a good college, and now seemed like the right time to bring it up again.

"Kyle, you are an outstanding student and I don't need to preach the importance of education, but I want to stress the importance of expanding your horizons. In the United States everyone has choices and opportunities, and it is important to make the best of them. I am sure you realize how lucky you are to be growing up in this country. Hungary is a tiny country with only ten million people that does not offer her people the same opportunities. It was the homeland of many great achievers, but sadly they had to leave "home" to pursue their dreams. We will never know if the great accomplishments by these people would have been achieved if they had stayed in Hungary."

"What do you mean, Zsuzsi? Where did those people go?"

"To tell you the truth, Kyle, before I began the research for my talk to your class, I didn't realize the extent of the Hungarians' contribution myself. As I discovered more information, I wondered how the world might be today without the achievements of these talented people.

My own life was indirectly affected by one of them, Dr. Ignatz Semmelweiss, who discovered the importance of physicians' disinfecting their hands before childbirth or surgery. As the department chief of a Maternity Hospital in Vienna, he discovered that during childbirth, ten percent of the mothers died from puerperal, or "childbed fever"—a fatal infection occurring in wards staffed by medical students. But, in wards staffed by midwives, handling childbirth only, the mortality rate was only three percent.

He discovered that medical students went straight from the autopsy chambers to laboring mothers without washing their hands, and instead, would wipe them on aprons already coated with body fluids. When Dr. Semmelweiss uncovered this, he then required students to wash their hands with soap and water and rinse them in chlorinated lime solution before entering maternity wards. The death rate for birthing mothers dropped to less than 1.5%. When the hand-washing procedure was not followed, death rates increased to the previous high levels."

"Really, that's amazing, Zsuzsi. I guess that's how important discoveries happen. Today they have to use gloves, even in the dentist's office. Just washing your hands is not enough anymore."

"That's correct. However, in spite of clear evidence that these deaths were caused by the spread of the bacteria, Streptococcus pyogenes, his colleagues responded to Dr. Semmelweiss's findings with scathing attacks on his character. They refused to believe that their own hands were the vehicle for transporting disease.

Due to his radical ideas, Semmelweiss's academic rank was lowered and his hospital privileges restricted. The taunting and insults he received from the medical community destroyed his career and his spirit. He became despondent and mentally ill to the point that he was eventually committed to an insane asylum, where he died of blood poisoning, a disease not unlike the puerperal fever he had tried to conquer. It was many years after his death before his theory was proven and accepted."

"That is so sad that his great discovery was ignored. The poor man could have lived longer if they had just studied his theory."

"Some of the world's leading scientists were born in Hungary. Among the most prominent are physicists, Edward Teller and Leo Szilard, co-developers of the Atomic Bomb. Teller is also called the father of the H-Bomb. And, there was John von Neumann, born Janos Lajos Margitta Neumann, a mathematician, physicist, and computing pioneer. He was known as the father of the Binary Code and the Stored Program Computer; the keys to modern computer programming as we know it today."

"Can you imagine, Kyle? A Hungarian was responsible for that?" Robert joins in the conversation, "And you know, Kyle, in the computer world today we have Charles Simonyi, a chief architect at Microsoft Corporation, and Andy Grove, computer scientist, co-founder, and chairman of the computer giant, Intel. Another Hungarian was the father of Supersonic Flight, Todor von Karman, an aeronautical engineer and mathematician."

"In the financial world, George Soros has played a major role in American as well as international finance. Can you imagine what we would do today without ballpoint pens? They were developed by Joseph Laszlo Biro, an inventor, who also collaborated on the development and production of color television, LP records, the first modern contact lenses, modern electric trains, safety matches, the blimp Zeppelin, and even the design of the Model T and Model A Fords. Can you imagine, Kyle, he worked on the first cars?"

"There are so many Hungarians who contributed to our comfortable lifestyle, I am truly surprised, myself. Another, Dr. Albert Fono, received the first patent on airplane jet propulsion. Dr. Bela Schick invented the safety razor and also introduced the "Schick test" for determining susceptibility to diphtheria. Joseph Petzval is remembered for his work on optical lenses, which allowed for the construction of modern cameras. The Petzval curvature is named after him.

Several of these brilliant thinkers have received the Nobel Prize in science, while the 1986 Nobel Peace Prize went to another famous Hungarian, Holocaust survivor and author, Ellie Wiesel."

"I didn't know he was from Hungary," Kyle says, "And I cannot believe so many of these people whose names I have heard were actually born there. Many of them were really ahead of their time, or they were just brilliant."

"I think it's both. I bet you also didn't know that many from the early days of the film and entertainment industry were Hungarians. There is Adolph Zukor, producer and founder of Paramount Pictures, Joseph Pulitzer, the publisher, and William Fox, producer and founder of Fox Studios. Joe Pasternak was instrumental in the successful revival of Universal Studios with a series of hit musicals, and is also credited with discovering Judy Garland. That's a little trivia for you.

There were also many actors, and I'm sure one of them you are also familiar with, Bela Lugosi, whose most famous role was Count Dracula. Harry Houdini, the greatest magician that ever lived, also came from Hungary.

In the music field there were many composers and famous conductors. In fact, America's giant conductors, Fritz Reiner, Eugene Ormandy, George Szell, Sir George Solti, and Antal Dorati, were all born in Hungary, but moved to the United States and directed major orchestras here during the late 60's and 70's.

"Many of these names may not sound familiar to you now, but I am sure as you grow up, Kyle, you will hear more about them and how their accomplishments affected all of our lives.

What will you discover, Kyle? Are you thinking about any inventions? Did these people inspire you? Will you make history like they have? I know you can, and just think how you could make a difference in the world? When Michelle was your age and even earlier, we used to talk a lot to her and she lovingly nicknamed Robert, 'Channel RR,' for Robert Reyto. When Michelle had heard enough from your grandpa, she used to say, "Dad can we turn off Channel RR?" Well, I don't want to be nicknamed Channel SR, but you know how strongly we feel about education, and that includes more than just learning from books. We want you to remain the outstanding student you are, and we know you will succeed in whatever field you choose to pursue."

"I'll do my best," Kyle replies. "Talking about all these people makes me wonder where we would be if these people didn't contribute their knowledge and accomplishments to our society."

Michelle joins in the discussion, "Mom, I'm sure he understands. I am glad you told him about these people and I learned a lot, too. I didn't know much about them and certainly didn't realize the enormous influence they played in our lives."

"It's clear that Hungary suffered a major brain loss when all of these incredibly talented people left their homeland in pursuit of freedom. However, we are all blessed to have been the recipients of their great achievements. As a former Hungarian citizen, it makes me proud, but also sad, to know that a country which could produce such a wealth of world-renowned people, was also an active participant in regimes that cut short many more such blossoming lives."

As we continue our dialogue around the dinner table, Nicole imitates Mother and her accent. "Vait a minute. No vay. You're velcome." We all smile and find it amazing that a six-year-old can recognize it.

"Talking about accents, I have to tell you, kids, whenever Dad and I meet new people they always ask about our accents. Hearing how different we sound, they don't believe that we originally came from the same place. Once we explain, soon the conversations turn to inquiring about how Robert and I feel about Hungary. They often pose the question, "When did you last go home?" which always elicits a negative response from us. It's almost an insult when people refer to Hungary as our home. We left Hungary of our own free will, and became American citizens as soon as we could. For us, America has always been home, and a very good one at that. While we speak the language, when we travel to Hungary we think of ourselves as visiting a foreign country.

Similar reactions are evoked when people tell us that they recently returned from "your homeland." People are taken aback when we reply, "America is our homeland. Hungary was only the place of our birth." At the same time, we do not deny our European roots and rich culture.

"When you graduate from high school, Kyle, perhaps we can go to Hungary as a family, and show you around, so that all you've heard from us will come alive for you. We took Michelle when she was thirteen, and when you graduate, Nicole will be old enough to learn from the experience as well."

CHAPTER 33

THE GOLD TRAIN

MY DISCUSSION IN KYLE'S SCHOOL was very meaningful for Michelle as well. She had heard and seen many holocaust-related stories, but had not known much about life under Communism. That day made her much more aware and interested in what had really happened in my early life. From weekend to weekend, Mother, Robert, and I can hardly wait to spend time with Michelle, Steve, Kyle, and Nicole.

Sunday, September 1st, 2002, was no exception. Arriving at their house, Nicole opens the door and greets us with a big kiss and a hug. Kyle is not at home, but Michelle greets us with a question, "Have you seen today's Los Angeles Times yet?" "We have not," I say. Without saying a word she shows us the article.

HOLOCAUST SUIT ACCUSING U.S. CLEARS OBSTACLE

Courts ruling for Hungarian survivors who seek reparation for Nazi loot army seized, rejects government's immunity claim . . . .

But U.S. district judge ... ruled that the plaintiffs were entitled to have the statute of limitations waived. ...

The plaintiffs claim that the U.S. knew or easily could have learned the provenance of much of the stolen goods and acted illegally by failing to return them to their rightful owners. ...

Department attorneys contended that because Hungarian Jews knew as early as 1947 that the U.S. army had taken possession of the gold train, the six-year statute of limitations had expired no later than 1963. ...

The suit relies in part on reports issued in October 1999 and December 2000 by the president's advisory commission on holocaust assets, which cited previously classified U.S. government documents.

The reports state that Maj. Gen. Harry J. Collins, the chief U.S. military official in western Austria at the end of World War II, placed orders from a U.S. military warehouse in Salzburg, Austria, for enough china and silver for forty-five people, as well as a dozen silver candlesticks, glassware, thirty sets of table linens, carpets and furs for his villa, and a personal railroad car.

Collins died in 1963, and is buried in Salzburg." ...

"Can you believe this? Let me scan the article" I say. While I am reading, the whole family is sitting around discussing it. I cannot wait to join in. "Isn't this something, I was so amazed when I uncovered some of the details at the library. I even have copies of the *New York Times* articles from 1948. Listen to Rozsi and you'll learn more about it."

The Gold Train contained the unlawfully seized jewels and other valuables of 800,000 Hungarian Jews. To collect money and rob Jews of all their possessions, the Nazis set up laws demanding the Jewish population submit a list of their real estate holdings and deposit all valuables with the authorities. These included gold jewelry, diamonds, and other precious stones, as well as gold coins. We had to submit even wedding bands to designated banks or a specific Nazi office. The demand notices were distributed through newspaper and radio announcements and signs on the streets. People who went out from the protected houses brought back the news to those of us who hardly ever went outside.

To make it look official, the Nazis gave meaningless receipts for the confiscated valuables, and none of them were ever returned. In addition to what they collected through this procedure, the Nazis were aware of the location of prominent Jewish homes, which they simply walked in and ransacked, taking all of the valuables. This included silverware, porcelains, linens, rugs, paintings, and personal belongings such as clothes and furs. The Nazi Party and their leaders appropriated part of the belongings for their own use, and the remainder was stored.

In 1945, during the liberation process, as the Soviet troops were approaching, this loot was loaded into boxcars for transport to the West by members of the pro-Nazi Hungarian Government of Szalasi. The wagons were filled with jewelry, art, and other treasures including paintings, Persian and Oriental rugs, fur coats made of rare and valuable furs, stamp collections, and miscellaneous heirlooms. This became known as the "Gold Train." The forty-four-car train was spirited westward under military escort, headed toward Germany or neutral Switzerland, but was captured by the American Army in May 1945, in the town of Werfen, about sixty miles south of Salzburg, Austria.

The United States Military Authorities took under

their control a huge part of this find. Can you imagine?
I have a list of what was included: ten cases each filled
with 45kg of gold, one case filled with about 100kg of
gold coins, eighteen cases each filled with 35kg of gold
jewelry, and thirty two cases, weighing anywhere from
30 to 60kg each, containing gold watches. There was
also a trunk containing miscellaneous foreign currency,
as well as a sealed package containing diamonds. There
were 1,560 cases containing silver items, one case con-
taining silver bricks, plus one hundred paintings, and
about 3,000 Persian and Oriental rugs. Two of the
train's wagons contained other assorted valuables, such
as clothing, furs, stamp collections, cameras, Bohemian
cut colored glassware, and the finest porcelains of
Dresden, Meissen, Rosenthal, and Herend. According to
the documents, in addition to the assets captured by U.S.
troops, thirty-six cases containing gold, gold coins, and
watches, and ten cases of diamonds and pearls were
transported into the French Zone, where they were
seized by French troops in St. Anton.

When I think about it I still cannot believe it all. The
U.S. forces removed the assets from the train and moved
them to storage facilities in Salzburg, Austria, the major-
ity of which were stored in the Military Government
Warehouse. After examining the items, the Commanding
General of U.S. Forces in Austria, General Mark Clark,
along with other military authorities, determined that
the owners as well as the country of origin were uniden-
tifiable. This was ridiculous, because the origin of the
trainload was known, coming directly from Hungary,
and there were itemized lists attached. Based on their
assertion, the officials claimed that restitution to
Hungary was not feasible. It was hushed up then, but

now there is so much information available. I wish we
could have known some of it sooner, possibly we could
have submitted claims for it—particularly, since I hap-
pen to have original documents listing many of our valu-
ables. In researching this part of our past, Zsuzsi has
uncovered a lot of documents that tell the full story.

With the declassification of the documents, I had no problem finding information relating to the Gold Train. In 1946, the United States signed two international agreements concerning the contents of the Gold Train assets, the Final Act of the Reparation Conference and the Five-Power Agreement for Non-Repatriable Victims of Germany. In accordance with these agreements, carloads of non-cultural property were transferred to the United Nations International Refugee Organization (IRO) for disposal. This permitted the sale of the non-monetary gold and other ownerless property for the benefit of non-repatriable refugees. A different policy was followed for the return of cultural properties; these were to be returned to their country of origin.

A document marked "Confidential Security Information" was prepared six years later, on March 26, 1952. That document, titled *Hungarian Cultural Property* in U.S. Custody proposed that the cultural property be held indefinitely for eventual return to its rightful owners. According to this document, this cultural property included: (1) Contents from the Hungarian library, under seizure by the Alien Property Custodian, stored at Columbia University; (2) 1176 paintings from the Hungarian Gold Train now in U.S. control, stored in the Residenz Depot, Salzburg, Austria; and (3) The Crown of St. Stephens and related objects. The St. Stephen's crown was actually returned to Hungary in 1978 from the U.S., where it had been stored since the end of World War II. It is now on display in the rotunda of the Parliament in Budapest.

Despite numerous requests by the Hungarian Jewish Community to return the properties to the 200,000 Hungarian Jews who survived and returned or remained in Hungary after the war, the victims' assets were designated "unidentifiable" by some high government officials. Then to hurt us even more, the decision was made to dispose of all items by auction, and the proceeds were to be turned over to the IRO. Crates of Jewish property started to arrive at Staten Island in the middle of December 1947. This was only two years after the war, when no efforts were made to identify former owners. The first auctions took place in June 1948 at the Parke-Bernet Galleries in New York. According to *New York Times* articles published on June 25th, 1948, the auction proceeds far surpassed expectations. On June 23rd, there is even an advertisement for three sessions of the auction.

According to a November 6th, 1945 document titled *Purchase of Merchandise,* the Army Exchange Service in Austria purchased merchandise to be sold at Army Exchange stores. Due to challenges by the Army Legal Division, the first attempt to dispose of the Gold Train Property through the Army PX's did not succeed. A year later in November 1946 it was approved and then it contained a more extensive inventory.

By 1947, when it became well known in the international community that the U.S. government was planning to sell certain contents at auction and turn over the benefit to the IRO, the Hungarian Jewish community protested. A telegram from the Central Board of Jews to the Department of State on February 21st, 1947 stated:

"Undersigned legal representative bodies of the Hungarian Jewry were informed with deep consternation of the fact that the United States government is planning to transfer the value of so-called golden train which form the property of Hungarian Jewry to the refugee committee of the UNO."

The Central Board requested emphatically for the valu-ables to be placed in their hands for disposition, acting as the legal representative of Hungarian Jewry. A second letter in late February followed on humanitarian grounds, requesting the same action. The United States ignored the pleas, and in a reply on May 19th, 1947, the U.S. Legation replied, defend-ing the original decision.

"With the approval of the United States government, the commanding general, U.S. forces, Austria, determined that the property should be turned over to the Intergovernmental Committee of Refugees for Relief ..."

Despite every attempt to reverse the decision, certain con-tents of the Gold Train were auctioned in New York in 1948 and other parts disposed of in various manners.

It is fortunate that the Gold Train was captured by the U.S troops before its contents fell permanently into Nazi hands, but the hastily made decisions to sell, and the inappropriate distrib-ution of valuables and money has yet to be adequately addressed. To this day there remains no convincing explanation for why the confiscated property of the Hungarian Jewish com-munity was so readily dispersed so soon after the end of the war. The fact remains that the property was never returned to its rightful owners.

An undated document in the United States National Archives titled, List of Material Loaned from *Property Control Warehouse* states, "numerous high-ranking officers of the American Forces in Austria appropriated Hungarian Jewish treasures ... for the decoration of their residences. For example, Major General Harry J. Collins requisitioned a specific list of household furnishings for his home, and a list of decorative items for his railroad car and villa. General Laude received ... for his Salzburg home; General Hume received ... General Howard received ... to decorate his Vienna apartment; and Brigadier General Linden received ... for his quarters on the von Trapp Estate." In addition to their personal use, in a report on March 8th, 1946, General Collins expressed interest in providing proper quarters and furnishings for military families settling in Austria, and to that end, "quite probably demands might be made upon property in the warehouse."

As of 1996, declassified U.S. State Department documents show that two tons of TGC gold are still being held at the U.S. Federal Reserve Bank in New York ($28 million estimated value in 1996), and that the Bank of England is still in possession of twice that amount. The contents of the Hungarian Gold Train make up a portion of this amount.

Reflecting on my family's experiences and the hardships they endured, I keep asking Mother, who has always been a very active problem solver and fighter, why people gave up instead of fighting to regain their holdings.

I am grateful that some of these documents were released, because for all these years, since the end of the war, we have wondered what could have happened. I truly believe that after the war people wanted to put their past behind them and build a new life, to channel all their energy toward the future. Information and research were not easily available. Documents were sealed as 'confidential.' Today though, since the documents have been declassified, there are many questions. Personally, I had to make a decision when I was solicited in 1999 to join the class action suit against the United States Government. The first step in the process was to remove the Statute of Limitations to allow the issue to be heard. Although I even have documents to prove the confiscation of property, I didn't join the suit. I love this country and I didn't want to sue the government. But now, knowing that there is a chance for at least a moral reparation, I might join and help the case. I was told that only a few people have documents and that will likely be a key issue. If nothing else, perhaps we will get answers to the many questions, and I hope I'll be around to hear them.

It seems that Mother and I, and many other Jews have the same questions:

Did General Clark represent the U.S. Government?

Did General Clark have so much power to act unilaterally in making his decision to declare the contents of the train unidentifiable? The Gold Train was unique, because the contents were *not* collected from Jews all over Europe, but very specifically from the Jews of Hungary, and mainly from Budapest.

Who determined how to dispose of the valuables? Who authorized the sale through Army Exchange Stores? Why Army Exchange Stores?

Why was gross misappropriation by Generals allowed?

To whom were those Generals accountable?

And the main question, why was it necessary to dispose of the loot so soon after the end of the war, disregarding numerous requests from Hungary's Jewish Community, disregarding those who survived and without giving them the opportunity to submit claims?

It seems that there is no single explanation for why the contents of the Gold Train were so readily dispersed. The fact remains that various policies and agreements prevented the property from being returned to its right-

ful owners. What we know is that lost valuables ended up in inappropriate hands, and now with the world at our fingertips, investigating the mystery of the Gold Train is not only a genuine possibility but also a must.

After resigning ourselves to our losses we were thankful to be alive. We set out to rebuild and hoped to enjoy the fruits of our labor. Our hope was short lived, and only after three years we fell into the hands of the Communists, and experienced similar oppression and confiscation, the stealing of our property yet again. It is ironic that after almost sixty years we know the facts, but it is still impossible to locate and distribute the properties to its rightful owners.

CHAPTER 34
EPILOGUE

REFLECTING ON OUR LIVES we realize how history seems to repeat itself, and unfortunately hatred has not ceased despite the passage of time. We lament that the frequency of these political upheavals has accelerated drastically in our lifetime, and in less than sixty years there is yet another threat facing us, this time from terrorists.

For my mother, the horrors of the bombings, the ghetto, the lack of food, the fear and suffering we endured during the Nazi occupation still remain vivid memories. As I was an infant during the Nazi atrocities, it is only through my mother's recollections that I have relived those terrifying days and months. Despite all the oppression and deprivation, my parents had the will to keep their hopes alive. They always emphasized the positive and were able to instill in me that we can learn from every moment of hardship and use that knowledge to our advantage. It seems that somehow I must have known this at an early age, for I have always recognized the importance of looking ahead. Now as an adult who has gone through so much, I am deeply aware that without adversity one cannot appreciate the good, and without hope there is no future.

During the past few years there have been many films showing the suffering and hardship people had to endure during
World War II. Documentaries appear on TV, and Holocaust
Museums have opened throughout the world. The Shoah
Foundation's videotaping of life histories of Holocaust survivors
has brought a greater awareness to the general public. More
people are now able and willing to share their personal experiences. My awareness increased by reading, looking at photographs, watching films, and discussing the atrocities with
people who also experienced them. My friend, Myrna, recently
told me that thirty-seven years ago when we met, she inquired
several times about my early life experiences, but I always
responded with, "Not now, I'll tell you some other time." While
she was disappointed, she accepted my decision and respected
my privacy. She is glad that she will finally get her answers. It
took all these years for me to be comfortable enough to talk
about it. I am fortunate to be still young enough to make this
awareness my mission, and make a difference in the world. I am
grateful to Kyle for encouraging me to relate my life experiences
to young people, and fortunately, after many years, now I am
able to talk about it.

My mission now is to raise awareness of both oppressions,
which occurred in my lifetime. The reason being, that in contrast
to the Nazi era, there is considerably less information and less
discussion on the suffering endured during the Communist
oppression, despite the length and extent of their cruelty. Russia
and the Eastern Bloc countries were closed societies, and news
was kept from the population within, but even more importantly, to the outside world. It seems that people who were
fortunate to leave or escape to the West preferred to concentrate
on their new lives rather than dwell on the past.

As I reflect on the journey of my life, I realize that in the past
thirty years I have traveled to many countries, but consciously

avoided returning to Hungary. Robert and I spent two short days visiting in 1979, when Michelle was thirteen, as we wanted to show her where we had grown up. She was the same age as I was when we left Hungary, and we felt it would be educational and beneficial for her. Hungary was still under Communism then.

After checking in at our hotel we had to leave our passports with the front desk and they were not returned to us until we left. The two days felt like two years and when we had to surrender our passports we felt like we wanted to leave right away. As we checked in Michelle got very upset when she heard the discussion between the front desk clerk and I regarding our passports. She understood most of the discussion in Hungarian and saw my concern but I repeated it in English, and told her that I couldn't explain it in front of others. I was afraid to express my feelings publicly and tried to control my emotions.

This was a lesson in life under Communism for Michelle, and a chance for us to teach her about tolerance and lack of freedom of expression—a very small taste of what we had to live with every day during the Communist era. Outside we felt very uncomfortable just walking on the streets. We felt like we were being watched and followed. And perhaps we were. When we walked near my parents' old apartment we were afraid to go too close for fear of being accused of trespassing. On Hungarian soil, we were considered Hungarians, and we would have been too close to Biszku's home. Our American passports could not completely protect Robert and me.

Michelle was safer because she was born in America. It was difficult to explain that to Michelle. It was her introduction to an oppressive society, a society without individual rights. That stay made us even more determined never to return, and Robert and I did not go there again until 1994. That visit was different. Hungary was no longer under Communist control. Since the fall of Communism in 1989, the world has changed and Hungary has changed with it. We were quite curious to see how those changes had affected life there.

Robert was invited to lecture at the very same dental school that he had attended as a student prior to leaving the country. This was a more positive visit than our first visit in 1979, but the experience was still bittersweet. The changes were happening slowly. People were still unhappy, still didn't have everything they wanted. Few repairs had been made to the bombed out buildings from World War II or the bullet holes from the revolutionary days. The country simply did not have the financial resources for restoration.

Implementing political changes took a while, but now, several years later, with the influence of Western-style politics, Hungary has become more inviting for returning visitors and the traveling public. Filled with magnificent architecture, much of which is undergoing renovation, Hungary is an open, friendly country. Budapest, a scenically beautiful city, appears to be on its way to once again deserving of its title "The Pearl of the East."

The city was built in a unique architectural style, known as Hungarian Art Nouveau, which is a local variation on the international Secession style that reached Hungary at the turn of the last century. There are also a number of Baroque and Renaissance-style relics, one of which is the Renaissance style State Opera House, which was opened in 1884 and remained the center of cultural life throughout the upheavals in Hungary's history. The Opera House went through extensive renovations and was reopened in 1994, the year of its centenary. The architecture of this building is very similar to that of the old Paris Opera House, and in many ways the whole city is a visual reminder of Paris.

The Dohany Synagogue, a magnificent structure built in 1859 in the Moorish style with tall twin towers, is the largest synagogue in Europe, and the second largest in the world, after New York's Temple Emmanuel. During the Communist era this temple complex housed the only Jewish Seminary for training rabbis in the Communist bloc countries. It is still a major source of Jewish culture and heritage for Eastern European countries, housing a museum whose collections represent the life and suffering of Hungary's Jews.

Dohany Synagogue was recently reopened after extensive renovations and visitors are welcome to view both the structures and a small cemetery park behind the main building. Theodore Herzl, the visionary of Zionism, was born in Budapest in 1860. As a youngster, he lived next door to the synagogue and celebrated his Bar Mitzvah there. In 1878 his family moved to Vienna, where he received his doctorate of law degree and lived until his death in 1904.

In the courtyard behind the synagogue, in the Raoul Wallenberg Memorial Park, stands The Emmanuel Holocaust Memorial, also known as the Victims' Memorial Tree. It is a magnificent contemporary metal sculpture, formed in the shape of a weeping willow, each leaf symbolizing a victim of the Holocaust, with their names inscribed on the leaves. Names are constantly added, as family members dedicate the engraved leaves in memory of lost loved ones. In addition to this memorial, there is also a much-deserved monument honoring Raoul Wallenberg in the nearby Szent Istvan Park, and a memorial to Carl Lutz, located in the former Jewish quarter of the city, within walking distance from the synagogue.

For me, the Dohany Temple is meaningful for several reasons. My parents were married there in 1941. After leaving Hungary, they remained in contact with the Chief Rabbi of Hungary, Rabbi Schreiber, who was the senior Rabbi of this synagogue. My parents continuously supported him whenever he requested temple supplies. In fact, in the late seventies, my parents furnished the Memorial Chapel behind the Temple in memory of our family members who had died. To us, this represented more than just a place of worship; it was filled with memories and gave us a sense of community.

In May 2000, Mother and I returned to the Dohany Temple and spent a morning worshiping there, almost sixty years after her wedding. She and I went back together, because after my uncle Janos's death, officials rummaged through his house for any relatives or contact information; and they found my parents' address from prior correspondence between Janos and Mother. She received an official notification of Janos's death.

In the past, receiving any official correspondence from the Hungarian Government would have created major concerns; we had received only arrest warrants or other decrees from them before. Now, fifty years later, this communication brought a letter of benefit, because I became the beneficiary of his estate. He never had children and I was the only blood relative through my father. How times have changed. When we lived there, we would have been shaking from fear while opening any official letter.

Another important part of my traveling experience was the enjoyment of the local cuisine. Since I do not eat much Hungarian food, the visits offered a great opportunity to sample and enjoy foods and tastes, which I remember from many years ago. The cuisine used to be quite heavy, but to accommodate modern tastes, the new style of cooking is much lighter. The result is equally tasty, however. No flavor was lost in the conversion to contemporary cooking.

With the influx of a significant number of tourists, many of the theaters we remember so fondly have been refurbished and brought back to their original grandeur. Many nights while visiting Budapest, we enjoyed fabulous performances. We often wished we could better understand the new political satires, but unfortunately, we were unfamiliar with many of the characters involved, as well as with the modern expressions in contemporary Hungarian language. Nevertheless, we appreciated the use of humor to make political statements.

Indeed, it is often humor that helps us cope with adversity. This is probably what gave my parents and many others the extra strength and courage to make the best of situations. They laughed, even in the worst of times, and they never gave up their dreams. So often we felt helpless, but we were never hopeless. They have always been very strong role models for me, and I sincerely hope that I have set a similar example for my daughter.

As I reflect on my parents' inner strength and their ability to cope, I think of a conversation with a friend about accepting hardships. We realized if there were never any tears we could not appreciate the laughter.

I feel very strongly that history repeats itself, and ignorance is often our biggest enemy. With all the hateful acts occurring around the world, we should strive to become informed about our own past. The poet Robert Graves once said, "If we don't learn from the past, we are doomed to repeat it."

We must educate and remind the younger generations who are growing up in this land of plenty, sheltered and shielded from atrocities committed for personal agendas or power. By being informed they are better equipped to resist the encroachment of evil, and know what it is that they must prevent.

I know the youngsters I talked to learned from my experiences, and I am very glad I could contribute to their education. Although each child was affected by a different episode, they all came away enriched. They understood about life beyond their own: past history can teach them and touch their lives now. I will always treasure their thank you notes:

Dear Mrs Reyto:

Thank you for coming to talk about your life. It was very interesting; I wish I could learn more about it. You should write a book about it. I think it would sell.

...

I learned a lot that I didn't know before. You really made me think about how people must have struggled.

...

I learned a lot and it reminded me of how lucky I am to live today without having to worry about being captured by Nazis or Communists.

...

I thought it was really interesting to hear about fake passports and other things everyone did to survive. Thank you very much for giving us a better view.

...

I really learned more about the Holocaust and it really got me feeling how all the Jews did then. I will never forget how horrible it must have been for you. And for you to share it with us is really cool.

...

I will always remember what you said about people. Not all people are bad.

The one thing I remember a lot is the people turning on the gas. That will stick with me for a long time.

...

I went home and told the story to my family; they were really interested and enjoyed it as well, but not as much as I did. I hope you can come back in a few years and talk to my little sister when she is in 8th grade.

...

It taught me to be grateful for all the things I have in life. I do not take things for granted. I was on the edge of my seat the whole time. I kind of had an idea what it must have been for you growing up, but I learned a lot more.

...

Something that you said about hearing something on the news. It's not all true. When you told our class this, it really got to me.

...

I have a totally new perspective on the whole Holocaust and Jews.

...

I am not Jewish but to learn about another person's perspective on something so evil is very cool. I could never survive something like that."

Having everything in life without some struggle causes people to take things for granted. The accomplishment of achieving one's goals is the greatest fulfillment, and conquering an obstacle is the ultimate euphoria.

My father passed away in 1994, but Mother has remained my inspirational leader, and now the leading figure in a family of four generations. Mother and I share strong feelings about promoting education, awareness, and philanthropy. She and I remain involved in our community, and we are dedicated supporters of many causes.

Mother often talks to the children about helping those less fortunate than themselves. She even gives Nicole and Kyle checks to send to organizations themselves. She has them address the envelopes and has them mail them. Most organizations send back thank you notes to the children, and she hopes that those will remind Nicole and Kyle of their meaningful support, even at an early age. Whenever she can, she even goes to the mailbox with them so they can mail it all together.

As I write this, I cannot help but think about the events of September 11th, 2001. The over 3,000 deaths and the continued aggression of fanatics keep reminding us of how drastically this event has forever affected our lives. Beyond any doubt, it was a turning point for everyone in the free world, but especially in the United States. Many people who may not have thought about it before now realize the importance of working hard to prevent evil and eliminate the forces of oppression.

Those fortunate enough to have grown up in this wonderful, free country, have never had to deal so personally with global adversity and confrontations with evil forces. Now, however, we are all aware that with hateful, fanatic people alive in the world, we must never let our guard down. The surprise attack of September 11th proves that we must be prepared, both to prevent, and if need be, handle attacks.

Yet, more than ever, we must learn to live beyond fear and subscribe to the idea of not waiting, and do what we can today. I remember my father-in-law always putting things off, claiming he would get to them after he retired. Unfortunately, he passed away before he had the opportunity to enjoy most of them.

During the year we attend temple services irregularly, but the High Holidays we always observe. Recently our Rabbi in one of his sermons during the High Holidays made a powerful statement:

> "You must have faith in yourself and be able to change. Every day brings new challenges and it is our responsibility to implement them in our daily lives. If we are not willing to learn from each day and its challenges, there is no reason for tomorrow."

It is our obligation to work for a better tomorrow and our duty to teach our youngsters how to build a better world. They must realize that the good life is a privilege and not simply something to which they are entitled. We must take responsibility for our own actions and strive to achieve our goals. It is equally important to help those less fortunate. Ultimately, the joys and rewards of giving are our own. Every generation seems to be threatened by external forces, some more obvious than others. But with knowledge, awareness, and commitment we can defeat threats and obstacles and achieve our dreams.

This chronicle of my journey from oppression to freedom demonstrates that a life dominated by hatred and persecution can turn into one filled with hope and dreams. There were many stops, reversals, and transfers along the way, but the destination was worth all the effort. The dictionary defines a dream as "something that somebody hopes, longs, or is ambitious for, usually something difficult to attain or far removed from present circumstances." It is my dream that my experiences become the foundation for higher awareness, and a model of one's ability to overcome agony and misery.

Dream what you want to dream,
Go where you want to go,
Be what you want to be,
Because you have only one life
And only one chance
To do all the things you want to do.
—ANONYMOUS

Nicole, Susanne, Rozsi and Michelle, 2003

ABOUT THE AUTHOR

SUSANNE REYTO is an author and speaker on the turbulent years in Hungary after WWII. She brings a rich tapestry of experience and wisdom to all her endeavors. Her often harrowing childhood and her ultimate escape from Communist Hungary in the late 1950's left an indelible mark on her spirit. Instead of allowing the horrors she endured to defeat her, Susanne maintained a sense of optimism and persevered in the pursuit of her dreams. That is the message she spreads to her audiences, young and old.

Susanne founded a travel agency that rose to international prominence, and she gained recognition as a consultant to corporations. Her work and writing have been featured in major newspapers and she has appeared on television shows in the United States and Canada. Susanne lives a life balanced between family, business, political activism, music, theater, and philanthropy. She was active in Beverly Hills politics and has given generously of her time and money to causes ranging from the Girl Scouts to the City of Hope. When she is not traveling the world with her husband, Susanne Reyto lives and writes in Los Angeles and thrives on spending time with her family and bringing her important message to future generations.

For speaking engagements,
please contact Susanne at:
susanne@pursuitoffreedom.com

BUDAPEST 1944–1949

GYOR – Passed through on the way to border, Dec. 1949
SOPRON – Wagon ride towards border, Dec. 1949
SZOMBATHELY – Hearing prior to sentencing, Dec. 1949
BALASSAGYARMAT – Manci and Pista, Feb - Aug. 1950
SATORALJAYJHELY – My parents' imprisonment, Dec. 1949 - Dec. 1950

SZOLNOK — transfer from train to horse drawn wagon - May 1951
KOTELEK — Internment May 1951 - Jan 1953
KUNSZENTMARTON — Jan - Sept 1953
BUDAPEST — Return from internment Sept 1953 - March 1957

U S S R

• Satoraljaujhely

48°

• Balassagyarmat

⊃Budapest

• Szolnok
• Kotelek

• Kunszentmarton

R O M A N I A

46°

www.PursuitofFreedom.com